Discovering Psychology

This publication forms part of the Open University module DSE141 Discovering psychology. Details of this and other Open University modules can be obtained from the Student Registration and Enquiry Service, The Open University, PO Box 197, Milton Keynes MK7 6BJ, United Kingdom (tel. +44 (0)845 300 60 90; email general-enquiries@open.ac. uk).

Alternatively, you may visit the Open University website at www.open.ac.uk where you can learn more about the wide range of modules and packs offered at all levels by The Open University. To purchase a selection of Open University materials visit www.ouw.co.uk, or contact Open University Worldwide, Walton Hall, Milton Keynes MK7 6AA, United Kingdom for a brochure (tel. +44 (0)1908 858793; fax +44 (0)1908 858787; email ouw-customer-services@open.ac. uk).

Discovering Psychology

Edited by Nicola Brace and Jovan Byford

The Open University Walton Hall, Milton Keynes MK7 6AA

First published 2010.

Edited and designed by The Open University.

Typeset by The Open University.

Printed in the United Kingdom by Bell & Bain Ltd, Glasgow

The paper used in this publication is procured from forests independently certified to the level of Forest Stewardship Council (FSC) principles and criteria. Chain of custody certification allows the tracing of this paper back to specific forest-management units (see www.fsc.org).

978-1-84873-466-1

1.1

Mixed Sources
Product group from well-managed forests and other controlled sources
www.fsc.org Cert no. TT-COC-002769
© 1996 Forest Stewardship Council

Contents

General introduction

Defining psychology

Here you are at the start of a book entitled *Discovering Psychology*. As you have chosen to study psychology, it is likely that you have an idea about what the subject is about. It could well be that some of what you know about psychology, and why you are interested in it, has come from the newspapers or television. Psychology and psychologists have become a regular feature in the media in relation to a broad range of issues. Consider the following examples:

- 'Curling up for an afternoon nap can improve the brain's ability to learn by clearing out cluttered memory space, psychologists say.' (The *Guardian,* 22 February 2010)

- 'A "dark side" to the internet suggests a strong link between time spent surfing the web and depression, psychologists have claimed.' (*Daily Telegraph*, 3 February 2010)

- 'Primary school pupils are better behaved within the classroom than in the 1970s, says a long-term study by educational psychologists.' (BBC News online, 24 November 2008)

This is just a small glimpse of what has been reported in the press. Psychologists regularly appear on television, either on news programmes or in documentaries, to comment on a host of issues, such as the influence of the internet, child development, attraction, animal behaviour, ageing, stress, mental health, personality, differences between men and women, reasons for committing crimes, offender rehabilitation, and the belief in the paranormal.

So psychologists seem to comment on just about anything to do with humans – their behaviour, personality characteristics, mental state and abilities. This gives us a hint as to what psychology is and what psychologists do. Psychology could be defined as the scientific study of behaviour and mind.

Psychology as a scientific endeavour

When you listen to a psychologist or read about what they do, the claims they tend to make are often associated with the terms 'evidence' or 'research'. Even if psychologists sometimes say things that sound common-sensical, their arguments are almost always made on the basis of the results of studies. In other words, psychologists will usually present arguments based on *evidence* gathered through *research*.

Let us look at the three news reports again and explore how the specific conclusions about the benefits of napping, the link between internet use and happiness, and behaviour in the classroom were arrived at.

In relation to the benefits of an afternoon nap, this newspaper article reported a study by Matthew Walker and colleagues from the University of California, Berkeley. In this study, thirty-nine healthy young adults who agreed to take part were split into two groups of approximately equal size. One group became the 'nap' group and the other the 'no-nap' group. In the first phase of the study, all thirty-nine volunteers completed a learning task designed to test their memory. They completed the task at noon, and both the 'nap' and 'no-nap' groups performed equally well. Two hours later, at 2 p.m., the 'nap' group had a 90-minute sleep, whilst the 'no-nap' group remained awake. Then, at 6 p.m., both groups participated in more learning tasks. The researchers found that those who were in the 'nap' group performed better than those in the 'no-nap' group. The explanation offered is that the 90 minutes of sleep allowed the brain of those in the 'nap' group to 'store' the learning that took place at noon, thus making room for the new learning that occurred at 6 p.m.

This type of investigation is known as an *experiment*. You may remember carrying out experiments at school for scientific subjects such as chemistry, biology and physics. But experiments are not limited to the natural sciences; psychologists make extensive use of them too. In fact, an experiment doesn't require test tubes and other laboratory apparatus. It involves, instead, carefully manipulating whatever it is you are interested in studying and then measuring the effect that this manipulation has had on something else. In the above example, the psychologists manipulated the volunteers' experience so that half had a nap and the other half did not, and then they measured the effect this had on learning.

Throughout this book, you will be introduced to this method of investigation in more detail, and learn about some very well-known, 'classic' experiments that have been conducted to investigate a number of different issues, including obedience, learning, attention and memory. However, experiments are just one of many types of method that psychologists use when carrying out their investigations.

The second newspaper article used a different method to explore the link between the amount of time spent online and happiness. This claim was based on a study conducted by psychologists Catriona Morrison and Helen Gore from the University of Leeds. Their study involved the use of a questionnaire which was sent out to 1319 young people and adults. Of this number, eighteen individuals were deemed to be addicted to the internet. A high proportion of these internet addicts were found to be depressed.

This research finding was therefore based on a type of investigation that involved asking people to respond to a list of questions. In fact, they were asked several sets of questions, including one set about what they used the internet for, another set about how much they used the internet, and a third that had been designed specifically to measure whether or not they suffered from depression. By comparing the answers to the different sets of questions, researchers were able to draw conclusions about possible links between internet use and depression.

So, *questionnaires* are another type of method that psychologists can use. In the first chapter of this book, you will read more about the construction and use of questionnaires. An important point to consider is what type of conclusions can be drawn from questionnaire-based studies. In the above case, for example, it is difficult to tell whether internet addiction causes depression, or the other way around. As Catriona Morrison explains (*Daily Telegraph*, 3 February 2010): 'Our research indicates that excessive internet use is associated with depression, but what we don't know is which comes first – are depressed people drawn to the internet or does the internet cause depression?' This issue of causality is an important one in psychological research and is discussed in several chapters of *Discovering Psychology*.

What about the claim in the third article, concerning pupils' behaviour in the classroom? The investigation was led by Brian Apter, an educational psychologist employed by the Wolverhampton City Council. With his collaborators he studied the behaviour of primary school pupils in 141 classrooms. Their findings were then compared with those obtained in earlier studies of classroom behaviour that have been routinely conducted since the 1970s. From these comparisons, it was possible to infer an improvement in classroom behaviour that began in the mid 1980s and that then continued for the following two decades. The reason for this improvement was thought to be better teaching and more verbal engagement with pupils.

This study used a method of investigation known as *observation*. Information regarding the pupils' behaviour was obtained by *observing* and recording the number of pupils who were 'on-task' and following the teacher's instructions, and the number of pupils who were deemed to be 'off-task' and not following the teacher's directions. In several chapters you will read about studies that used observations, and learn more about how this method can be used to arrive at reliable conclusions about the behaviour that is being investigated.

Diversity within psychology

The previous section described three different methods that are used in psychological investigations: experiments, questionnaires and observation. As you progress through the chapters of this book you will come across other methods. For example, in Chapter 1 you will read about the use of *interviews* to gather information about people's views on a range of topics, including their childhood. This particular approach can be used to obtain a much more in-depth understanding of people's attitudes, beliefs and dispositions, and is one that is increasingly adopted in psychology.

Therefore, psychologists vary in the approach they take to their research, with some adopting the experimental method typical of the natural sciences, and others engaging in the sorts of investigation (such as questionnaires and interviews) that are more typical of the social sciences. Crucially, however, this is not the only kind of variability that exists within psychology. There are also many sub-disciplines, which differ in respect of their main focus of study. As you progress through the chapters, you will be introduced to some of the main sub-disciplines, including social psychology, developmental psychology, biological psychology, cognitive psychology and the psychology of individual differences. Although there is some overlap between them, each sub-discipline focuses on a different aspect of human behaviour, characteristics, mental states or abilities, and draws on methods of investigation that are appropriate to its particular focus.

The structure of this book

The primary aim of *Discovering Psychology* is to illustrate how psychologists go about their investigations and to give you a taste of the range of topics they address. The book is divided into three parts, each consisting of three chapters and a short introduction and conclusion. Each part has a common theme running through the chapters. Part 1 looks at what makes people do harm to others. Part 2 considers how other people influence or shape what we do, while Part 3 explores internal mental processes, namely language, attention and memory, and looks at different ways in which they can be investigated.

Each chapter follows a common structure and is divided into five parts:

- Section 1 introduces the specific topic explored in the chapter, and how this relates to a particular problem relevant to everyday life.
- Section 2 describes a pioneering study, one that is regarded today as being a classic piece of psychological research.
- Section 3 explores in more detail a particular feature or underlying assumption of the classic study that is of broader relevance to psychology.
- Section 4 considers developments in psychology since the classic study was completed.
- Section 5 reflects on the broader relevance of the classic study and the more recent findings to the particular problem set out in Section 1.

The studies explored in the book are a very small subset of the research conducted by psychologists to date. However, the material has been carefully chosen to provide a taster of the main sub-disciplines and the range of methods used by psychologists. By exploring in detail nine classic studies in distinct areas of psychology and by describing the work that followed, we hope to give you an insight into the diverse nature of the discipline. Also, you will notice that included in the book are studies conducted as early as the nineteenth century, across the twentieth century and into the twenty-first century. So, in reading the chapters you will get a sense of how psychology has evolved over the years, and how our understanding of the human mind and behaviour has become more sophisticated, although many questions remain unanswered.

In addition to the five sections, each chapter contains activities that you are invited to undertake. These should not take very long to complete and they will increase your engagement with, as well your understanding of, the material covered in the chapter. There are also two boxes in each chapter, focusing on specific points relevant to the topic under discussion. One of these, entitled 'Why do it this way?', explores the reasons or assumptions underpinning the method used in the classic study described in that chapter, and highlights some broader issues relevant to psychological research more generally.

Finally, the classic study covered in each chapter addresses a particular everyday or real-world issue. For instance, Chapters 1 and 2 explore whether the conduct of Nazi war criminals is best explained in terms of personality or situational influences, Chapter 5 examines a number of important questions related to the nature of an infant's attachment to their caregiver, while Chapter 8 considers if it is safe to drive while using a mobile phone. This link to everyday concerns will help you to get a sense of the broader relevance of psychological research, and the fact that psychology has always been responsive to practical problems faced by society as a whole.

We hope that you will enjoy finding out about what psychologists do, and how their research sheds light on everyday life.

Jovan Byford and Nicola Brace

Part 1

My Lai Massacre

Freud

Adorno

Bandura

Milgram

Goldberg personality

Extraversion/Introversion

Psychoanalysis

Mein Kampf

F Scale.

Introduction

'What makes people do harm to others?' This might sound like a strange and somewhat negative question with which to begin the journey of discovering psychology. Why not look at more positive themes – love, happiness, friendship or altruism? Psychology must have something to say about these, inherently psychological, yet more affirmative and upbeat topics.

While this might be the case, it is also true that within psychology there has traditionally been a greater emphasis on trying to explain, account for and suggest ways of changing the more *negative* aspects of human behaviour. This is in part because society as a whole tends to call upon experts, psychologists included, when things go wrong. At the same time, psychologists and their research interests are, as you will see, deeply rooted in the historical and social context. Scholarly attention is often drawn to the problems and challenges facing society, so the questions that psychologists choose to address, as well as the way they go about seeking answers, are determined by the world that they inhabit.

It is therefore not surprising that after 1945, when the world became aware of the atrocities committed by the Nazis and their allies during the Second World War, psychologists became particularly aware of the need to investigate and explain the potential psychological roots of the excesses of human violence and aggression, including mass murder and genocide. Subsequent events, such as the massacre of civilians in the village of My Lai in Vietnam committed by a US military unit in 1968, or the genocides in Cambodia (1975–79), Rwanda (1994) and Bosnia (1995), suggested that the events of the Second World War were in fact not an isolated case, but that the tendency to cause harm to other human beings on a massive scale has become a stable aspect of the human condition. What is more, people do harm to others also on a more 'mundane', everyday level, and not just in war. Horseplay in the schoolyard can deteriorate into bullying, aggressive intimidation and violence. Violence of one kind or another takes place regularly in city centres, schools, playgrounds, and homes. Although the media often exaggerate the frequency of anti-social behaviour and violent crime, these phenomena are nevertheless around us and represent a cause for concern.

One thing that people often ponder over when hearing of stories of aggression and violence are the origins of the perpetrators' actions, and the question from the beginning of this introduction gets posed: 'What makes people do harm to others?' Significantly, the explanations that spring to mind are mainly psychological. Is it personality? Are there certain kinds of people who are more likely to harm others because of their character and inbuilt dispositions? Or is the situation to blame? Is the context in which an individual might find themselves the main determinant of their behaviour? If so, *how* does the environment influence an individual? Also, how do people *become* violent? Are the roots of violence to be sought in early childhood, in the relationship with parents and caregivers? Or is violence simply learned, from watching others and from living in a society in which it is increasingly difficult to avoid violent films and computer games?

These are some of the issues that are considered in Part 1 of *Discovering Psychology*. In Chapter 1, Jean McAvoy examines the research on the authoritarian personality which was carried out in the 1940s by a group of researchers in the USA. Theodor Adorno, Else Frenkel-Brunswik, Daniel Levinson and Nevitt Sanford were keen to uncover aspects of personality that make some people predisposed to embrace the kind of extremist, violent and racist ideology that was espoused in Germany under Hitler. In their quest for this *authoritarian personality* they used a complex method involving thousands of questionnaires and more than a hundred in-depth interviews. The study will be used to illustrate two issues relevant to research on personality: first, how personality can be *measured*, and, second, how these differences in personality *develop* and where they come from. As you will see, to address the latter question, Adorno and colleagues drew on the psychoanalytic theory of Sigmund Freud. Jean McAvoy also explores some contemporary developments in the study of authoritarianism which account for this phenomenon in very different ways.

Chapter 2, by Philip Banyard, examines one of the best-known studies in the history of psychology, the obedience studies carried out by Stanley Milgram in the 1960s. In his research Milgram demonstrated the lengths to which people are willing to go just because someone tells them to do something. The focus of Milgram's work was on the power of the situation and the extent to which doing harm is a function not so much of *who* we are, but of the circumstances we find ourselves in. Philip Banyard also discusses the ethics of Milgram's research, specifically whether the author of the study took sufficient precautions to protect the integrity and well-being of the participants in the experiment. The chapter also considers developments in obedience research since Milgram, and in particular how psychologists have tried to overcome the ethical issues posed by Milgram's obedience studies. How does one investigate obedience without compromising the well-being of participants?

In Chapter 3 John Oates explores the work of Albert Bandura on the effects on children of the media's portrayal of violence. Through a discussion of a classic study, John Oates introduces the broader notion of *social learning* – learning through observation and imitation. Chapter 3 also discusses the role that psychologists can, should and do play in informing government policy on regulating the portrayal of violence in the media, especially given the attention that the media itself places on the apparent causal link between youth crime and aggression and exposure to violent games and films.

We hope that you will enjoy the chapters and that you will gain not just a greater understanding of what makes people do harm to others, but also an appreciation of what psychologists do and of the challenges they face as they seek to explain and understand human behaviour.

Chapter 1
Exposing the authoritarian personality

Jean McAvoy

Contents

Aims and objectives

By the end of this chapter you should be able to:

- outline what psychologists mean when they refer to the term 'personality'
- describe the notion of the 'authoritarian personality' and how it has been measured
- discuss the methodological problems of using scales to measure personality
- outline alternative approaches which have sought to explain 'authoritarian' behaviour.

1. Introduction

A central task for psychology is to try to explain people's behaviour. A lot of what psychologists do involves addressing the question: 'Why do people do the things they do?' An important factor in human behaviour which psychologists have traditionally been interested in is **personality**. There are many definitions of personality but, in general terms, it refers to a set of stable and enduring individual characteristics or inner dispositions that lead people to behave in a steady way over time and maintain a consistent orientation to other people and the world around them.

Activity 1.1

Spend a few minutes thinking about someone you know. How would you describe their personality? Do you think their personality influences the way they behave? Think about some of the things they do that you consider are down to their personality.

What kinds of things did you come up with? What personality characteristics does the person you have chosen have? What terms did you use to describe him or her? Did you use terms like 'extrovert', 'serious', 'competitive', 'bossy', 'liberal', 'realistic' or 'a good listener'? You probably came up with a completely different set of terms. This is unsurprising given that there are thousands of words available to us that relate to aspects of personality, and people use them in everyday life to describe themselves and others, attribute motives for behaviour, and make sense of the world. The fact that there are so many different terms to describe personality is in itself illustrative of its importance. It has been found, for instance, that people, especially in Western societies, have a tendency to attribute causes of someone's behaviour to their personality, rather than to the situation, even in instances where there is overwhelming evidence that a situation is more important (Ross, 1977). For example, if people see a stranger slip and fall in the street, they are more likely to attribute the accident to the person's 'clumsiness' or 'carelessness' (a feature of their personality) than to the fact that the ground is slippery (an aspect of the situation). They will tend to do so even when a situational explanation would have been more appropriate (such as if the pavement is visibly wet). Lee Ross (1977) has called this preference towards a personality-based explanation for behaviour the **fundamental attribution error**. Personality therefore appears to be

Personality
A person's stable and enduring traits and characteristics, which lead them to behave in a steady way over time.

Fundamental attribution error
The tendency to explain the causes of other people's behaviour as a product of their internal characteristics and dispositions rather than external situational factors.

central to the way in which, in everyday life, many people view and interpret the causes of other people's actions, attitudes, choices, etc.

Figure 1.1 Prior to the 1983 general election, Neil Kinnock, then leader of the Labour Party, was walking on the beach when he tripped and fell during a photo opportunity. Political commentators suggested the incident contributed to Kinnock's party losing the general election because people saw his fall as a reflection of his character

Psychologists tend to be more cautious about the role of personality in human behaviour. Very few psychologists today would claim that behaviour can be explained exclusively in terms of personality characteristics, and, instead, they have warned against the dangers of focusing too much on personality. Nevertheless, personality is widely acknowledged as playing an important role in shaping the way people are and how they interact with the world around them.

1.1 Approaches to personality

Individual differences
Any characteristics that are susceptible to variation between individuals; for example, personality or intelligence.

For psychologists interested in personality, the first task has been to define, categorise and measure personality. Because the term 'personality' encompasses characteristics and dispositions that are susceptible to individual variation (no two people have identical personalities), the efforts to define and measure personality are part of a sub-discipline of psychology concerned with the study of **individual differences**. As mentioned previously, there are thousands of words describing personality characteristics. Can these be reduced to a smaller and therefore more manageable cluster of personality traits? For instance, if it could be established that people who are 'affectionate' tend also to be 'generous', 'gentle' and 'modest', then maybe all these different terms to describe that aspect of a person's personality are not necessary. Instead, 'agreeableness' could be used as a broader category that encompasses a range of characteristics, including how 'gentle' or 'generous' or 'affectionate' someone is. If this rule is followed, it is possible to reduce the vast number of terms to a small number of categories that can be used to describe and measure human personality.

This is precisely the approach taken by Lewis R. Goldberg, for example, who, in the 1980s, devised what are known as the 'Big Five' personality factors (Goldberg, 1981). According to Goldberg, personality can be divided into five dimensions, namely Extraversion (which covers things like sociability, assertiveness, adventurousness), Agreeableness (mentioned above), Conscientiousness (things like orderliness and reliability), Emotional stability (things like security, irritability, emotionality) and Intellect (imagination, perceptiveness, etc.). The assumption here is that each of the five factors is a continuum (a seamless progression ranging from extreme extraversion to extreme introversion, for example, or emotional stability to emotional instability) with each person's personality being definable in terms of where they are along each of the five dimensions. As well as categorising and defining personality in terms of a smaller number of factors, Goldberg also devised a way of measuring personality. He developed a questionnaire which is used to establish how extrovert, agreeable, emotionally stable, etc. a person is.

Other psychologists researching personality have also tried to reduce personality to a smaller number of core characteristics, but have come up with different dimensions. The **personality theory** put forward by Paul Costa and Robert McCrae (1992), for instance, also has five factors, but theirs are slightly different from those of Goldberg. Hans Eysenck (1967), on the other hand, has put forward a theory which states that personality consists of just three dimensions. There is some overlap between the different theories – Costa and McCrae, Eysenck and Goldberg all have **Extraversion** as a factor – but there are also differences. How many dimensions a theory proposes and how these are defined depends very much on the method that the researcher uses to derive them and the various assumptions that guide their research.

Importantly, however, psychologists have not just been interested in describing people's personalities or measuring them. They also looked at

Personality Theory
A set of propositions about the structure and/or development of personality that forms the basis of a coherent, evidence-based explanation.

Extraversion
A personality type characterised by outgoing and gregarious behaviour. It forms an extraversion–introversion continuum with introversion, at the opposite pole, typified by reserved and inward-looking behaviour.

how personality is formed. Why do people have different personalities? What causes particular personality characteristics to develop in certain people but not others?

A classic example of a personality theory that focused on development rather than on measurement is the work of Sigmund Freud. Freud was a psychoanalyst working in Vienna in the first half of the twentieth century and is credited as the father of the psychoanalytic movement. **Psychoanalysis** is an approach within psychology that explores the ways in which human behaviour and thinking are influenced by unconscious processes. Although Freud's immediate concern was the mental health of his patients, he also used his therapeutic practice to think about the human mind more generally and about what makes us who we are. Notably, Freud lived before psychologists became interested in the details of categorising and measuring personality. He was interested instead in where personality comes from, and used his extensive experience as a psychoanalyst to theorise about the development of personality.

Psychoanalysis
A set of theories and therapeutic methods exploring the unconscious processes influencing human behaviour.

Figure 1.2 Sigmund Freud (1856–1939)

The main tenet of Freud's theory is that personality consists of two broad elements: the *conscious* and the *unconscious*. He argued that much of what a person is like (i.e. their outward personality of the kind measured by personality tests) is determined by drives, impulses and motivations that are not accessible to conscious awareness. Outward manifestations of personality are therefore just the tip of the iceberg, one that lies at the top of a much larger structure – the unconscious.

Also, Freud stipulated that personality is formed in childhood through the way an individual experiences and reacts to people around them. According to psychoanalytic theory, the growing child goes through several stages of development. At each stage he or she experiences gratifications and frustrations. For example, according to Freudian theory the first stage of development is the 'oral stage' when a baby's interaction with the outside world is limited to the satisfaction of its basic need: the need to eat. At this stage, the baby concentrates on learning about its mouth, and all the pleasures and discomforts associated with it – such as sucking, biting or hunger. Normally the child will progress from this stage after weaning. However, if a child encounters some difficulty at the oral stage, and its progress through it is inhibited in some way, the child will become 'fixated' at this stage and this will shape its adult personality. Thus, if an infant is weaned too early, for example, she or he might grow into an adult who is unconsciously motivated to seek extra oral gratification, such as to overeat, for example. Now, I have presented this in quite a simplistic way. You might not be surprised to hear that Freud's theories are a lot more complicated and sophisticated than this, but this just introduces two assumptions underpinning the psychoanalytic theory of personality. First, infant and early childhood experiences (including the relationship with parents) have a strong influence on personality formation. Second, besides the conscious aspect of personality, and the visible traits, behavioural tendencies and dispositions, there is also the world of the unconscious, which is inaccessible to conscious awareness.

1.2 Personality and 'authoritarianism'

This chapter examines a specific theory of personality, one that, rather than looking at personality generally, sought to describe, measure and explain a specific kind of personality: the **authoritarian personality**. During the Second World War, the world witnessed atrocities on a horrific scale. Millions of people were murdered by the Nazis in the most brutal ways. Among them were six million European Jews, most of whom were systematically murdered in Nazi concentration camps. After the war, psychologists sought to explain what it is that leads some people to take part in such extreme violence. One question that they

Authoritarian personality
A kind of personality typified by obedience to authority, strict adherence to rules, and hostility towards anyone different from oneself.

23

asked is whether there is a particular kind of person who is more likely to commit this kind of aggression.

Figure 1.3 Do violent and destructive movements and ideologies such as Nazism attract only certain kinds of people?

An answer to this question was proposed by a group of researchers working at the University of California, Berkeley, in the 1940s. Theodor Adorno, Else Frenkel-Brunswik, Daniel Levinson and Nevitt Sanford suggested that some people have a specific kind of personality that makes them susceptible to extremist ideologies and predisposes them to commit acts of aggression and murder in the name of political ideology. They called this the *authoritarian personality*. In this chapter you will read about the idea of authoritarian personality in more detail. How did Adorno and colleagues go about looking for the authoritarian personality? How did they measure it, and most importantly how did they explain its roots? What is it that makes people become authoritarian? Finally, how valid is the claim that participation in mass violence is attributable to a particular kind of personality?

Summary

- Psychologists largely agree that personality plays an important part in how people behave.
- Many theories have been developed that try to define and measure personality.
- Freud argued that personality consists of two main elements: the *conscious* and the *unconscious*.
- After the Second World War, Adorno and colleagues examined what makes people susceptible to extreme ideologies such as Nazism. Their research led to the concept of the authoritarian personality.

2   The authoritarian personality

In the 1940s, Nevitt Sanford was a psychology professor working at the University of California at Berkeley. He recruited a PhD student, Daniel Levinson, to work on constructing a method of measuring **anti-Semitism** (Smith, 1997). Later, Sanford invited Else Frenkel-Brunswik and Theodor Adorno to join his project and collaborate with him as part of a research team. Both Adorno and Frenkel-Brunswik had witnessed the rise of **fascism** and anti-Semitism first hand. Adorno was an eminent sociologist in Germany, and Frenkel-Brunswick was a child psychologist in Austria. Both of them fled Germany in the 1930s and made their way to America. Like many scholars at this time, especially those who had been affected personally by the events in Europe leading up to and during the Second World War, the research team were trying to explain how it was that the Second World War saw so many people join in such extraordinary inhumanities and on such a large scale.

But, while the research team were motivated by the desire to understand what had happened in Europe between 1933 and 1945, they conducted their research in the United States, in the years after Nazism had already been defeated. Their starting point was that anti-Semitism and fascism were not solely a 'German' problem, as some had speculated. Instead, as Adorno and his colleagues soon realised, they had no difficulty in finding Americans whose outlook was such as to indicate that they would readily accept fascism if it should become a strong or respectable social movement. In other words, people with a predisposition to accept violence towards anyone different from themselves or embrace an extremist political ideology were to be found anywhere, not just in Germany. It is this predisposition for fascism that Adorno and colleagues called the *authoritarian personality*.

This study by Adorno, Frenkel-Brunswick, Levinson and Sanford, published in 1950, quickly had an enormous impact. A review by Brewster Smith in 1950 described it as 'certainly the most extensive and sophisticated research on [anti-Semitism] yet contributed by psychologists' (quoted in Smith, 1997, p. 160). Today, the description of someone as 'authoritarian' has entered the colloquial language, and is used to describe the kind of attitudes and dispositions that Adorno et al. (1950) sought to explain. In the following sections I will look at *how* Adorno, Frenkel-Brunswick, Levinson and Sanford conducted their investigation, and *why* they did it the way they did.

Anti-Semitism
Prejudice and hostility towards Jews.

Fascism
A political ideology or regime marked by extreme nationalism and racism, centralisation of authority and the suppression of political opposition.

Before doing so, it is worth drawing attention to the issue of authorship in the authoritarian personality study. Theodor Adorno has become almost synonymous with the research on the authoritarian personality. And yet it was Nevitt Sanford who instigated this research, with Adorno joining the project last, after Levinson and Frenkel-Brunswik. The reason why the study is known under Adorno's name is purely and simply because 'A' comes first in the alphabet! When they were preparing the almost 1000-page book in which they published the results of their work, the authors took the decision to list the researchers' names alphabetically. So the study became known as Adorno et al. (1950). There is a particular irony in this, though. A little while earlier Adorno had changed his name, shortening it from Wiesengrund-Adorno to simply Adorno. But for this change, Adorno would have been the fourth named author on the study and we might now be referring to authoritarian personality as the work of 'Frenkel-Brunswick and colleagues' (Altemeyer, 1996).

Figure 1.4 Theodor Adorno's name became principally associated with the authoritarian personality study, although he was not the main contributor

2.1   Measuring personalities

The idea of 'measuring' personality is quite a strange one in some ways. Think back to the description of someone you know which you provided for Activity 1.1. Perhaps describing the personality of the person you chose felt reasonably straightforward. But how would you go about 'measuring' their personality? In your description, did you use words like *quite* bold, *very* conscientious, *always* enthusiastic, or *sometimes* relaxed? These kinds of words help us get some rough sense of how much someone might exhibit a particular characteristic, but they are quite broad terms, and not very precise. More importantly, they are based on impression rather than objective measurement. In order to make meaningful comparisons between two people's personalities (for instance, John is more 'extrovert' than Judy) or assess an individual's personality in relation to the population as a whole (William is more 'agreeable' than the average person), psychologists need quite precise methods for actually measuring different aspects of personality.

Measurement was the first issue that Adorno and colleagues set out to resolve. They began with the assumption, common in research on personality, that people's **attitudes** are a reflection of their underlying personality characteristics. Adorno and his colleagues argued that a way of tapping into an aspect of human personality is by measuring corresponding attitudes. So they began by trying to measure *attitudes*, in order to draw some conclusions about underlying *personality*.

Attitudes
A person's beliefs and feelings about issues, events, objects or people, which are thought to influence behaviour.

Adorno and colleagues were interested in characteristics that they believed accounted for much that happened in Europe during the Second World War. Jewish people had been a particular target under the violent Nazi regime so Adorno et al. developed ways of measuring attitudes towards Jews in particular, but also towards anyone ethnically different, as well as attitudes towards traditional, conservative political beliefs.

Adorno et al. (1950) argued that these three attitude sets were all intrinsically related to one another so that people who endorse conservative political beliefs tend also to exhibit intolerance towards those who belong to other ethnic groups, as well as towards Jews.

Scale
A set of items such as questions on a questionnaire which combine to measure a bigger construct (e.g. a personality characteristic) that cannot be measured directly.

To measure these attitude sets, Adorno et al. used **scales**. In psychological research a scale refers to a set of items – statements – to which participants are asked to respond. The individual items on the scale are all related in meaning and together they combine to add up to a bigger construct. So, for example, in the ethnocentrism scale devised by Adorno et al., there are a set of statements about people from minority ethnic groups and about people from the dominant American, white, Christian group in the 1940s and 1950s (see Table 1.1 for examples). Participants in the study were asked to rate how much they agree with each statement. These individual statements are said to combine to represent a bigger characteristic – **ethnocentrism** – meaning favouring one's own group at the expense of another. The combined ratings on individual items are then used to derive each participant's ethnocentrism score.

Ethnocentrism
Belief in the superiority of one's own ethnic group or culture.

Table 1.1 Examples from the three attitude scales devised for the authoritarian personality study

From the Anti-Semitism scale (AS-scale):
It is wrong for Jews and Gentiles to intermarry.
It is sometimes alright to ban Jews from certain apartment houses.
The best way to eliminate the communist menace in this country is to control the Jewish element which guides it.
From the Ethnocentrism scale (E-scale):
In view of the present national emergency, it is highly important to limit responsible government jobs to native, white, Christian Americans.
There will always be superior and inferior nations in the world and, in the interests of all concerned, it is best that the superior ones be in control of world affairs.
There will always be wars because, for one thing, there will always be races who ruthlessly try to grab more than their share.
From the Politico-Economic Conservatism scale (PEC-scale):
Young people sometimes get rebellious ideas, but as they grow up they ought to get over them and settle down.
In general, full economic security is harmful; most men wouldn't work if they didn't need the money for eating and living.
Character, honesty, and ability will tell in the long run; most people get pretty much what they deserve.

Source: Adorno et al., 1950, pp. 69–70, 110–11, 158

Table 1.1 shows some examples of the kinds of statement included in the attitude scales. Remember, Adorno and his colleagues were trying to find out the extent to which ordinary American citizens would agree with overtly anti-Semitic, ethnocentric and conservative ideas.

Participants were presented with the scales in the form of questionnaires and were asked to indicate their own levels of agreement or disagreement with each item, saying whether they felt 'slight support' for the statement, 'moderate support', 'strong support', 'slight opposition', 'moderate opposition' or 'strong opposition'.

You may have noticed that these options do not invite participants to offer any kind of 'neutral' response. The researchers argued that when surveys such as this allow space for neutral responses, such as 'neither support nor oppose' or 'don't know', this middle-ground option tends to attract a lot of responses from participants. The researchers here wanted to 'force' participants to take a position either in favour of or against the statements and therefore omitted this 'neutral' category.

Once participants had completed the scales indicating their levels of agreement or disagreement, the researchers scored participants' responses on a range from 1 to 7:

Strong opposition	1 point
Moderate opposition	2 points
Slight opposition	3 points
Slight support	5 points
Moderate support	6 points
Strong support	7 points

You can see that points run from 1 to 7, with the middle point – 4 – being omitted. Four points were assigned only when participants did not register any response to an item. Thus, although participants were not given the option of a neutral response, their failure (or refusal) to rate a statement was interpreted as neutrality and was therefore awarded the score of 4.

The ratings of individual items within a scale were then added up to give an overall score for each participant. The higher the score, the more the person was said to exhibit the characteristic in question. So, a person who tends to agree with (indicate support for) the statements in the ethnocentrism scale would receive a high score, indicating a high level of prejudice towards people from ethnic groups other than that to which that person belonged.

Figure 1.5 Absence of ethnocentrism: choosing to mix together with other ethnic groups

Having established scales to measure attitudes towards Jews, other ethnic groups and conservative political ideas, Adorno et al. developed an additional scale, the potential for fascism scale. This scale, known as the **F-scale**, was central to Adorno et al.'s study. It included items that made no explicit reference to racial or ethnic minorities, or conservative politics. It was a measure not of attitudes but of personality characteristics underpinning potential for fascism.

F-scale
A measure of personality characteristics underpinning potential for fascism.

How did Adorno et al. go about developing the F-scale? Their starting point was that this personality measure, while containing items that do not mention explicitly either Jews or other ethnic groups, would nevertheless yield scores that correspond to those obtained on the various attitude measures. This is because, they argued, there is a strong relationship between the potential for fascism and prejudiced attitudes: a person who scores highly on the anti-Semitism and ethnocentrism scales should also obtain a high score on the F-scale, and vice versa. (They were less concerned with the political and economic attitudes, as these were believed to be less directly linked to potential for fascism, as a personality measure.) So, Adorno et al. came up with a large number of more general statements about obedience, respect for authority and traditions, resistance to novel or unusual lifestyles, disapproval of sexual freedoms and gender equality, and so on (see Table 1.2 for examples). These statements were administered in a questionnaire to over 2000 respondents, along with the other three scales, the ones that measured anti-Semitism, ethnocentrism and political and economic attitudes. Based on the responses that they collected, Adorno et al. identified those items on the potential for fascism measure that were most strongly related to the anti-Semitism and ethnocentrism scores. This enabled them to draw together a final version of the F-scale containing those items that best predicted a person's anti-Semitism and ethnocentrism score. The F-scale, which measured the potential for fascism, lay at the core of the authoritarian personality.

Table 1.2 Examples from the Potential for Fascism scale (or F-scale) devised for the authoritarian personality study

No insult to our honor should ever go unpunished.
Obedience and respect for authority are the most important virtues children should learn.
Books and movies ought not to deal so much with the sordid and seamy side of life; they ought to concentrate on themes that are entertaining or uplifting.

Source: Adorno et al., 1950, pp. 226–7

The authors of the study were eager to make it clear, however, that what the F-scale was measuring was the *potential* for fascism, not fascism itself. After all, they were not conducting research on active members of a fascist movement or German Nazis, but white, middle-class Americans from around San Francisco. What they wanted to tap into, therefore, are the kinds of personality characteristics that predispose individuals to become seduced by fascist ideology. The investigators argued that the score on the F-scale can determine the extent to which a participant exhibits personality characteristics – namely authoritarianism – that would make them likely to support oppression and violence towards minority groups.

2.2 Interpreting the scales: composing an authoritarian personality

Adorno et al. argued that participants scoring highly on the F-scale were revealing an authoritarian personality; and, in contrast, those with low scores were revealing a non-authoritarian, more liberal, personality. The authoritarian personality was described as consisting of nine characteristics. These included things such as deference to authority, obedience to rules, rigid adherence to 'traditional' values, the rejection of anything unconventional, rigid thinking and hostility to others, especially those appearing weaker in some way. Also linked to authoritarianism were some less obvious characteristics. For instance, people with an authoritarian personality tend to perceive the outside world as threatening, and they are said to be more superstitious, and overly concerned with sexual propriety.

According to Adorno et al. (1950, p. 228), these characteristics were interconnected and formed a 'single … more or less enduring structure in the person'. This 'structure' – the authoritarian personality – provides the framework through which some people make sense of the world and through which their actions are shaped. More importantly, it predisposes individuals to prejudice, and makes them receptive to anti-democratic, fascist and right-wing ideologies.

Crucially, Adorno et al. were not saying that everyone who scored highly on the authoritarian personality scale *was* a fascist; or that everyone with an authoritarian personality *would* commit violent acts against others in the name of political ideals. Rather, they were saying that, where people high in authoritarian characteristics found themselves in a society that tolerated prejudice towards weaker others, they would be the ones most likely to endorse those prejudiced ideas, be swayed by arguments that suggested the ideas were reasonable, and then act on them. So authoritarianism was a predisposition for fascism which would become realised if the political climate of the day made right-wing ideologies socially acceptable.

2.3 Explaining the causes of 'authoritarianism'

So far, you have read about the way Adorno et al. set out to discover people's attitudes, and used these to say something about their personalities. However, you may also have noticed that while the scales were able to *measure* authoritarianism and locate people on a range from 'low in authoritarian tendencies' to 'high in authoritarian tendencies', these measures do not explain *where* the differences come from. They do not tell us why some people present these characteristics suggesting an authoritarian personality, and others do not. So, where does an authoritarian personality come from?

To answer this question, Adorno et al. decided they needed a more in-depth, individual approach. In the first phase of the study, in which they

Interview
A 'conversation with a purpose', designed to gather in-depth information from research participants. Interviews may be structured, asking the same questions of all participants, or semi-structured or unstructured, allowing interviewers to adapt questions according to participants' responses.

developed the F-scale and looked at how it is related to prejudice, Adorno et al. administered questionnaires. In the second phase, where they looked for the underlying causes of authoritarianism, they decided to conduct **interviews**. Adorno et al. (1950, p. 291) argued that an interview allows the researcher to ask the participant open questions about 'what he thinks about himself, about his hopes, fears and goals, about his childhood and his parents, about members of the other sex, about people in general'. The interviews therefore offered the participant in the study the necessary 'scope and freedom of expression' (p. 291).

As you can imagine, interviews are much more time-consuming than questionnaires. In the first phase of the study, Adorno et al. administered the questionnaires to more than 2000 respondents. It would have been impossible to interview all of them. Instead, they picked a sample of 150. Roughly half were from those who scored highly on the authoritarianism scale, and half from those who obtained low scores. This gave the researchers two distinct groups to work with so that they could look for patterns of similarities and differences between them. These 150 participants were interviewed in depth to find out *why* they had or had not developed an authoritarian personality. As Adorno and colleagues put it, they wanted to find out the following:

> Does the family constellation differ in the typical prejudiced home as compared with the typical unprejudiced home? Do prejudiced individuals tend to have different images of their parents than do unprejudiced ones? How does the handling of discipline vary in this respect? Do prejudiced and unprejudiced individuals differ in their sex life, their way of choosing friends, their values, their general cognitive and emotional approach to life?
>
> (Adorno et al., 1950, pp. 291–2)

The interviews lasted an average of two hours each. They covered wide-ranging questions. Participants were asked about their work, income and religion, and questioned about politics and attitudes to minority groups. But the questions that interested the researchers most were those about the participants' families, their early childhoods, and their sexual and social relationships. This was because the researchers were heavily influenced by psychoanalysis. Psychoanalytic theory argues that the importance of childhood and parenting practices is crucial to the way personality develops. Moreover, the relationship styles developed in early childhood become the template for adult relationships too. Therefore, the research team set out to explore connections between the adult scores on authoritarian personality scales and information gleaned from interviews about early childhood relationships.

By comparing the interview data from the two groups, Adorno et al. observed that respondents who scored highly on authoritarianism tended to report growing up in stricter family environments, compared with those who exhibited low authoritarianism. They were also more likely to report having parents (or other primary caregivers) who had been harsher disciplinarians, who demanded obedience, and who were quick to punish infractions. Adorno and colleagues argued that, in response to this harsher upbringing, children developed feelings of both love and hate towards their strict parents. How and why this happened was explained in terms of the psychoanalytic theory. The researchers argued that children experienced a deep desire to please much-loved parents; but the strict and quick discipline they received also induced a hatred and resentment towards the disciplining parent. This tension between simultaneous love and hate produced strong and conflicting emotions in children, which were both psychically uncomfortable to bear and difficult to reconcile. As a consequence, the feelings of hate for the parents were repressed; that is, buried in the unconscious. The outcome of this process is that the child was left idealising and revering the harsh parent. Crucially, however, Adorno et al. argued that the feelings of anger and hostility, although hidden away in the unconscious, continued to have influence. They were displaced on to others – especially those whom it was 'safer' or easier to hate and despise – in other words, anyone who was seen as weaker and more vulnerable than the self.

Figure 1.6 Roots of authoritarianism?

Perhaps you can see the way this argument is going? Children of strict authoritarian parents, in order to deal with their environment, underwent a number of unconscious processes which resulted in their idealising the authority figures that were their parents, and redirecting hatred, fear and aggression to weaker others. This, according to the way Adorno et al. interpreted psychoanalytic theory, became the enduring, albeit unconscious, pattern for organising their future *adult* relationships too. Authority is to be revered and anyone perceived as weaker, or unconventional, could become the target for hate and aggression.

Box 1.1   Why do it this way?

Adorno et al. (1950) used a mixture of methods, using both scale measures and in-depth interviews. The scales allowed the researchers to test large numbers of people quickly and systematically and the questions could all be presented in the same way to all participants. Then, scoring responses along a numerical scale allowed the researchers to transform a complex series of questions about beliefs and attitudes into a single numerical score. The fact that this method involved some kind of measurement means that the data collected was **quantitative data**. Transforming people's responses into scores (i.e. numbers) made it possible to make direct comparisons with others' scores.

The interviews, on the other hand, allowed the researchers to collect much 'richer' data. The scales had constrained participants to responding only to those items presented by the researchers, and limited them to simple indications of levels of agreement or disagreement. In contrast, the interviews allowed participants to present, in their own words, their life histories, their experiences, their own ideas and thoughts. Data collected in this way is referred to as **qualitative data**.

The two different methods used by Adorno et al. reflected the two traditions in psychology that influenced the researchers. One was psychoanalysis, which uses clinical interviews and free-flowing conversation as a way of investigating the human mind, and the other was the approach to studying personality, which focuses on measurement and quantification.

Quantitative data
Data that can be measured, counted, or expressed in numerical terms, for example, scores, ratings or percentages.

Qualitative data
Data that is not in numerical form. There are different kinds of qualitative data, for instance interview material, written text such as newspaper articles, or diaries.

Summary

- Adorno et al. used a series of questionnaires to measure attitudes to Jews, minority groups and conservative beliefs, and the potential for fascism.
- The researchers also used interviews informed by psychoanalytic theory to identify the causes of these authoritarian personalities.
- Adorno et al. argued that harsh discipline in early childhood caused children to unconsciously project feelings of hate onto people different from themselves, and this became the template for their adult relationships.

Work out why
Nazis r bad

Dissocial
Personality

Hitler
Communism
P. 48
Rokeach
Milgram
Define Authoritarianism
Blood & Honour
Combat 18

3   Exercising caution: evaluating the 'authoritarian personality' study

The authoritarian personality study has had tremendous impact since its publication in 1950. Over 2000 articles were published in response in the first forty years alone (Meloen, 1991). On the other hand, the idea of the authoritarian personality has been subject to sustained criticism. This criticism takes two main forms: a critique of the methods Adorno et al. used, and a critique of their interpretations of the data. I will now examine these in turn.

3.1 Focusing on method: the questionnaires

The first of the main criticisms of Adorno et al.'s method centres on the construction of the F-scale. Psychologists who have used questionnaires and scales to measure attitudes and personality have uncovered something called the **acquiescence response bias**. They found that participants can show a tendency to agree with statements presented in attitude scales, regardless of the topic. There is, in other words, an inclination, among some people, to simply 'go along' with the ideas expressed in the questionnaire items. The possibility that people may exhibit an acquiescence response bias is sufficiently well established that it is now a major concern for the way questionnaires are constructed.

Acquiescence response bias
A tendency to agree with statements presented in scales, regardless of content.

Why is acquiescence a problem for scale construction? How is it relevant to Adorno et al.'s study? Recall that the F-scale was designed by the authors so that all the statements run in the same direction. If you look back at examples in Table 1.2, you will see that each statement is worded in such a way that agreement always points towards authoritarianism. Because of the acquiescence response bias, it is impossible to determine, from looking at the scores, if participants who scored highly on the scale really are particularly authoritarian, or whether they are simply the sort of people who agree to any statement encountered in questionnaires. Therefore, it cannot be ascertained for sure whether the scale in fact measures what Adorno et al. assumed that it measures, namely authoritarianism.

Box 1.2   Acquiescence response and the problem of bias

Questionnaires have been popular in psychology and the social sciences more generally partly because they are easy to administer to a large number of people, they can generate a great amount of data relatively quickly, and they are relatively inexpensive. However, none of this is much use if the questionnaire is not well constructed in the first place. Any bias resulting from the way a questionnaire is constructed undermines the conclusions that can be drawn from it. The F-scale underpinning the authoritarian personality study has been criticised for eliciting just such a bias: the 'acquiescence response'. This refers to a tendency people have to agree with statements put to them by researchers. Consequently, the extent to which people might really agree with the items in the questionnaire may be artificially inflated by the acquiescence response.

This has serious implications for the F-scale. Participants were asked to complete the scale by saying to what extent they agreed or disagreed with a series of statements. But, on the F-scale, items were all worded in such a way that 'authoritarian' views were always represented by agreement with the content. Are participants indicating agreement with an authoritarian statement because this is actually their opinion? Or are they just going along with the ideas expressed? If there was any 'acquiescence response' in the original F-scale responses it would have biased the results and exaggerated the appearance of commitment to authoritarian ideas.

Activity 1.2

Think for a moment how you might solve the problem outlined in Box 1.2. What could the researchers do to control the possibility that acquiescence responses might bias the scores on the scale? Remember, the problem is that all the items on the scale run in one direction and 'acquiescing' would score the same as 'agreeing' with authoritarian items.

The solution to this problem of acquiescence bias is to include a mix of 'positive' and 'reverse' statements. This means rewording some scale items in such a way that a participant would have to disagree with a statement in order to exhibit authoritarian ideas. Several studies have done just this. In one example, Bernard Bass (1955) reversed half of the items on the F-scale. The column on the left shows some of the original F-scale statements. The column on the right shows the same statements, but this time in the reversed form:

Table 1.3

Examples from the F-scale devised by Adorno et al. (1950)	Examples from Bass's (1955) reversed F-scale
Familiarity breeds contempt.	Familiarity does not breed contempt.
No weakness or difficulty can hold us back if we have enough will power.	Weaknesses and difficulties can hold us back; will power is not enough.
If people would talk less and work more, everybody would be better off.	If people would discuss matters more before acting, everybody would be better off.

On Bass's revised scale, if participants are being consistent in their support for authoritarian ideas, they would agree with the statements on the left, which run in favour of authoritarian ideas; but they would disagree with the statements on the right, which run counter to authoritarian ideas. Any tendency towards an acquiescence response bias has been balanced out across both negative and positive statements.

So, if the responses overall continue to show support for authoritarian ideas, investigators can be more confident that they have identified a pattern in participants' thinking rather than simply a tendency to 'go along'.

As Table 1.3 shows, the acquiescence response bias can be avoided if statements that run in different directions are included, within the same scale. This has since become established practice in psychology. In the case of authoritarian personality, this means that the F-scale would include some statements that are worded in such a way that *disagreement* points to authoritarianism. Several subsequent studies did precisely this and found that once the effect of the acquiescence bias is removed, participants tend to score lower on the F-scale, and therefore exhibit fewer specifically authoritarian tendencies (Christie, 1991). Nevertheless, many of these later studies continued to find substantial support for the idea of authoritarianism, and authoritarian personality, although these tendencies were less pronounced than Adorno et al. originally thought. So, while the acquiescence response bias clearly influenced Adorno et al.'s findings, it did not completely invalidate the idea of authoritarian personality.

3.2 Focusing on method: the interviews

A second criticism of the authoritarian personality study refers to the interviews conducted by Adorno et al. in the second stage of the study. Robert Rosenthal (1966) raised the concern that the researchers' findings were affected by **confirmatory bias**. Confirmatory bias refers to the way in which researchers can unintentionally (or otherwise) shape the outcomes of their study to match the expectations they had at the start. Remember that the interviews were conducted with two sets of respondents: one group was selected because they scored highly on the authoritarianism scale, with the second consisting of participants who obtained low scores. The methodological concern raised by Rosenthal (1966) and indeed by others is that researchers who conducted the interviews knew, for each and every interviewee, whether they belonged to the high-scoring or low-scoring group. What is more, they knew the basic hypothesis of the research; that is, the types of difference that Adorno et al. *expected* to find. This knowledge may have affected, even if only inadvertently, the content of the interview and the interpretation of what the participants said. Note that there is no suggestion here that Adorno et al. sought to fix the results of their findings. The confirmatory bias often takes a very subtle form, and occurs without the researcher's conscious intent. This is why it is common practice today to introduce what are known as **double blind** procedures. This means that both the interviewer and the interviewee would be unaware of (or be 'blind' to) both the hypothesis of the study and which group the interviewee belongs to. That way, the results could not be affected by the interviewer's (or the interviewee's) pre-existing knowledge of, or assumptions about, the study.

Confirmatory bias
A tendency to pay most attention to those features of a phenomenon that appear to confirm prior expectations.

Double blind
A research design where neither the participants nor the investigator know which group the participants belong to, thus reducing the risk of bias in measures and interpretations.

3.3 Authoritarianism as personality?

Criticism of Adorno et al.'s study was not limited to methodological issues. There were those who questioned whether the phenomenon that the authors of the study sought to identify, measure and explain is an enduring feature of personality at all. Others challenged the assumption that the authoritarian personality is useful in shedding light on the type of behaviour that led Adorno et al. to embark on their research in the first place.

Let's look at the second criticism first, before returning to the first one in Section 4. If authoritarianism was the main cause of the events in Nazi Germany between 1933 and 1945, then it means that there was a higher prevalence of authoritarian personalities in Germany compared with other countries where Nazism did not develop. Given that the authoritarian personality was researched after the end of the war, this proposition could not be tested directly. However, Thomas Pettigrew (1958) conducted a study in which he explored the levels of authoritarian personality in South Africa and in different parts of the USA. He wanted to see if there was a difference in levels of authoritarianism between: apartheid South Africa, where racist policies permeated every level of society; the southern USA where the policy of segregation was still in place; and the northern USA where racial discrimination was less prominent. If Adorno and colleagues were right, and prejudice within a society can be accounted for by authoritarianism among the population, then there should be differences between the three contexts. What did the study reveal? Pettigrew found that, while participants in the southern USA and South Africa were more racist than their counterparts in the northern parts of the USA, authoritarian personality levels, as measured by the F-scale, were similar across the three groups. In each context, only around 10 to 15 per cent of the population could be described as having an 'authoritarian personality'. So, there was little evidence of a link between the prevalence of authoritarian personalities and actual levels of prejudice within a society (Duckitt, 1989). Authoritarianism alone was not sufficient to account for the differences in prejudice and the levels of support for racial discrimination.

Figure 1.7 Racial segregation in South Africa and the American South in the 1950s

This finding is important because it suggested that the prevalence of high authoritarianism or potential for fascism as measured by the F-scale is not necessary to produce fascist movements or sustain racist regimes or political cultures. Pettigrew's research appears to suggest that the potential for fascism exists as a personality characteristic in every society, and only in a minority of cases. But how then does fascism become a *mass* movement? When Hitler came to power in 1933, he attracted nearly 44 per cent of the popular vote. Even if it could be assumed that all 10–15 per cent of the German population who were authoritarian voted for Hitler, this only accounts for one-third of his overall support, and means that two-thirds of his supporters were not authoritarian (Billig, 1978). There was clearly something above and beyond authoritarianism that accounts for the support which existed in Germany in the 1930s for a fascist political party, its programme and its leader.

A related criticism has been directed at the psychoanalytic interpretation of the causes of authoritarianism. According to the original study, the reasons why people act as they do are said to be hidden in the unconscious. Crucially, because the processes underpinning authoritarianism are unconscious, people are prevented from being able to direct them at will, and the ability to exercise choice and agency is limited. Unconscious processes keep individuals fixed in particular kinds of personality, and lead them to repeat the same kinds of behaviour. If this is so, then once formed, authoritarian personalities would tend to remain that way.

There is, however, substantial evidence suggesting that deference to authority, prejudiced thinking and other features of the authoritarian personality fluctuate in any given population. Gerda Lederer (1993), for instance, noted that authoritarian tendencies diminished in Western Germany after the Second World War, when that country began its transition towards democracy. If authoritarian personality is a stable quality, as Adorno et al. suggested, then sudden reductions in authoritarianism would be difficult to account for. Similarly, authoritarianism can vary according to experience: it can increase or diminish in response to specific social events or situations, sometimes even within a short period of time (Minard, 1952; Pettigrew, 1958). An explanation based on the idea of personality – which implies stable predispositions and patterns of behaviour – does not seem to be able to account adequately for such fluctuations.

These criticisms of the authoritarian personality are important for a number of reasons. They all seem to point to the fact that, although Adorno et al. were clearly onto something with the idea of authoritarianism, an authoritarian personality appeared to be neither necessary nor sufficient for explaining prejudice, discrimination or violence towards minorities. Evidently, social environment, cultural norms and political context all have a key role to play. Remember, however, that Adorno et al. argued from the outset that authoritarian personality was a predisposition, something that is likely to manifest itself only in certain socio-economic and political conditions. So they were aware of the dynamic interplay between personality and context, but prioritised personality. The balance of evidence appears to suggest, however, that it is other factors, above and beyond personality, which are the more important determinants of prejudice.

The criticisms of the authoritarian personality study should not detract from its importance in the history of psychology. While echoing many of these criticisms, Michael Billig (1978, p. 36) referred to the work of Adorno et al. as 'the single most important contribution to the psychology of fascism' and, more importantly, as 'a major landmark in the history of psychology'. This is because of the study's sheer scope, ambition and scale, and the fact that it sought to bridge the gulf that separated the psychoanalytic tradition and the quantitative approaches to personality (see Box 1.1). In that sense, Adorno et al. were pioneers, keen to explain what they considered to be the most destructive phenomenon in the history of the world. Therefore, they should be evaluated on the basis not only of how much they got right, but of how much they inspired others to think about prejudice and develop new theories about the phenomenon they wanted to understand.

Summary

- The authoritarian personality study has been criticised both for the methods used and for the interpretations put on the results.

- Subsequent research that addressed the issue of the acquiescence response bias in the design of the F-scale found that authoritarianism is a valid phenomenon and that some individuals display characteristics associated with authoritarian personality.

- Confirmatory bias was identified as a potential problem during the interviews because the interviewers knew participants' scores from the surveys.

- Later research questioned whether authoritarian personality is either necessary or sufficient to explain events such as those in Nazi Germany.

4   Revivals and revisions of the authoritarian personality

Soon after Adorno et al. completed their study, American society, and the Western world more generally, found itself fighting another war, this time a cold war with the communist Soviet Union. While Adorno et al. had believed that fascism posed the greatest threat to society, others argued that the threat of a possible nuclear war involving the USA and the Soviet Union meant that *communism* posed the greater threat. So, from a psychological perspective, authoritarianism needed to be explained when it appeared both on the right of the political spectrum (linked with racism, anti-Semitism and conservative attitudes), and also on the left, which was seen as equally 'authoritarian', inflexible and undemocratic, but not 'fascist' in the conventional sense.

Figure 1.8 Communist Soviet Union: a new threat to the Western world

To address this issue, Milton Rokeach (1960) reconceptualised the idea of 'potential for fascism' (as measured by the F-scale) as a more general authoritarianism termed 'dogmatism', a concept which could encompass both right-wing conservatism and left-wing communism. More importantly, Rokeach rejected the psychoanalytic explanation, originally

Cognitive style
The habitual way a person processes information.

proposed by Adorno et al. He argued that the various features of authoritarianism were the product not of unconscious processes but of a distinct **cognitive style**, a particular way of structuring and processing information. Those high in authoritarianism, or dogmatism, were said to be closed-minded. This means that they were less able to evaluate new information and more likely to maintain contradictory beliefs depending on the authority behind the message. In other words, they tended to look at the source of the message rather than its logic or plausibility. So, if an authority figure presented inconsistent information it would be endorsed purely because of the status of that figure. In contrast, those low in authoritarianism/dogmatism were more open-minded, meaning they would be more able to evaluate information independently, recognise inconsistencies, and be more swayed by the content of the message rather than the authority of the source. In essence, open and closed cognitive styles were characterised by 'the ability (or inability) to discriminate substantive information from information about the source, and to assess the two separately' (Rokeach, 1960, p. 60). Crucially, dogmatism was seen as a process of cognitive function – of information processing and reasoning – rather than as anything to do with personality, unconscious processes or political ideologies.

Rokeach's approach had the advantage of extending exploration of extremes of prejudice and hatred to other dogmas. However, it was still essentially a personality theory, in that it located the roots of dogmatism within the individual and their relatively stable cognitive style. For many critics, though, this emphasis on personality did not address the main shortcoming of the Adorno et al. study, namely the issue of the interplay between the person and the context.

4.1 Altemeyer and right-wing authoritarianism

By the mid 1960s research into authoritarianism had begun to wane. By that time, researchers were looking beyond the concepts of an authoritarian personality for explanations of prejudice. Also, research by Stanley Milgram, which you will read about in Chapter 2, showed that tendencies to engage in acts of mass violence of the kind that Adorno et al. sought to explain might not be attributable to personality at all. Instead, it might be more to do with the situation in which people find themselves.

However, the idea of authoritarianism has not been completely superseded by other explanations and approaches. Although there were clear problems with the original study, there were those who were reluctant to abandon the concept altogether. There were aspects of the idea of 'authoritarianism' that were worth retaining.

The person most responsible for rekindling the interest in authoritarianism in recent decades is Bob Altemeyer, who revised and updated Adorno et al.'s original work. Like Adorno et al., Altemeyer was interested only in authoritarianism on the right. Altemeyer (1981) argued, however, that the definition of authoritarianism in the work of Adorno and colleagues was too broad. As you will remember, the original study proposed that authoritarianism consisted of a wide range of characteristics, including things like superstition, interest in sexual propriety, etc. Altemeyer argued that it is possible for someone to be superstitious without being authoritarian, just as someone could be authoritarian without being overly concerned about sexual behaviour.

Altemeyer went on to revise the original F-scale and develop his own measure – the right-wing authoritarianism scale. This new and updated measure addressed the methodological flaws of the original scale, balancing positive and reversed items. In addition, Altemeyer's definition of authoritarianism was much simpler, consisting of just three characteristics:

- *authoritarian submission*, which means deference to authority, such as government officials and religious leaders
- *authoritarian aggression*, which means supporting extreme action against anyone who deviates from what is considered 'normal'
- *conventionalism*, which means a preference for established ideas and practices and a resistance to anything that might appear new or different.

Altemeyer found that people who scored highly on the right-wing authoritarianism scale tended to be conservative, favour conventional gender roles, support harsh punishment for criminals, and express hostility to homosexuality and prejudice against people from groups other than their own. In that sense, the similarities between right-wing authoritarianism and the original idea about authoritarian personality are clear. However, there is a key difference in the way the two studies explain the causes of authoritarianism. Like Rokeach (1960), Altemeyer rejected the psychoanalytic explanation of authoritarianism which emphasised the role of the unconscious. Instead, Altemeyer proposed an explanation based on the idea of 'social learning'. You will read more about social learning in Chapter 3. For the time being, it is sufficient to know that for Altemeyer the attitudes revealed on the right-wing authoritarianism scale were reflections of values observed and learned in childhood from strongly disciplinarian parents. No unconscious processes were involved. Instead, children adopted certain patterns of behaviour from their parents, including placing a high value on obedience to authority and displaying intolerance and aggression towards anyone and anything unconventional. More importantly, Altemeyer does not see right-wing authoritarianism as fixed in a person's personality, but more as a cluster of attitudes that are learned in childhood. Also, he argued that how, where and when these attitudes – that is, right-wing authoritarianism – will be demonstrated depends on the context and situational factors that bring them to the surface.

Activity 1.3

Pause for a moment and think again about the work of Rokeach and Altemeyer. How do their ideas differ from those of Adorno et al.? Are there any similarities in the way in which they approached their research question?

An important similarity is that, just as in the original study by Adorno et al. (1950), subsequent research also took a two-pronged approach. Both Rokeach and Altemeyer sought to *measure* the specific aspect of personality underpinning authoritarianism and then to *explain* why some people are more or less authoritarian or, in the case of Rokeach, 'dogmatic'. You probably noticed also that a major difference between the three is in the domain of the *explanation*. Adorno favoured the psychoanalytic explanation, focusing on what happens in the unconscious. Rokeach interpreted 'dogmatism' as a reflection of a specific way of processing information. Altemeyer adopted a social learning approach. What this demonstrates is that these three researchers have been influenced by different theories, and that, as is often the case in psychology, the same problem can be approached from different perspectives.

However, all three studies also share common shortcomings. They are all, ultimately, more descriptive than explanatory (Jones, 2002). They describe what authoritarianism looks like, but have all struggled to explain clearly and convincingly where it comes from. In fact, evidence to support the social learning, cognitive style or psychoanalytic explanations has been at best circumstantial.

Also, none of the three explanations has been able to adequately explain the key question that underlies much of the discussion in Part 1 of the book. What is the relative importance of personality in determining human behaviour, and how important are other factors, such as the situation or a person's social environment? While the importance of these other factors is acknowledged in the accounts of authoritarianism (although often indirectly), how they interact with personality is seldom addressed in any detailed way.

Summary

- Rokeach suggested that both right- and left-wing authoritarianism were based on a closed-minded cognitive style, rather than the unconscious.

- In the 1980s, Altemeyer devised a 'right-wing authoritarian scale' and offered a revised description of the authoritarian personality that he attributed to social learning.

- Critics argue that these studies overemphasise personality explanations for behaviour and that more attention should be given to the context in which behaviour occurs.

5   Final thoughts

The chapter has posed the question: to what extent could the extreme Nazi violence towards European Jews in the Second World War be explained in terms of a particular personality type? You read about the pioneering work of Adorno et al., which sought to measure and explain personality characteristics that predispose individuals to become part of far-right, fascist movements. You also read about subsequent research that moved away from personality-based explanations and also broadened Adorno et al.'s work to cover left-wing as well as right-wing authoritarianism.

So, can the causes of mass violence be understood in terms of personal characteristics of the perpetrators? While the work on authoritarianism goes some way to explaining the tendency in some people to support totalitarian political ideologies, the authoritarian personality has been shown to be neither a sufficient nor a necessary factor in determining whether someone will take part in violence. Although Adorno et al.'s study has been criticised both on methodological grounds and for its emphasis on personality, it has nevertheless been influential in highlighting the need for psychology to investigate phenomena such as authoritarianism, fascism and genocide.

Although Adorno et al. were interested in explaining the root causes of Nazi atrocities, their work has a distinct contemporary relevance. The defeat of the Nazis in 1945 did not bring an end to fascist ideology. Today, almost seventy years later, there are still extremist neo-Nazi groups – the skinheads, Blood & Honour, Combat 18 and others – who promote the ideas of racial superiority and violence towards minority groups. At the time of writing, a number of European countries have witnessed a rise in the popularity of right-wing political parties who espouse extremist views and maintain links with violent neo-Nazi groups. In the UK, the British National Party, a party whose leaders promote racist, anti-Semitic and homophobic views, won almost a million votes at the 2009 European elections and won three seats in the European Parliament. Explaining fascism, or what Adorno et al. called authoritarianism, is therefore something that remains of relevance today.

Figure 1.9 Fascism today

The key issue, however, is whether the explanation for fascism should be sought, as Adorno et al. suggested, in personality. In many ways their attempt at explaining fascism was a product of the historical time that they inhabited. Evidence of the Holocaust that emerged after the war was so shocking that people wanted to believe that the Nazi perpetrators were quite different from anyone else; that they were particular kinds of people with profoundly flawed personalities. But a personality explanation has been shown to be problematic. Personality is understood to be quite a stable property, in which case personality theories of prejudice struggle to account for the rapid rise in anti-Semitism after Hitler came to power in Germany, and the reduced levels after the war.

All of the studies referred to in this chapter tried to find ways to measure attitudes to authority. The results were then interpreted in psychoanalytic terms, in terms of how information is processed, or by reference to socially learned attitudes and patterns of behaviour. However, scoring highly on a particular scale does not mean that individuals will go on to act in particular ways. Pettigrew showed that individuals with the same apparent traits might behave differently depending on the culture in which they live, so responses are about opportunity and cultural values as well as about the individual.

[Handwritten margin notes:] CULTURE — Personality / Situational / Personality / Situational. UPBRINGING — Hitler / Commander / Soldier — SITUATION²

Also, authoritarianism poses a problem in society as part of a group phenomenon. It manifests itself in far-right movements, religious cults, neo-Nazi groups, radical political parties, etc., many of which continue to exercise influence in contemporary society. Authoritarian *individuals* are therefore much less of a concern than authoritarian *movements* or groups. What this suggests is that a perspective moving away from the individual, towards exploring the context in which authoritarianism appears, and how it is fostered within groups and institutions, might be more fruitful. As Richard Schermerhorn (1970, p. 6), one of the critics of the individualist approach, argues, 'prejudice is a product of situations, historical situations, economic situations, political situations … and not a little demon that emerges in people simply because they are depraved'.

As you have been reading about the authoritarian personality in this chapter you may have thought that it is characterised by a collection of extremely negative traits. Many commentators would agree with you (Oesterreich, 2005). Indeed, the term 'authoritarianism' is used today not just to describe various right-wing extremist groups such as the neo-Nazis or the skinheads but also as a term of insult. The traits associated with authoritarianism appear to be so negative that the temptation is to imagine that 'authoritarians' are always other people, never 'us'. It would be comforting to suppose that ordinary people were not like these extraordinary authoritarians, the ones who are susceptible to obeying the extreme demands of authority figures. However, psychological research has shown us that, in certain circumstances, obedience to the punitive demands of authority figures is a feature of quite ordinary people. The next chapter will take up this story.

Summary

- Fascism and right-wing extremism are still present in most Western societies, which means that the study of authoritarianism has a contemporary relevance.
- Any explanation of authoritarianism needs to take into account historical, political and ideological factors and not just those located within the individual.

References

Adorno, T.W., Frenkel-Brunswik, E., Levinson, D.J. and Sanford, R.N. (1950) *The Authoritarian Personality*, New York, NY, Harper.

Altemeyer, B. (1996) *The Authoritarian Specter*, Cambridge, MA, Harvard University Press.

Altemeyer, B. (1981) *Right-wing Authoritarianism*, Winnipeg, University of Manitoba Press.

Bass, B.M. (1955) 'Authoritarianism or acquiescence', *Journal of Abnormal and Social Psychology*, vol. 51, no. 3, pp. 616–23.

Billig, M. (1978) *Fascists: A Social Psychological View of the National Front*, London, Harcourt Brace Jovanovich.

Christie, R. (1991) 'Authoritarianism and related constructs' in Robinson, J.P., Shaver P.R. and Wrightsman L.S. (eds) *Measures of Personality and Social Psychological Attitudes*, San Diego, CA, Academic Press.

Costa, P.T. and McCrae, R.R. (1992) *NEO PI-R Professional Manual*, Odessa, FL, Psychological Assessment Resources.

Duckitt, J. (1989) 'Authoritarianism and group identification: a new view of an old construct.' *Political Psychology*, vol. 10, no. 1, pp. 63–84.

Eysenck, H.J. (1967) *The Biological Basis of Personality*, Springfield, IL, Thomas.

Goldberg, L.R. (1981) 'Language and individual differences: the search for universals in personality lexicons' in Wheeler, L. (ed.) *Review of Personality and Social Psychology*, vol. 2, London, Sage.

Jones, M. (2002) *Social Psychology of Prejudice*, Upper Saddle River, NJ, Pearson Education.

Lederer, G. (1993) 'Authoritarianism in German adolescents' in Stone, W.F., Lederer, G. and Christie, R. (eds) *Strength and Weakness*, New York, NY, Springer.

Meloen, J.D. (1991) 'The fortieth anniversary of "The Authoritarian Personality"', *Politics and the Individual*, vol. 1, no. 1, pp. 119–27.

Minard, R.D. (1952) 'Race relations in the Pocahontas coal field', *Journal of Social Issues*, vol. 8, no. 1, pp. 29–44.

Oesterreich, D. (2005) 'Flight into security: a new approach and measure of the authoritarian personality', *Political Psychology*, vol. 26, no. 2, pp. 275–97.

Pettigrew, T.F. (1958) 'Personality and socio-cultural factors in intergroup attitudes: a cross-national comparison', *Journal of Conflict Resolution*, vol. 2, no. 1, pp. 29–42.

Rokeach, M. (1960) *The Open and Closed Mind*, New York, NY, Basic Books.

Rosenthal, R. (1966) *Experimenter Effects in Behavioural Research*, New York, NY, Appleton-Century-Crofts.

Ross, L. (1977) 'The intuitive psychologist and his shortcomings: distortions in the attribution process' in Berkowitz, L. (ed.) *Advances in Experimental Social Psychology*, vol. 10, New York, NY, Academic Press.

Schermerhorn, R.A. (1970) *Comparative Ethnic Relations*, New York, NY, Random House.

Smith, M.B. (1997) '"The authoritarian personality": A re-review 46 years later', *Political Psychology*, vol. 18, no. 1, pp. 159–63.

Chapter 2
Just following orders?

Philip Banyard

Contents

Aims and objectives

By the end of this chapter you should be able to:

- describe the research of Stanley Milgram on obedience
- outline some of the ethical challenges psychologists encounter when devising studies on human behaviour
- discuss the relative importance of situational influences on human behaviour
- appreciate how Milgram's studies have informed the debate on the phenomenon of obedience, and social behaviour more generally.

1 Introduction

Figure 2.1 Doing what is expected: the power of the situation

Activity 2.1

Take a closer look at the three photographs in Figure 2.1 and describe
what you see. All three photographs show people engaged in some sort
of action. The first shows soldiers in battle, who are charging having
been instructed to do so by an officer. The second image is from a
football match and shows Nottingham Forest supporters chanting and
waving their arms in a uniform fashion. The third, taken in China, shows

a group of cyclists waiting for the signal from a traffic warden before crossing a junction. What do you think accounts for the behaviour of these individuals? What is it about being in the military that makes people willing to put themselves in harm's way, or take the lives of others, just because someone else issues an order? Do you think that football fans behave in the way shown here when watching the game at home on the TV? What is it about the traffic wardens that makes people listen to their commands and obey?

In all three situations depicted in the photographs, people appear to know what is expected of them in the situation in which they find themselves, and are behaving accordingly. This is not in itself surprising. Even in the most mundane situations in everyday life, people seem to realise that situations, and the presence of others, impose different demands on their conduct. For example, if they think that someone can see them, most people behave differently from how they behave if they are alone. Schoolchildren's behaviour will change, often instantly and in a dramatic way, as soon as the teacher leaves the classroom. There are also places, such as airports, where people, regardless of their personality characteristics or political views, appear to be especially ready to accept unquestioningly the authority of uniformed personnel and follow instructions to take off their shoes, open their bags, be searched, etc.

Obedience
Complying with the demands of others, usually those in positions of authority.

In Chapter 1 you learned about the role that personality plays in determining behaviour. What the examples in the previous paragraph appear to suggest is that people's actions can be accounted for by other factors, including the situation in which they find themselves, and who else is present. In this chapter I explore the issue of situational influence in more detail, using as an example the work on **obedience** to authority by Stanley Milgram. There are very few studies in psychology that demonstrate, in such a dramatic and disturbing way, the power of the situation.

1.1 Early influences

Stanley Milgram was born in New York City in 1933 to working-class Jewish parents who had emigrated to the USA from Europe. His first degree was in political science but after a crash course in psychology he started a doctorate in psychology at Harvard University in 1954. In 1961 Milgram began work on a study that would define social psychology for the next fifty years. The key question that Milgram wanted to explore is what makes people do evil things. He devised a unique task, an experiment, that placed people in a **moral dilemma** where they had to choose between doing what they were told and doing the 'right thing'. The reason his research became so well known is that it held up a mirror for people to see themselves in, and the image was not as nice as they expected.

Moral dilemma
A situation in which each possible course of action breaches some otherwise binding moral principle.

Figure 2.2   Stanley Milgram (1933 1984)

Just like Adorno et al.'s (1950) study, Milgram's work was inspired by the big moral question in the middle of the twentieth century, namely how the horrors of the Second World War could have happened and how they could be prevented in the future. The question concerned the behaviour of the Nazis and their allies who carried out the mass slaughter throughout Europe. An important aspect of the crimes committed by the Nazis was their systematic nature. Millions of victims of Nazism perished in large concentration camps which were essentially factories of death. How could people go about carrying out the systematic murder of thousands of other human beings? Given that among the victims of Nazism were over six million European Jews, this was a personal question as well as a scientific one for Milgram, who was very conscious of his Jewish heritage. In a letter from France to a school friend he wrote:

> My true spiritual home is Central Europe. … I should have been born into the German-speaking Jewish community of Prague in 1922 and died in a gas chamber some twenty years later. How I came to be born in the Bronx Hospital I'll never quite understand.

> (Quoted in Blass, 2009, p. 39)

Who were the people who carried out the atrocities against Jews in concentration camps? Were they 'monsters'? A widespread assumption at the time was that those behind the Holocaust must have been different from most of humanity, otherwise the world would be full of evil. The work of Adorno and others, which you read about in Chapter 1, reflected this view: the Nazis, it was assumed, had a distinct, identifiable and measurable personality, one that was rooted in childhood development. The implication of this assumption was that people who carried out those atrocities, who have an authoritarian personality, were somehow 'different'. This was in many ways a comforting explanation as it implied that the inclination towards such evil acts was limited to a small majority of the population: those who would score high on the 'F-scale'.

1.2   Adolf Eichmann and the banality of evil

At the time of Milgram's studies a trial was taking place in Jerusalem of one of the Nazi leaders involved in the Holocaust. Adolf Eichmann had been part of this project from the beginning, and in 1942 he was given the job of transportation administrator, which put him in charge of all the trains that carried Jews from around occupied Europe to a small number of death camps in Poland. After the war, Eichmann fled to Argentina where he was captured in 1960, and a year later he was put on trial in Israel. He was found guilty and hanged.

The question that Milgram asked, and that also became the centre of Eichmann's trial, concerned what sort of person could carry out such evil actions. The analysis of the trial that interested Milgram was the writing by Hannah Arendt, a well-known philosopher and writer who reported on the trial for *The New Yorker*. In her reports, Arendt focused on how ordinary Eichmann appeared to be. She had expected the person who carried out monstrous acts to look and behave like a monster, but the reality, as observed by her, was very far from this. Eichmann came across as a bland, simple and passionless man – not a monster at all but an ordinary, petty bureaucrat who claimed to have been 'doing his job', which in his case involved killing hundreds of thousands of people. This observation led Arendt (1963) to refer to the 'banality of evil'. Evil acts, she argued, do not require people to be intrinsically 'evil'. All that is needed is for people to be prepared to carry out orders, and obey authority. Interestingly, this was the essence of Eichmann's defence: he claimed that he was just following orders.

Figure 2.3   Adolf Eichmann: an evil man or an efficient bureaucrat who was merely 'following orders'?

Since Arendt's reports were published as a book, the notion of the 'banality of evil' has received some criticism, especially in relation to Eichmann. It turned out that Arendt attended only the start of the trial, and heard Eichmann and his defence team as they tried to convince the court that he was merely following orders. If she had stayed to witness more of the court case, she would have come to a very different conclusion. As it turned out, Eichmann was not just following orders but was an innovator in ways to transport people to their deaths more efficiently. He had, at times, gone beyond his remit and continued with the slaughter of Jews even after he was ordered by his superiors to stop. He was also aware that other people considered his actions to be wrong, but even when the war was over he failed to show any remorse (Haslam and Reicher, 2008). Eichmann was evidently not an ordinary man. Nevertheless, Milgram was intrigued by Arendt's writing and saw a similarity between the idea of the 'banality of evil' and a phenomenon that he observed in his research in the psychology laboratory at Yale University in Connecticut, USA. The topic of his research was obedience to authority.

Summary

- Behaviour may be influenced by the situation a person finds themselves in, as well as by personality.

- The 'banality of evil' hypothesis suggests that in certain circumstances ordinary people can carry out extraordinary crimes, and that this may have been the case with some Nazi officials.

- Stanley Milgram's research explored obedience to authority.

2   Milgram's obedience study

Milgram was one of the most innovative and productive social psychologists of his generation, who undertook a variety of studies that explored social psychological aspects of everyday life. However, he is largely remembered for one dramatic piece of work – the obedience studies. The best way to get inside this study is to imagine that you are one of the participants taking part in Milgram's experiment. So read on with that in mind.

2.1   The set-up

It's 1961 and you are arriving at the doors of the Psychology Department of the prestigious Yale University in the USA. The reason you are here is that you replied to an advert in the local paper asking for volunteers to take part in a study on memory. The advert (see Figure 2.4) offered a fee plus expenses and said that you would be paid on arrival at the laboratory.

As you walk through the doors you are met by a serious-looking man in a laboratory coat who turns out to be the experimenter. He introduces you to a genial middle-aged man who is described as a fellow volunteer. The experimenter explains that the study will involve one of the volunteers taking on the role of a 'teacher' and the other taking on the role of a 'learner'. As part of the experiment, the 'teacher' will engage the 'learner' in a simple memory task. The 'learner' and the 'teacher' will be in different rooms and will communicate through microphones (see Figure 2.5). The experimenter reveals that the study is designed to investigate the effect of punishment on learning. The 'teacher' will be asked to administer an electric shock to the 'learner' every time the latter makes an incorrect response on the memory task.

To select who will be the 'teacher' and who will be the 'learner', you draw slips of paper. You pick out the 'teacher' slip. You then watch as the 'learner' is strapped into a chair, and you hear the experimenter tell him that 'although the shocks can be extremely painful, they cause no permanent tissue damage'. The experimenter now gives *you* a sample shock of 45 volts to show you what the 'learner' will experience during the study. The shock is unpleasant, but short of being painful.

Public Announcement

WE WILL PAY YOU $4.00 FOR ONE HOUR OF YOUR TIME

Persons Needed for a Study of Memory

*We will pay five hundred New Haven men to help us complete a scientific study of memory and learning. The study is being done at Yale University.

*Each person who participates will be paid $4.00 (plus 50c carfare) for approximately 1 hour's time. We need you for only one hour: there are no further obligations. You may choose the time you would like to come (evenings, weekdays, or weekends).

*No special training, education, or experience is needed. We want:

Factory workers	Businessmen	Construction workers
City employees	Clerks	Salespeople
Laborers	Professional people	White-collar workers
Barbers	Telephone workers	Others

All persons must be between the ages of 20 and 50. High school and college students cannot be used.

*If you meet these qualifications, fill out the coupon below and mail it now to Professor Stanley Milgram, Department of Psychology, Yale University, New Haven. You will be notified later of the specific time and place of the study. We reserve the right to decline any application.

*You will be paid $4.00 (plus 50c carfare) as soon as you arrive at the laboratory.

- -

TO:
PROF. STANLEY MILGRAM, DEPARTMENT OF PSYCHOLOGY, YALE UNIVERSITY, NEW HAVEN, CONN. I want to take part in this study of memory and learning. I am between the ages of 20 and 50. I will be paid $4.00 (plus 50c carfare) if I participate.

NAME (Please Print). . . . .

ADDRESS . . . .

TELEPHONE NO. . . . . Best time to call you . . . .

AGE . . . . OCCUPATION . . . . SEX . . . . . .
CAN YOU COME:

WEEKDAYS . . . . EVENINGS . . . . . . WEEKENDS . . . .

Figure 2.4   The advert used to recruit volunteers for Milgram's study

The experimenter then takes you into the adjacent room and sits you down in front of an impressive-looking apparatus that will be used to administer the shocks (see Figure 2.6).

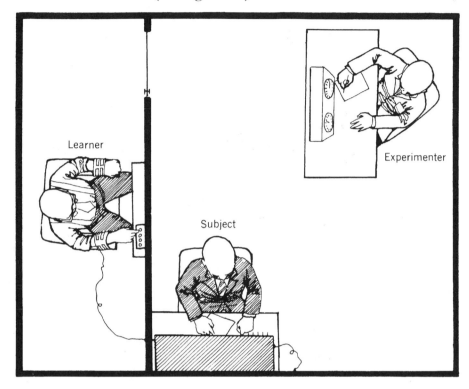

Figure 2.5   The layout of the experiment at the Yale laboratory

The shock generator consists of a row of switches that run in 15 volt increments from 15 volts through to 450 volts. Under the label for each switch are some descriptive words, such as 'slight shock' (15 volts), 'moderate shock' (75 volts), 'strong shock' (135 volts), 'very strong shock' (195 volts), 'intense shock' (225 volts), 'extremely intense shock' (315 volts), 'danger: severe shock' (375 volts) and finally 'XXX' (435 volts). Suddenly, this looks quite serious and you probably hope that you don't have to go very far up the scale. This is especially so given that you received the 45-volt shock, and you know that this was unpleasant enough. The last switch on the shock generator administers an electric impulse ten times as strong!

Figure 2.6   The 'shock generator' used in Milgram's experiment

In the first phase of the experiment, the experimenter asks you, the 'teacher', to read a series of word pairs to the 'learner' who is expected to memorise them (for instance, 'green-grass' , 'blue-sky', 'nice-day'). In the second phase, the test phase, you are asked to read out the first word of the pairs (e.g. 'green'), followed by four possible responses ('grass, hat, ink, apple'). If the 'learner' identifies the paired word correctly, you are to move on to the next word pair on the list. If the answer is wrong you have to tell the 'learner' the correct answer, indicate the level of punishment you are going to give them (starting with 15 volts), and flick the appropriate switch on the shock generator. For every subsequent incorrect answer, you are told to move one switch up the scale of shocks.

The experiment starts. To begin with everything is fine and the 'learner' gets most of the answers right. You have only used the shock generator a couple of times, and at this stage the shocks are mild. Then the 'learner' starts to get the answers wrong and you are moving up the shock scale into the 'strong shock' range. Although you cannot see the 'learner' you can hear him and as the shocks increase he starts to shout out. You have heard him grunt at the low voltage but now he is starting to ask to be let out. At 120 volts you hear him shout out in an agitated tone, complaining that he is in pain, and at 150 volts he asks to be released.

Suddenly, you feel uncomfortable and you decide to stop. The experimenter, the man in the grey coat, objects and asks you to carry on, in spite of the 'learner's' protestations.

Activity 2.2

What do you think you would do in this situation? At what point would you stop? 200 volts? 150 volts? Would you respond to the cries of your fellow volunteer or would you complete the job you agreed to do and carry out the instructions of the experimenter?

How many people do you think would continue to follow the orders? At what point do you think people would stop?

Before Milgram carried out the study, he posed the same questions as in Activity 2.2 to different groups of people, including ordinary members of the public, college students, psychologists and psychiatrists. He asked them to speculate on how far they thought most people would go if asked to administer shocks. Most ordinary people said that participants would generally refuse to administer shock, or at least not go very far beyond the point where the 'learner' experienced pain. Also, most said that participants *should* rebel, and that they should not continue beyond around 150 volts. Among the professional groups, there was widespread agreement that nobody taking part in the study go all the way.

You will be relieved to know that in the actual study carried out by Milgram, no person was hurt during the procedure, and the only actual shock administered was the 45-volt 'tester' given to the 'teacher'. In fact, the whole situation was staged. The role of 'experimenter' was played by a 31-year-old biology teacher. The 'learner', presented as a 'fellow volunteer', was in on the deception and was merely playing the part. In reality, he was a 47-year-old accountant, who was chosen for the role because he appeared mild-mannered and likeable. He was not the sort of person one would want to see hurt. The drawing of slips of paper was fixed to ensure that the 'naive participant' was always cast in the role of the 'teacher', and the 'shock generator' was simply a simulator. The sounds (the moans and cries) that the participants heard were a recording played from the adjacent room. Importantly, however, the deception was so good that participants believed that they were actually administering shocks. So the study presented an ingenious way of discovering how far people would be willing to go, just because a psychological experiment on 'the effects of punishment on learning' demanded it. Most people like to think that they (and people around them) would not go very far. But what happened when Milgram actually placed people in that position?

2.2 The results

In the first instance Milgram conducted the study on a sample of forty participants, all of them male. Each played the role of 'teacher' in the situation described in Section 2.1. Each participant went through the identical experimental procedure: all forty heard the same instructions, encountered the same 'experimenter' and 'learner', heard identical (pre-recorded) cries from the next room. The 'experimenter' in the grey lab coat offered the same words of encouragement. The sessions were filmed and notes were taken by observers looking through an observation mirror.

Figure 2.7   Scenes from the Milgram study

Milgram found that, of the forty participants who took part in the study, all obeyed up to 300 volts, the twentieth switch on the shock generator. This is the point at which the 'learner' was heard screaming: 'I absolutely refuse to answer any more. Get me out of here. You can't hold me here. Get me out. Get me out of here.' However, only five of the forty participants refused to continue beyond this point. Four gave only one more shock before breaking off, with an additional five stopping between 315 volts and 435 volts. But as many as twenty-six continued to the end of the scale and administered the maximum 450 volts. This is despite the fact that, at 330 volts, they had already heard intense and prolonged screaming: 'Let me out of here. Let me out of here. ... Let me out of here. You have no right to hold me here. Let me out! Let me out!' Shocks beyond 330 volts were accompanied by eerie silence. Nevertheless, twenty-six ordinary members of the public from Connecticut administered the maximum shock and continued to do so until the experimenter called a halt to the proceedings.

As well as counting the number of participants who went all the way on the shock generator, Milgram also observed their reactions. Participants who took part in the study generally displayed signs of nervousness and tension. Many were visibly uncomfortable and probably would not have continued had they not heard the experimenter say things like 'Please continue', 'Please carry on', 'It is absolutely essential that you continue' or 'You have no choice; you must go on'. At the end of the study, many of the obedient participants heaved sighs of relief or shook their heads in apparent regret. Some even had laughing fits during the experiment, probably brought on by anxiety. Milgram (1963, p. 375) wrote that 'full-blown, uncontrollable seizures were observed for 3 subjects. On one occasion we observed a seizure so violently convulsive that it was necessary to call a halt to the experiment'. (You may have noticed that in this quote Milgram refers to people who took part in his study as 'subjects'. This was common practice in psychology in the 1960s. Today the word 'participant' is used instead as the word 'subject' is considered demeaning, and lacking in respect towards volunteers on whose participation much of psychological research ultimately depends.)

Do Milgram's findings seem plausible to you? Ordinary members of the public were prepared to administer electric shocks to another person on the mere (albeit persistent) request of a man in a laboratory coat. They did so despite the protests from the 'victim' and continued even after the supposed recipient of the shocks went quiet. Before the study, when Milgram asked his fellow professionals to predict how many participants would refuse to go all the way, they said that all of them would do so. In reality only 35 per cent did. In Milgram's study, the average voltage at which participants stopped shocking the 'learner' was 368 volts Members of the public predicted that people would stop at around 140 volts. This is a remarkable discrepancy. It is therefore not surprising that Milgram's research went on to provoke considerable debate.

Box 2.1 Why do it this way?

Milgram's obedience work is remarkable, not only because of the important questions it sought to explore, but also because it is a fine example of good experimental procedure in social psychology.

The most important feature of any laboratory experiment is its *controlled* nature. Note that every person who took part in Milgram's research underwent an identical experience. All participants received the same instructions, encountered the same individuals (the 'experimenter' and the fellow 'volunteer') and heard identical cries and protestations from the 'learner'. To ensure consistency in the experimental procedure, Milgram even recorded the anguished cries in advance, and played them to participants from a tape.

This equivalence of experience across the forty participants was essential if meaningful comparisons were to be made. It ensured that any difference in behaviour observed in the study could not be attributed, for instance, to the fact that some participants heard louder or more desperate cries than others. For similar reasons, Milgram used the same 'learner' and 'experimenter' with each participant. He wanted to ensure that none of the results could be accounted for by differences in the personality or the demeanour of the confederates.

Another interesting aspect of Milgram's research is that he recruited participants from the general public, using a newspaper advert. At the time (and still now in many psychology departments) participants tended to be recruited mainly from among the student population. However, Milgram was interested in exploring the level of obedience to scientific authority among ordinary members of the public – that is, people with no direct link to the university or research environment – and so he recruited from the general public.

Finally, in Milgram's original study, all forty participants were male. Why do you think this was the case? This was not because Milgram wanted to exclude women from his research. He later conducted further studies in which he explored gender differences in obedience. In the initial study, however, he decided to control for the potential effects of gender on the findings by limiting the sample to men.

2.3   The variations

The findings of Milgram's original study highlighted the phenomenon of obedience, but it could not reveal what it is about the situation that made participants administer potentially lethal shocks to a fellow human being. To address this question Milgram carried out further research in which he introduced subtle variations to the original procedure. By examining the effects of these variations on levels of obedience, he was able to isolate specific aspects of the situation that might influence whether participants obey or not.

By the time Milgram completed his research in 1962 he had processed 800 people through nineteen variations of the original design. For instance, in one variation, Milgram introduced into the proceedings a dialogue about a heart attack. He wanted to see whether alerting the participants to the impact of the shocks on the 'learner's' health might reduce obedience. Note that all other aspects of the original study were preserved. Interestingly, the conversation about the heart attack made no real difference. Twenty six out of the forty participants still continued to 450 volts, although those who stopped did so at a lower voltage with five stopping as soon as the 'learner' asked to be let out. So, the reference to the heart attack made those who disobeyed do so earlier, but it did not prevent the more obedient participants from going all the way.

Milgram also varied the proximity of the 'learner' and 'teacher'. In one variation he put them in the same room, while in another he required the 'teacher' to hold the 'learner's' arm down on a plate to receive the electric shock. This manipulation had a clear effect. Milgram found that the closer you place the 'teacher' to the 'learner', the fewer shocks the 'teacher' is likely to administer. Equally, the further you place the 'learner' away from the 'teacher', the less the impact their pleas are likely to have.

Equally crucial was the presence of the authority figure. In one variation, the 'experimenter' in the grey coat pretended to have to leave the experiment owing to some emergency and was replaced by a person in plain clothes, who was not a scientist. Only 20 per cent of participants went all the way and gave the 'learner' 450-volt shocks. Similar results were obtained when orders were given by phone. The physical presence of an authority figure was therefore crucial.

In another variation Milgram placed two 'experimenters' in the room. One told the participants to continue (as in the original study), while the other told them to stop. In this variation, all the participants stopped giving the shocks very early on. This showed that an absence of a *clear* authority figure reduces obedience.

Milgram also conducted a version of the experiment in which he placed a second 'teacher' in the room, although this one was a stooge instructed to obey until the end. In this variation all the participants went along with the confederate and shocked up to 450 volts! So the mere presence of another obedient 'volunteer' made all the participants go all the way.

One of the main conclusions of Milgram's work was that under certain conditions involving the presence of authority, people suspend their capacity to make informed moral judgments and defer responsibility for their actions to those in authority. When people are in this particular frame of mind, the nature of the task that they are asked to perform becomes largely irrelevant, and the main determinant of their actions is the commands of the authority figure.

Summary

- Milgram found that most people would administer potentially lethal levels of shock to another human being, just because they were told to do so by an authority figure.

- The use of a controlled experimental procedure enabled Milgram to explore different aspects of the situation that influence the extent to which people will obey authority.

- Two key factors in obedience are the presence of a clear authority figure, and the distance between the person administering the shock and the 'victim'.

3   Milgram's study and ethics

At the beginning of Section 2 you were asked to put yourself in the shoes of one of the participants in Milgram's research. How do you think being a participant in the study felt? As you already read, many of the participants were visibly uncomfortable during the procedure. This is one of the reasons why the study created a storm, starting with a hostile review of the research in a newspaper, the *St. Louis Post-Dispatch*. The newspaper criticised Milgram and Yale University for putting the participants in such a stressful situation. It claimed that Milgram violated the rules of ethics which guide psychological research. The charge was repeated in academic circles, and led to Milgram's application to join the American Psychological Association being put on hold for a year. Milgram made a robust rebuttal of the charges and the debate about the issues led to the introduction of new codes of good practice for psychologists.

3.1   Ethics

Before we look at the arguments that swirled around the obedience study we need to consider what we mean by **ethics**. It all starts with *morals,* which are rules to guide our behaviour. These rules are based on a number of socially agreed principles which are used to develop clear and logical guidelines to direct behaviour. They also contain ideas about what is good and desirable in human behaviour. *Ethics*, in the context of psychological research, refers to a moral framework that governs what psychologists can and cannot do.

Ethics
Priciples that determine right and wrong conduct. In psychological research, ethics refers to the codes and principles that researchers should adhere to.

The first generally accepted code of ethics for research on humans was devised in 1947 as a response to the very events that provoked Milgram's research. During the Second World War (1939–45), under the Nazi regime, research was carried out on human beings that led to many deaths, deformities and long-term injuries. Revelations about this research were as great a shock for the post-war world as the death camps, because these acts of brutality and murder were conducted by doctors and scientists.

After the war the victors held a series of trials, in the German city of Nuremberg, of people who had taken part in the worst excesses of the horrors that had swept across Europe. Among them were twenty-three doctors involved in the brutal experiments. Sixteen of them were found guilty, of whom seven were sentenced to death. Significantly, the judgement included a statement about how scientists should behave when experimenting on other humans. This is referred to as the Nuremberg Code (see Table 2.1) and it became the basis for future ethical codes in medicine and psychology.

Table 2.1   The Nuremberg Code (1946)

1	The voluntary consent of the human subject is absolutely essential
2	The experiment should yield fruitful results for the good of society, that cannot be obtained by other means
3	The experiment should be based on previous research so that the anticipated results can justify the research
4	All unnecessary physical and mental suffering should be avoided
5	No experiment should be conducted where there is reason to believe that death or disabling injury may be the result
6	The degree of risk should also be less than the potential humanitarian importance of the research
7	Adequate precautions should be in place to protect the subjects against any possible injury
8	Experiments should only be conducted by qualified persons
9	The human subject should always be at liberty to end the experiment
10	The scientist in charge should be prepared to terminate any experiment if there is probable cause to believe that continuation is likely to result in injury or death

Source: adapted from Katz, 1972, pp. 305–6

Informed consent
The principle in psychological research whereby participants must be given comprehensive information concerning the nature and purpose of the research and their role in it, in order that they can make an informed decision about whether to participate.

Four key principles emerged from the Nuremberg Code. First, participants must be able to give **informed consent** to the procedure. Second, they must retain the *right to withdraw* from the study whenever they want. Third, the *welfare of the participant* must be protected wherever possible. The fourth principle is the most difficult to interpret because it concerns the *costs and benefits* of the study. It says that any risks to the participants must be greatly outweighed by the possible benefits for the greater good.

3.2   The case against Milgram

Activity 2.3

Before you go on to read about the criticism of Milgram's obedience studies, try to think through all the issues relating to ethics that are raised by this work. In what way were the participants deceived, or harmed? Did they have the right to withdraw? Do you think that in Milgram's case the ends justify the means? Do the benefits of the study justify the costs? Do you think that the results of the study are worth the pain and discomfort caused to the participants?

Among those who were highly critical of Milgram's study was fellow psychologist Diana Baumrind. She started her critique by noting the dilemma that all research psychologists face: 'Certain problems in psychological research require the experimenter to balance his career and scientific interests against the interests of his prospective subjects' (Baumrind, 1964, p. 421).

Baumrind challenged Milgram on whether he had properly protected the *welfare of the participants*. She used direct quotes from Milgram's original report to illustrate the lack of regard she said was shown to the participants. In particular, she noted the detached manner in which Milgram described the emotional turmoil experienced by the volunteers. For example:

> In a large number of cases the degree of tension [in the participants] reached extremes that are rarely seen in sociopsychological laboratory studies. Subjects were observed to sweat, tremble, stutter, bite their lips, groan, and dig their fingernails into their flesh. These were characteristic rather than exceptional responses to the experiment.
>
> (Milgram, 1963, p. 375)

In Baumrind's view, and in the view of numerous others, the levels of anxiety experienced by participants were enough to warrant halting the experiment. What is more, just because someone volunteers to take part in the study (i.e. gives informed consent at the start of the study), it does not mean that the researcher no longer has responsibilities towards them and their well-being. On the *principle of cost–benefit*, Baumrind challenged the view that the scientific worth of the study balanced out the distress caused to the participants. She acknowledged that some harm to participants might be a necessary part of some research – for example, when testing out new medical procedures – as in those cases results cannot be achieved in any other way. Social psychology, however, is not in the same game as medicine and is unlikely to produce life-saving results. The strength of the conclusions does not, therefore, justify harming participants. Milgram related his study to the behaviour of people who worked in the Nazi death camps and suggested that his study illuminated the way that ordinary people living ordinary lives are capable of playing a part in destructive and cruel acts. Baumrind dismissed this justification for the study and suggested there are few, if any, parallels between the behaviour in the study and the behaviour in the death camps.

Baumrind went on to make a further criticism by considering the effect of this work on the public image of psychology, and suggested that it would be damaged because the general public would judge that the participants were not protected or respected.

A further potential problem with Milgram's experiment concerns the participants' *right to withdraw*. Do you think that this principle, embedded in the Nuremberg Code, was sufficiently observed in Milgram's research? Recall that one of the key aspects of the experimental procedure was that whenever a participant demonstrated a reluctance to carry on with administering the shocks, they were told by the 'experimenter' in the grey coat 'you must go on', or 'you have no choice; you must go on'. It might be argued that telling a participant that they 'have no choice' but to continue with the experiment contravenes the right to withdraw, which is enshrined in the ethics code. To be fair, fourteen of the forty participants in the original study did withdraw, in spite of being told that they had no choice, so it could be argued that, ultimately, the participants did have a choice. It is just that making that choice was made more difficult by the presence of the 'experimenter' and by his prods. After all, the study was about obedience, and the instructions from the 'experimenter' were essential to the investigation. Exercising or not exercising the right to withdraw is what the study was about.

3.3   The case for the defence

Milgram made a series of robust defences for the study, starting with a response to the newspaper article that first raised concerns. He dismissed the accusation that participants were severely traumatised by the experience. He argued that 'relatively few subjects experienced greater tension than a nail-biting patron at a good Hitchcock thriller' (quoted in Blass, 2007). This was rather disingenuous, given his other descriptions of their reactions (see above). However, Milgram made a more measured response to the academic arguments. He pointed out, for instance, that he could not have known the outcome of the research before he started. As you already read, before embarking on the study he asked fellow professionals how they expected people to behave, and they predicted that participants would not continue to obey and administer severe shocks to the 'learner'.

More importantly, Milgram was not oblivious to the psychological needs of his participants and was aware of the potential harm caused by the study. Immediately after the study, its true purpose was revealed to the participants. They were interviewed and given questionnaires to check they were all right. A friendly reconciliation was also arranged with the 'victim' whom they thought they had shocked. This procedure, known as **debriefing**, is commonplace today, but this was not the case in the 1960s. So, in this respect at least, Milgram was ahead of the game in terms of ethics procedures (Blass, 2004).

Debrief
A post-research interview designed to inform the participant of the true nature of the study. It may also be used to gain useful feedback about the procedures in the study.

Milgram also conducted a follow-up survey of the participants one year after the study, to ensure that there was no long-term harm (Colman, 1987). The results showed that 84 per cent said they were 'glad to have been in the experiment', and only 1.3 per cent said they were very sorry to have taken part. Milgram also described how the participants had been examined by a psychiatrist who was unable to find a single participant who showed signs of long-term harm. Morris Braverman, a 39-year-old social worker, was one of the participants in Milgram's experiment who continued to give shocks until the maximum was reached. He claimed, when interviewed a year after the experiment, that he had learned something of personal importance as a result of being in the experiment. His wife said, with reference to his willingness to obey orders, 'You can call yourself an Eichmann' (Milgram, 1974, p. 54).

Milgram's basic defence was that the harm to the participants was not as great as it might appear, and for some of them the change in their understanding of their own behaviour and the behaviour of others was a positive event. He makes a further defence that we have to treat all people with respect and that this involves allowing them to make choices even if those choices are not always for the best. In direct response to Baumrind's criticisms he wrote:

> I started with the belief that every person who came to the laboratory was free to accept or to reject the dictates of authority. This view sustains a conception of human dignity insofar as it sees in each man a capacity for *choosing* his own behavior.

(Milgram, 1964, p. 851)

3.4   The judgement

So what do you think should be the final judgement on the ethics of Milgram's study? As you can see from the debate between Milgram and Baumrind, ethics is something that psychologists debate and often disagree on. Ethics principles, like all rules, are subject to interpretation and disagreement.

And yet, while individuals might have their personal view about whether a piece of research is ethical or not, what really matters is the judgment of institutions that regulate the profession. In the USA the regulatory body is the American Psychological Association. Its equivalent in the UK is the British Psychological Society. These institutions have ethics committees which issue guidelines and codes of conduct related to ethics in research and can reprimand researchers who can be shown to have violated the rules. At the time of Milgram's study, his research was investigated by the ethics committee of the American Psychological Association, who eventually came to the conclusion that it was ethically acceptable. Notably, however, Milgram's studies could not be carried out today, as the ethics guidelines have become more restrictive since the 1960s.

Finally, one further issue regarding Milgram's study is worth pointing out. Although the ethics of Milgram's research have been questioned, it could be argued that the obedience study, more than any other study in psychology, demonstrated *why* ethics are important. Recall that what Milgram's study showed was that ordinary people were willing to harm another human being just because they were told to do so by a person they believed was a psychologist, and because doing so was supposedly 'required by the experiment'. This shows that people generally are ready to give scientists the benefit of the doubt and go along with what they are doing, even when it involves harming individuals. This in itself illustrates how important it is to have some moderation of scientific activity, and have limits imposed on what scientists can and cannot do.

Summary

- Psychologists have a duty of care towards participants and must ensure that their well-being is preserved throughout a study.

- Participants must be asked to give informed consent before taking part in research and have a right to withdraw at any point.

- Milgram's obedience studies kick-started an ethics debate in psychology and highlighted the need for the development of more stringent guidelines for the conduct of research psychologists.

- Although Milgram's obedience study was judged to be ethical at the time of publication, it would be in violation of the strict ethics guidelines in place today.

4 Obedience research after Milgram

4.1 Replications

Milgram's research was carried out in Connecticut in the 1960s, on a sample that consisted exclusively of men. Can we say, therefore, that Milgram's findings about obedience are limited to middle-aged American men, or were they, as he seemed to assume, universal? To address questions such as these, psychologists use **replication**: they carry out additional research, on different populations, in different historical and social contexts, and look at whether similar results can be obtained. For instance, Milgram himself addressed the gender issue by carrying out a study identical to the original one, but with female participants. He found that women were as likely to administer electric shocks as men.

Replication
When a result from a research study is found again in a subsequent study. Replication is important to establishing the veracity of a finding.

Further replications of Milgram's study have been conducted in many countries, obtaining a range of results. Peter Smith and Michael Bond (1993) produced a review of twelve of these studies and found a fair degree of cultural variation in obedience, ranging from 92 per cent obedience to only 12 per cent. Smith and Bond offered two conclusions from their review. First, substantial numbers of people from a variety of countries will harm other people on the instructions of an authority figure. Second, the variability in the levels of obedience can be explained by the social context of the study and by the often subtle differences in the wording of the orders given by the authority figure. This second factor confirms the basic finding of Milgram's study: people are not blindly obedient to authority, but respond to the specific social and physical context in which they receive the orders.

Other researchers sought to identify specific processes that encourage obedient behaviour. Don Mixon (1972) carried out a study in which he used a role-playing method. People taking part in the study acted out the parts of 'teacher' and 'learner'. There was obviously far less deception here (participants knew that they were taking part in role play), but it enabled those taking part to consider what might have gone through a participant's mind in the original study. One of the findings concerned the role in obedience of the laboratory-coated 'experimenter'. It emerged that, in evaluating the appropriateness of their own behaviour, participants often looked to the authority figure – the 'experimenter' – for clues. The calmness audible in the 'experimenter's' responses and verbal prods to the 'teacher' suggested that there was less of an emergency situation than appeared. The 'experimenter' showed no concern as the 'learner' started to scream. This inaction might have indicated to the 'teacher' that the screams were not unusual, or dangerous, especially as the 'teacher' is aware that the 'experimenter' had already carried out the study with other participants. Perhaps this is one of the features of the situation that encourages obedience in the 'teacher'.

Another challenge to Milgram is whether the study would work outside the laboratory. Would comparable levels of obedience be observed in real-life situations?

Activity 2.4

It is worth stopping at this point to reflect on the situations in everyday life where people are required to do as they are told. Think of two or three occasions in the last week where you complied with a request, or an order, to do, or stop doing, something. For example, perhaps you stopped at red traffic lights or agreed to work late to meet a deadline? Are there any occasions when you obeyed where you later wondered about whether that was the right course of action?

Also, can you think of particular professions where obedience is relevant and which involve people taking orders from others?

A particularly interesting study using a real-life work environment was carried out by Charles Hofling et al. (1966). They investigated how far nurses would go in administering a fatal dose of a medication on demand from a doctor. A bottle of dummy pills was labelled 'Astroten' (a non-existent drug) and placed in the ward medicine cabinet. The bottle had a label which said the usual daily dose was 5 mg and the maximum daily dose was 10 mg. The nurse on duty received a phone call from a Dr Smith asking her to give his patient 20 mg of Astroten straight away. He explained that he was in a hurry and wanted the drug to have taken effect before he saw the patient, and that he would sign the drug authorisation form when he came on the ward in about ten minutes' time.

This request broke hospital procedures because nurses were only to give drugs with written authorisation, were not to exceed the maximum dose, and were only to take instructions from people they knew. The nurses in this situation had not come across the drug before, nor 'Dr Smith'. Remarkably, twenty-one out of the twenty-two nurses who were given this request followed the instruction and prepared the drug for the patient. When they were interviewed afterwards, some commented that doctors frequently phoned instructions and became annoyed if the nurse protested. Half the nurses said they had not noticed what the maximum dosage was. Either way, it appears that the word of the authority figure was enough to override the rules governing appropriate conduct (and common-sense notions).

4.2 Recent work

The ethics issues raised by the original study have meant that complete replications have been impossible in university psychology departments. Recently, however, there have been two innovations that provide an opportunity for the research to continue. The first involves virtual worlds.

Avatar

A term used to describe an alternative virtual identity that is used in three-dimensional computer games, or an image used to represent oneself in online communication.

It is now common to have a virtual character. Many people in the UK have played on game consoles where you can create your own alternative, virtual identity known as an **avatar**, who is then the character that plays your part in computer (and even online) games. Online social networks and virtual worlds offer further opportunities to create avatars. But how 'real' are they to us and could they be used as part of a psychology study?

This is the question explored by Mel Slater and colleagues (2006) when they replicated the obedience study in a virtual environment. In their study, volunteers (who took the role of 'teacher') were required to interact with a female virtual character (the 'learner') who took part in a memory task (see Figure 2.8). As in the obedience study, when the 'learner' gave a wrong answer the 'teacher' had to administer a shock and with each subsequent wrong answer to turn up the voltage.

Figure 2.8   Obedience in cyberspace

In one variation of the experiment, where the 'teacher' communicated with the 'learner' by text and could not see her, all participants completed the procedure and administered the twenty shocks. In another variation, the 'teacher' spoke to the 'learner' and could see her responses. In this variation some of the 'teachers' would not complete the procedure. More importantly, on physiological measures such as heart rate, they showed significant signs of stress during the procedure, which was not the case when the communication was by text message.

In fact, the 'teacher's' response in this interactive 'virtual' encounter was not all that dissimilar to what it would have been if they were dealing with a real person. When the 'learner' in the experiment asked them to speak up, they spoke louder. Some of the 'teachers' showed frustration when the 'learner' got the answers wrong, and when she objected to the procedure some of the 'teachers' turned to the experimenter and asked for guidance.

Designing this 'virtual' encounter allowed the researchers to model the behaviour of people in real situations. The volunteers were always aware that it was a simulation but described a range of emotional responses to the situation. They felt genuine distress even though they knew they were not hurting anyone. This work gives an opportunity for further research into obedience and also raises a lot of questions about the impact on us of virtual people in virtual worlds.

A second recent innovation has been to replicate just part of Milgram's procedure. Jerry M. Burger (2009) argued that the 150-volt level in the original study was the key point at which most participants decided whether to continue to obey. It is at this point that the 'learner' started to scream and asked to be released. He argued that exploring how people respond at this point allows reasonable extrapolations to be made about their likely behaviour beyond this point. Burger put in a number of ethical safeguards including screening the volunteers and carrying out instant debriefing, and obtained approval for his study.

The measure of obedience in the Burger (2009) study was whether the 'teachers' would be prepared to go beyond 150 volts. The study modelled Milgram's original experiment and used his script, but it terminated after participants made their choice at 150 volts. Burger found that twelve 'teachers' stopped at that point and twenty-eight continued. Although this shows a little less obedience than the original study, it is a similar outcome.

Burger (2009), just like Slater et al., found a way to further explore the issue of obedience using a procedure similar to that devised by Milgram, but which addresses the main concerns about ethics. Both approaches to the study of obedience have been well received by scholars in the field.

Summary

- Replications of Milgram's study have found high levels of obedience.
- Concerns about ethics have made it difficult to replicate Milgram's original study, which has necessitated the invention of creative ways to study obedience.

5   The implications of Milgram's work on obedience

5.1   Situation vs personality

The big lesson that is commonly drawn from the obedience studies is that people are capable of acts of great inhumanity. Remember that one of Milgram's participants recalled his wife telling him that there was an 'Eichmann' inside him. The studies are often seen as suggesting that it is not so much who you are that defines your behaviour as *where* you are and who else is present (i.e. an authority figure). As Milgram writes (1974, p. 205), 'the social psychology of this century reveals a major lesson: often, it is not so much the kind of person a man is as the kind of situation in which he finds himself that determines how he will act'.

This was a shocking revelation at the time. When Milgram conducted his survey before the study, he found that most respondents believed that participants were not capable of inflicting lethal pain on another person, and they thought that people *should* and indeed *would* disobey. The popular press at the time also tended to label people who carried out evil acts as monsters and somehow intrinsically different from the ordinary man or woman. The obedience studies suggested otherwise.

However, is personality really irrelevant to obedience? Alan Elms, Milgram's research assistant, investigated this issue in more detail. He invited forty of Milgram's volunteers to return to the university to find out more about them and their personalities, and to look for differences between those who had been fully obedient and those who had defied authority. On standard personality measures, Elms found no differences between the two groups (Elms and Milgram, 1966; Elms, 1972). The only measure that suggested a difference between obedient and defiant participants was the authoritarian personality F-scale. This is not surprising given that, in Chapter 1, you learned that one of the key characteristics of the authoritarian personality is deference to authority figures. One could expect that obedient volunteers would show more authoritarian tendencies, and this is indeed what Elms found.

And yet, the difference in personality observed by Elms cannot explain fully the pattern of results that emerged from the obedience studies. People who obeyed in the original experiment did not do so solely because of their personality, although their authoritarianism was, it appears, a contributing factor. If personality was the sole cause of obedience, then none of the variations introduced by Milgram in subsequent studies would have made a difference. But they did. The greater proximity of the victim made participants less obedient, just as the presence of a uniformed 'experimenter' made them more so. This goes to show that behaviour, and specifically how we respond to authority, is not attributable to a single cause. Instead, it is the outcome of a complex interplay of a range of factors, including personality and the situation.

5.2 Just ordinary men?

If we go back to the Eichmann trial that was an influence on Milgram's research, the question that Milgram was asking, which also became the centre of Eichmann's trial, concerned what sort of person could carry out such evil actions. Eichmann's defence was that he was just following orders. Milgram's conclusion (1974, p. 189) was that 'a substantial proportion of people do what they are told to do, irrespective of the content of the act and without limitations of conscience, so long as they perceive that the command comes from legitimate authority'.

A similar argument was put forward by Christopher Browning (1992) to explain historical evidence related to the activities of Reserve Police Battalion 101. This was a German killing unit that is estimated to have murdered around 40,000 Polish Jews during the Second World War. However, unlike many other SS killing units, comprising hard core Nazi sympathisers and anti-Semites, the Reserve Battalion consisted of 'ordinary men', German conscripts most of whom had no allegiances to the Nazi Party or National Socialist ideology. And yet they took part in most brutal murders. In his book, entitled *Ordinary Men*, Browning draws on Milgram's work to explore how the specific situation in which members of the battalion were placed, together with the expectations placed upon them by their superiors, were enough to make mass murderers of them. So, not only was Milgram's research motivated by the events of the Second World War, but his work influenced the way in which historians view the actions of the perpetrators.

Figure 2.9   Just following orders? Deportation of Jews from the Warsaw Ghetto

The applicability of Milgram's work to the Holocaust has been challenged by David Mandel (1998), who claims that, by suggesting that obedient behaviour is inevitable in certain situations, Milgram provided an 'obedience alibi' to perpetrators. Milgram's emphasis on situational factors, Mandel argues, takes responsibility away from the individual and implies that they cannot be blamed for their actions. Mandel also argues that there is more to obedience than just obeying orders, and points to a specific incident described by Browning. On one occasion, Major Wilhelm Trapp, the commander of the Reserve Police Battalion 101, received orders for the battalion to carry out a mass killing of Jews, including women and children. Trapp was distressed by this assignment and told his men that those who did not feel up to it could be assigned to other duties. Only two per cent of the unit took up Trapp's offer. Mandel argues that, according to Milgram's research, more men should have taken up the offer because there was no direct command from authority to obey, because the task (shooting women and children) was presented by the superior officer as gruesome, and because there were other disobedient peers present.

Mandel's critique of Browning's application of Milgram's research to the actions of German military units is important because it points to the fact that there is more to obedience than deference to an authority figure issuing a direct order. An important additional factor is the broader context and the institutional arrangements in which people, in this case German soldiers, found themselves. In Milgram's original experiment, the fact that participants took part in a scientific experiment at a highly regarded institution, Yale University, invariably contributed to obedience levels. The obedience of nurses revealed in the study by Hofling et al. (1966) can be attributed, in part, to the institutionalised hierarchical organisation of hospitals and the fact that following instructions from doctors is embedded in the job description of nurses. In the specific episode discussed by Mandel, members of Reserve Police Battalion 101 were not responding just to the immediate authority of their superior officer, Major Trapp; their choice was embedded in a broader culture of the military which has its own standards of loyalty and solidarity. These included not just obeying orders, but also not abandoning fellow soldiers when the unit is faced with a gruesome task.

5.3   Conclusion

However Milgram's work is interpreted, it is undeniably one of the greatest and most influential sets of experiments in social psychology. It continues to challenge anyone who comes across it and still attracts academic and political interest.

Box 2.2   Milgram's other work

The impact of the obedience studies has been so great that most people are not aware of the other studies that Milgram carried out. They are remarkable for their originality and their breadth. Here are some examples, described in more detail in Milgram (1992).

Everyday obedience

Milgram explored obedience in everyday life and in one study asked strangers to give up their seat on the New York subway (see Figure 2.10).

Figure 2.10   Milgram on the New York subway

Familiar strangers

Milgram noticed that a strange phenomenon of city life is that we regularly see people whom we recognise but never talk to. He called these people 'familiar strangers'. They might be the person who always gets on the same bus as us, or whom we see in the corner shop. Milgram got his students to carry out a novel study on these familiar strangers. They chose a suburban railway platform and photographed commuters waiting for a train. A few weeks later the students gave the commuters the photograph and asked questions about the people depicted. On average, the commuters reported seeing four familiar strangers in the photograph, but the average number that they had ever spoken to was only 1.5. Other questions revealed that 47 per cent of the passengers had wondered about the familiar strangers although less than a third reported even feeling a slight inclination to start a conversation.

Dropped letter technique

Measuring attitudes and their effect on behaviour is very difficult but Milgram devised a delightful technique to explore this. He left un-posted letters in public places to see how many would be posted by the people who found them. The letters addressed to individuals or to socially admired organisations like medical research labs were most commonly posted (over 70 per cent returned), but most of those addressed to the Friends of the Nazi Party or the Friends of the Communist Party were never seen again (only 25 per cent returned).

Six degrees of separation

Milgram tested the 'it's a small world' hypothesis by asking some people from Kansas to send packages to a stranger in Massachusetts, several thousand miles away. The senders were told the stranger's name, occupation, and roughly where they lived. They were told to send the package to someone they knew on a first-name basis who they thought was most likely, out of all their friends, to know the target personally. That person would do the same, and so on, until the package was personally delivered to its target. Most of the packages didn't make it but the ones that did were able to get there in about six hops. This led to the famous phrase 'six degrees of separation', which suggests that any two people in the world can be connected by an average of six acquaintances.

Milgram's work represents social psychology at its boldest and most engaged with the bigger questions about human behaviour. However, concerns about ethics, and the controversy the experiments provoked, mean that attempting similar research is difficult. Nevertheless, as you read, this does not mean that obedience research has been abandoned. It is just that more imaginative ways of conducting research have to be created.

An important implication of Milgram's work, and obedience research conducted since, is that it is not reasonable to hope for simple answers to the puzzles of human behaviour, especially its more destructive aspects. One of the perplexing experiences of studying psychology is that the more you find out, the more you realise that there are further discoveries to be made. Don't despair! If you look back, even across only a hundred years, you will see that we now have a much better understanding of psychology. Just don't expect simple answers to questions concerning human mind and behaviour.

Summary

- Research on obedience suggests that human behaviour is the outcome of a complex interplay of a range of factors, including personality, the situation, and the broader social or institutional context.

- Milgram's work was not only motivated by a desire to understand the actions of perpetrators of the Holocaust, but has also influenced how some historians have interpreted their conduct.

References

Adorno, T.W., Frenkel-Brunswik, E., Levinson, D.J. and Sanford, R.N. (1950) *The Authoritarian Personality*. New York, NY, Harper.

Arendt, H. (1963) *Eichmann in Jerusalem*, London, Penguin.

Baumrind, D. (1964) 'Some thoughts on ethics of research: after reading Milgram's behavioural study of obedience', *American Psychologist*, vol. 19, no. 6, pp. 421–3.

Blass, T. (2004). *The Man Who Shocked the World: The Life and Legacy of Stanley Milgram*, New York, NY, Basic Books.

Blass, T. (2007) 'Memorable quotes' [online], The Stanley Milgram Website, www.stanleymilgram.com/quotes.php (Accessed 11 February 2010).

Blass, T. (2009) 'From New Haven to Santa Clara: a historical perspective on the Milgram obedience experiments', *American Psychologist*, vol. 64, no. 1, pp. 37–45.

Browning, C. (1992) *Ordinary Men*, London, Penguin.

Burger, J.M. (2009) 'Replicating Milgram: would people still obey today?', *American Psychologist*, vol. 64, no. 1, pp. 1–11.

Colman, A.M. (1987) *Facts, Fallacies and Frauds in Psychology*, London, Unwin Hyman.

Elms, A.C. (1972) *Social Psychology and Social Relevance*, Boston, MA, Little, Brown.

Elms, A.C. and Milgram, S. (1966) 'Personality characteristics associated with obedience and defiance toward authoritative command', *Journal of Experimental Research in Personality*, vol. 1, no. 4, pp. 1282–9.

Haslam, S.A. and Reicher, S. (2008) 'Questioning the banality of evil', *The Psychologist*, vol. 21, no. 1, pp. 16–19.

Hofling, K.C., Brotzman, E., Dalrymple, S., Graves, N. and Pierce, C.M. (1966) 'An experimental study in the nurse-physician relationship', *Journal of Nervous and Mental Disorders*, vol. 143, no. 2, pp. 171–80.

Katz, J. (1972) *Experimentation with Human Beings*, New York, NY, Russell Sage Foundation.

Mandel, D.R. (1998) 'The obedience alibi: Milgram's account of the Holocaust reconsidered', *Analyse und Kritik*, vol. 20, no. 1, pp. 74–94.

Milgram, S. (1963) 'Behavioral study of obedience', *Journal of Abnormal and Social Psychology*, vol. 67, no. 4, pp. 371–8.

Milgram, S. (1964) 'Issues in the study of obedience: a reply to Baumrind', *American Psychologist*, vol. 19, no. 11, pp. 848–52.

Milgram, S. (1974) *Obedience to Authority: An Experimental View*, London, Tavistock.

Milgram, S. (1992) (eds J. Sabini and M. Silver) *The Individual in a Social World: Essays and Experiments* (2nd edn), New York, NY, McGraw-Hill.

Mixon, D. (1972) 'Instead of deception', *Journal for the Theory of Social Behavior*, vol. 2, no. 2, pp. 145–77.

Slater, M., Antley, A., Davison, A., Swapp, D., Guger, C., Barker, C., Pistrang, N. and Sanchez-Vives, M.V. (2006) 'A virtual reprise of the Stanley Milgram obedience experiments, *PLoS ONE*, vol. 1, no. 1 [online], www.plosone.org/article/info:doi%2F10.1371%2Fjournal.pone.0000039 (Accessed 11 February 2010)

Smith, P.B. and Bond, M.H. (1993) *Social Psychology Across Cultures*, Hemel Hempstead, Harvester Wheatsheaf.

Chapter 3
Learning from watching

John Oates

Contents

Aims and objectives

After studying this chapter you should be able to:

- discuss how portrayals of violence in different media may affect human behaviour
- describe a key piece of research by Albert Bandura and colleagues into children's imitation of violent acts
- outline why findings of associations between events and behaviour do not provide conclusive evidence of cause-and-effect relationships
- outline how and why experiments can identify causes of behaviour
- summarise the findings of psychological research into the topic of media violence and behaviour
- outline the policies designed to protect children from negative effects of screen violence.

1 Introduction

You have read in the previous two chapters that explanations of why people do harm to others can be sought both in aspects of personality and in situational factors. Also, you read about some of the research that has given insights into how these different factors operate. There is, however, another important influence on human behaviour that was mentioned indirectly in earlier chapters. In Chapter 1, you encountered the suggestion that early childhood experiences have a strong influence on personality formation. Recognising that early experience can play a role opens the possibility that some form of learning is involved. This is precisely what Bob Altemeyer suggested when he proposed that the attitudes measured by his right-wing authoritarianism scale reflected the values observed and learned in childhood. You will read more about learning in Chapter 4, but here I would like to focus on the notion that children can learn new behaviours simply by observing other people's behaviour. This form of learning is known as **social learning**. Researchers exploring social learning found that their work was shedding new light on the way that different types of behaviour, including aggressive behaviour, are learned by children.

You read about Bob Altemeyer's work in Chapter 1, Section 4.1.

Social learning
A theory of learning based on observing and imitating the behaviours of others.

1.1 Multiple media and media violence

The advent of digital media and the proliferation of technologies that support their delivery, such as the internet, mean that children now have easy access to lots of information. This ranges from educational material, through various types of entertainment, to interactive online experiences.

The development of visual animation techniques, more recently through CGI (computer-generated imagery), has also led to the possibility of including sequences in films and games that show emotionally intense behaviour. For example, extreme violence can be portrayed in very realistic ways. Coupled with developments in computing power and the almost universal access to computers in developed nations, the growth of interactive gaming has opened up new possibilities for social interaction. Children and adults can now engage in activities that mimic those performed in the 'real world'. They can play in imaginary worlds through the medium of the computer screen, and also engage with actual others, either in simulation games or in virtual worlds.

Figure 3.1 Interactive gaming: a source of danger or an educational opportunity?

Engaging in simulation games can be of great educational benefit, as children are frequently asked to explore predictions and reflect on what they do and how they relate to others on screen. One example is a bridge-building game, which is designed to support children's understanding of physics. The aim is to build a bridge across a ravine and the challenge is to get the bridge structure right. Similarly, virtual worlds can provide a range of educational opportunities. The aim of one particular cartoon-like world, directed at 8-to-12-year-olds, is to teach them about road and traffic safety.

Activity 3.1

A national UK survey, looking at children's use of the internet (Livingstone and Bober, 2005), provided information on what children use the internet for. Below is a list of activities for which the internet can be used. Before reading on, scan the list. Which activity do you think would be most popular with children and which least popular?

- obtain information on things other than school work
- help with school/college work
- send and receive emails
- play games online
- send and receive instant messages

- download music
- look for information on careers and further education
- look for products and shop online
- read the news
- chat rooms.

Sonia Livingstone and Magdalena Bober (2005) conducted a survey of 1511 children and young people aged from 9 to 19, and, among other things, looked at their use of the internet. You might have judged the last activity (chat rooms) to be popular, but in Livingstone and Bober's study, among those respondents who reported using the internet daily or weekly, only 21 per cent said they accessed the internet to use chat rooms. In fact this was the least popular activity of all. Indeed, the activities above are listed according to their popularity, and so 'help with school work' was the second most popular activity – 90 per cent reported using the internet to do work for school or college, and 94 per cent to get information on other things.

A serious concern, however, is the dangers that participating in the digital world may present. One particular worry is the effects on children and young people if they are able to access media content that depicts violence. Since the early days of cinema, scenes of violence have been commonplace in feature films. In the 1930s, a study showed that crime was a major of theme of 25 per cent of the 1500 films that were analysed (Dale, 1935). There was also growing concern around this time about violence shown in comics. Behind these concerns lay a notion that there can be some sort of direct effect of viewing violent material on screen, an effect that either predisposes the viewer to change their attitude towards violence, for example by becoming more tolerant of violence, or renders them more likely to behave in violent ways themselves.

Exposure to media violence, either in films, on television or in computer games, is regularly cited as a possible factor causing violent behaviour in the real world. Several examples are explored in Box 3.1.

Box 3.1   Is media violence to blame?

Example 1

Following the murder of 2-year-old James Bulger by the 10-year-olds Jon Venables and Robert Thompson in Merseyside, England, in February 1993, there was widespread media speculation that the murder was linked to the viewing, by the murderers, of a violent video, *Child's Play 3*. It was being suggested that there were similarities between deaths portrayed in the film and James's death, although this was not the case. The *Sun* newspaper ran a front-page story, with a large image of Chucky, the murderous doll in the film, and a claim that the two 10-year-old boys had watched the film not long before they committed the murder of James Bulger. While there was no evidence that the boys had in fact watched this film, it did emerge that the father of one of the boys had rented it a week before the murder and that he had a collection of violent videos to which the boys probably had access. This case, and the widespread coverage of the suggestion that watching violent films had in some way contributed to the boys' aggression, led to a national debate, and several video rental companies withdrew the film.

Example 2

In 1999, two high-school students, Eric Harris and Dylan Klebold, walked through the corridors of the Columbine High School in Colorado, USA, carrying knives, guns and explosives. They attacked and killed twelve students and a teacher. One of the killers used a gun that he named Arlene, the same name as a character in the video game *Doom*, which he had been playing with his accomplice. Both teenagers spent a great deal of time playing and developing new levels for *Doom*, and there were suggestions that they had used a plan of the school for one of these. American newspapers also drew links with a scene from the 1995 film *The Basketball Diaries*, in which a trench-coated character shot several students in a school hallway (as in the Columbine tragedy).

Example 3

The parents of Stefan Pakeerah, who was murdered by Warren Leblanc in Leicester, England, in 2004, blamed a violent video game called *Manhunt*, which they thought Warren was obsessed with. The game, which is advertised as offering a 'psychological experience', awards the player points for killing characters on the screen. BBC News reported that a spokesman for the Entertainment and Leisure Software Publishers' Association said:

> We sympathise enormously with the family and parents of Stefan Pakeerah. However, we reject any suggestion of association between the tragic events and the sale of the video game *Manhunt*. The game in question is classified 18 by the British Board of Film Classification and therefore should not be in the possession of a juvenile. Simply being in someone's possession does not and should not lead to the conclusion that a game is responsible for these tragic events.
>
> (BBC News, 2004)

Figure 3.2 Exposure to violence in films and computer games: *Child's Play* and *Grand Theft Auto*

1.2 What's the mechanism?

If it is assumed, for now, that there is a tendency for people to 'copy' behaviour that they watch on screen, the psychological questions that can be asked are exactly how and why such a process operates, whether it always operates or whether it works in some situations and not in others. This is a series of questions about the 'mechanism' that lies behind the process. It's not difficult to agree that 'copying' other people's behaviour happens; after all, this is an essential part of most forms of training. 'Here, let me show you how to do it' must have been said billions of times in human history, quite apart from all the other copying of others' behaviour that takes place in everyday situations. But this sort of learning, for it is a form of learning, has proved to be something of a puzzle for psychologists to explain. It is one thing to observe that a process happens, but altogether something else to be able to *explain* it satisfactorily.

Summary

- An important form of learning involves observing other people.
- The increased availability of different media means that there are many more opportunities to observe other people's behaviour, both positive and negative.
- There is general concern that observing violent behaviour may encourage people who watch it to behave more violently.

2 Social learning

Classic research in the field of social learning theory, which has since become widely known as the 'Bobo doll studies', was carried out in the early 1960s by Albert Bandura and colleagues. Bandura was very interested in different forms of learning, especially social learning, and he predicted that in certain conditions children were likely to imitate aggressive acts that they had observed. To explore this issue, Bandura set up a series of laboratory experiments which involved looking at the effects that exposure to a violent model had on children's behaviour. As several experiments involved seeing a model act aggressively towards a 'Bobo doll', an inflated five-foot-tall toy, these became known as the 'Bobo doll studies'.

Albert Bandura was born in 1925, in Alberta, Canada. He studied psychology as an undergraduate at the University of British Columbia and as a postgraduate at the University of Iowa, in the USA. He took his first academic post at Stanford University, USA, in 1953, where he has stayed for his subsequent working life. Although he is perhaps best known for his classic studies of observational learning, he has also investigated other topics linked to social influence. He has recently been applying his work in this area to practical matters. He works with broadcasters in many countries, scripting public broadcasts on issues such as teenage pregnancy, the transmission of AIDS, and literacy.

2.1 The Bandura et al. (1963) experiment

The research conducted by Bandura and colleagues sought to explore the extent to which children would imitate aggressive behaviour that they saw performed by another person, referred to as a 'model'. They were also interested in investigating what factors would affect any imitation; for example, whether the child was male or female and whether or not the model was of the same gender as the child. In one study, which I will discuss in more detail next, Albert Bandura, Dorothea Ross and Sheila Ross (1963) explored whether children would be as likely to imitate the aggressive behaviour of a model depicted in a film as they would the aggressive behaviour of a live model. This study is therefore directly relevant to the debate about media and violence which is the focus of this chapter.

Figure 3.3   Albert Bandura

A total of ninety-six children (an equal numbers of boys and girls) participated in the experiment by Bandura et al. (1963), which was carried out at Stanford University. The children, all of whom attended the university nursery school, were aged between 35 and 69 months (about 3–6 years). Their average age was 4 years and 4 months.

Each child took part in the experiment individually. However, before the experiment began, Bandura and his colleagues allocated each child to one of four different groups. There were twenty-four children in each group. Although all ninety-six children underwent a similar procedure, the researchers introduced important variations in the procedure for each group, which enabled them to observe the effect of certain variables on children's behaviour. In psychological research, variations in the experimental situation are called **conditions**. So, the four groups could be referred to as the four conditions.

Condition
A variation in the experimental procedure. By comparing different conditions researchers can make inferences about the effects of one variable on another.

Let's look in more detail at what happened to the children who were in Group 1. A female experimenter took each child into a room and sat them at a table with multi-coloured stickers, coloured paper and potato prints, which they were shown how to play with. Shortly afterwards, the experimenter led another researcher, the model, into the room, seated them at another table with a toy set, a mallet and an inflated Bobo doll, and left the room. The model then played with the toys for a minute, before acting out, over a period of about 10 minutes, a series of aggressive behaviours towards the doll: sitting on the doll and punching it on the nose; hitting it on the head with the mallet; throwing the doll up in the air and kicking it. The model repeated these actions three times, each time saying things like 'Sock him in the nose', 'Hit him down', 'Throw him in the air', 'Kick him', 'Pow'.

Figure 3.4   Images from the Bandura et al. (1963) study. The aggressive behaviour of the adult model

The child was then taken to a second room, away from the first setting, where he or she encountered many attractive toys. The child was told that they could play with the toys, but, as soon as they started to play, the experimenter told them that these were 'the best toys' and that she was going to save them for some other children.

The child was told that they could play with toys in a third, adjoining room, to which they went next. In this room there was a Bobo doll, a mallet and a peg board, two dart guns and a hanging punchball. There was also a variety of 'non-aggressive' toys: a tea set, crayons and paper, dolls, toy bears, cars and trucks, and toy farm animals. All the toys were arranged in the same positions before each child entered. Children were allowed to play freely in this room for 20 minutes.

Have you guessed the purpose of this third room? Bandura and colleagues recorded the play behaviour of the children in this room, and this allowed them to see if the child was affected by the exposure to the modelled aggressive behaviours. What do you think was the purpose of the second room? What happened in this room was intended to subject the child to a mildly frustrating event (showing the children attractive toys that they were not allowed to play with) in order to, as the researchers put it, 'instigate aggression'.

The above procedure was repeated for each of the twenty-four children in Group 1.

Children in Group 2 underwent a similar experience with one important difference. Instead of being exposed to a live 'model' behaving in an aggressive way with the Bobo doll, the aggressive behaviour was shown in a film. The model and the behaviour were the same as those seen by Group 1, but they were shown on a TV screen.

Again, the children in Group 3 had a slightly different experience. After seating the child in the first room, the experimenter walked to a television in the room, said 'I guess I'll turn on the colour TV', and pretended to tune the TV to a cartoon channel. What was then shown was a film that started with music and some stage curtains being drawn and the title *Herman the Cat* appearing on the screen. The film contained footage of the same set of aggressive actions with the Bobo doll as in Groups 1 and 2, but performed by a model dressed as a black cat. The model moved in a 'cat-like' way, in a set with artificial grass, and a 'fantasy-land' background with brightly coloured trees, butterflies and birds. The same aggressive words were spoken, but in a high-pitched, cartoon-like voice.

The final group of twenty-four children (Group 4) were also introduced to the different rooms, but they were not exposed to any model behaving in an aggressive way with the Bobo doll.

To summarise:

- Group 1 observed a live model behaving aggressively towards the Bobo doll.
- Group 2 observed a film of the live model behaving aggressively towards the Bobo doll.
- Group 3 observed a film of a 'fantasy' model behaving aggressively towards the Bobo doll.
- Group 4 did not observe any aggressive behaviour towards the Bobo doll.

2.2 The design of the experiment

This was a carefully planned experiment. Each of the four groups of children experienced almost exactly the same set of events, in the same rooms with the same people and toys. There was one key element that varied across the groups: Bandura and colleagues varied the exposure to violence. In an experiment, when something is purposely manipulated in this way, it is called an **independent variable**. Recall that the four variations of the experimental situation are called conditions. The three conditions involving exposure to aggressive behaviour are defined as **experimental conditions** and the condition involving no exposure to aggressive behaviour is defined as the **control condition**.

You were introduced to the controlled nature of an experiment in Chapter 2, and you can see this approach being taken here too.

Independent variable
A variable that is manipulated by the experimenter to see what effect this has on another variable.

Experimental condition
A condition in an experiment where participants are exposed to a specific variation in the independent variable.

Control condition
The 'baseline' condition, against which experimental conditions can be compared.

Why was there a control condition? This is needed as a comparison, to see the extent to which children might behave aggressively towards the Bobo doll when they had not seen a model acting aggressively towards it. It is possible that providing children with a mallet means that they might use this to hit something even when they've not seen a model use it in this way. This is sometimes called the 'baseline' condition.

As well as manipulating exposure to violence, Bandura et al. made sure that:

- There were equal numbers of boys and girls in the study as a whole, and in each of the four groups.
- There was the same number of children in each group.
- The children across the groups were matched in terms of prior ratings of aggressive behaviour (i.e. how aggressive they were more generally).
- Half of the children saw a male model, the other half a female one. This meant that researchers used two different confederates, a man and a woman, who alternated throughout the study.

Activity 3.2

Take a couple of minutes to consider why it was necessary to take all these issues into consideration.

Making good decisions on features such as these can make all the difference between a poor research study and one that contributes significantly to new knowledge. Taking the above points in turn, it is important to note first that it may be that boys and girls differ in some way in how they respond to modelled behaviour. If there were only a few girls and lots of boys in the sample, it would not be possible to tell with any confidence whether there were real gender differences. Also, if boys and girls were not equally distributed across the conditions, it would be difficult to disentangle the effects of gender from the effects of the experimental manipulation. Similarly, if there were different numbers of children in each group, and a difference was found for one small group, that would make the finding difficult to interpret.

Examining prior levels of aggressive behaviour of the children is also important. Prior to the study, the children in each group were matched in respect of their aggressive behaviour with the children in the other groups. This was done on the basis of ratings that had previously been made, in their nursery school, of the levels of aggressive behaviour that they displayed, and also of how much they tended to inhibit their own aggressive impulses. This was another way in which the researchers tried to ensure that the groups differed only in respect of their manipulation of the independent variable. By matching the groups with regard to the participants' usual level of aggressive behaviour, the experimenters were controlling for it so as to reduce or eliminate its possible effects. Otherwise, it might confound the results. Variables that might influence the result, if they are not controlled for, are called **confounding variables**. It's very important for researchers to recognise what confounding variables there might be in a particular experiment and to control or eliminate them.

Confounding variable
A variable that is not controlled by the researcher but that can affect the results.

Finally, as well as manipulating the exposure to aggressive behaviour, Bandura and colleagues purposely varied the gender of the 'model'. In the experimental conditions, the part of the 'model' was played by either a male or a female researcher. The presentations were organised so that half the children in each condition experienced the modelling by the researcher of the same gender, and half experienced the modelling by the opposite-gender researcher. This enabled the authors of the study to explore whether children will be differently affected by a male model compared with a female model.

An important part of designing a research study is thinking about aspects like these. It is also important to bear these in mind when critically examining research findings. Whether or not researchers have taken this sort of care with designing a study can influence the validity of their findings and conclusions.

2.3   The findings

Now that the design of the experiment has been explained in full, I shall look at how the researchers obtained their data and at what they found. Remember that they observed each child's play in the third room for 20 minutes. They did this through a one-way mirror and the behaviour was video-recorded to permit thorough and careful analysis. The 20 minutes were broken down into 5-second units, and each unit was **coded** on the basis of the kind of behaviour the child was displaying. In total, for each child there were 240 **codings** (20 minutes equals 1200 seconds, and dividing 1200 by 5 gives you 240). These codings were intended to accurately capture the amounts of aggressive behaviour shown by the children. The amount of aggressive behaviour

Code/coding
A way of describing observed behaviour using a set of predetermined categories.

observed for each child was the **dependent variable**. It is referred to as a dependent variable because its level is expected to *depend* on the experimental manipulation of the independent variable.

In research such as that conducted by Bandura et al. (1963), it is necessary to define the behaviour being observed, before coding can start. Aggressive behaviour can take many forms, so the researchers identified four different types, and focused on these:

- *imitative aggression*: acts that were clear and complete repetitions of behaviour that had been performed by the model, such as punching or kicking the doll, and accompanied by the same or very similar utterances as in the first trials; for example, 'Kick him', 'Pow'.
- *partial imitative responses*: aggressive behaviour involving the use of the mallet on a toy other than the doll, or sitting on the doll but in a non-aggressive way.
- *nonimitative aggression*: any aggressive acts not observed in the model's behaviour.
- *aggressive gun play:* shooting or aiming the toy gun.

The number of times these behaviours were observed for each child was noted, and these were also added together to give a total aggression score.

You might be wondering how easy and reliable it is to code behaviour in this way. As a check, it is usual to have two people code some of the recording, and then to calculate the degree of consistency between them. This is what Bandura et al. (1963) did: 40 per cent of the trials were coded independently by two observers to examine how reliable the coding was. In more than nine out of ten observations the observers agreed, so this was taken to indicate that the coding was sufficiently reliable.

Dependent variable
A variable that is expected to change as a result of the manipulation of the independent variable.

Activity 3.3

The researchers wanted to explore whether the exposure to a violent model would increase the subsequent display of aggressive behaviour by the children. Before describing their findings, I would like you to try to predict what their observations revealed:

- Do you think that exposure to the aggressive model increased the amount of aggressive behaviour displayed by the children, compared with the control condition?

- Do you think there was a difference between the boys and the girls in the amount of aggressive behaviour they exhibited?
- Do you think that the male models had more influence on the children than the female ones?

The codings revealed that the children who participated in the three experimental conditions (i.e. Groups 1–3 who were exposed to an aggressive model) scored more highly in respect of the amount of aggressive behaviour than children in the control condition (i.e. Group 4). So, exposure to a violent model did increase the amount of aggressive behaviour exhibited by the children. However, it made no difference whether the model was seen live or on film. Also, in the conditions where children saw the model on film it made no difference whether the model was human or a fantasy, cat-like creature.

Figure 3.5. Images from the Bandura et al. (1963) study. Middle and bottom rows contain images of child participants replicating the behaviour of the adult 'model' shown in the top row

Also, it was found that in all conditions, including the control condition, the boys showed higher aggression scores than the girls. There were also gender differences in respect of the different types of aggressive behaviour (imitative aggression, partial imitative responses, nonimitative aggression and aggressive gun play). For example, boys displayed more gun play than girls in all conditions, while girls sat on the Bobo doll much more than the boys in all conditions, but were much less likely to punch it.

The researchers also found that the gender of the model made a difference. A higher level of aggression was observed among those children who saw the male model performing aggressive behaviour than among those exposed to the female model. This was true of both boys and girls.

Crucially, Bandura et al. were able to conclude that their findings supported the main prediction of their study, namely that both the live and the filmed displays of violence would increase the number of aggressive acts subsequently displayed by children.

Summary

- Albert Bandura and colleagues have investigated children's reactions to portrayals of aggressive behaviour.
- In an experiment by Bandura et al. (1963), children observed aggressive behaviour displayed by both live and filmed models.
- Exposure to the displays of aggression by both types of model led to greater subsequent aggressive behaviour.

3 Interpreting the results of the Bandura et al. (1963) experiment

From their results, the authors of this study concluded the following:

- Children's behaviour can indeed be influenced by seeing violent acts performed, and this influence manifests itself as increased levels of violent behaviour shortly after exposure.

- This influence differs depending on various factors, such as the gender of the child and of the person modelling the violent acts.

Generalise
To extend the findings of a single study to explain behaviour in other situations or settings.

However, the question then arises of whether these findings are generally applicable to all situations where aggression is observed, and to all children. Another way of phrasing this is: to what extent do the findings **generalise**? For example, this study was carried out with children in quite a limited age range and in a specific situation. It would be of interest to know if there are differences, in the amount of aggressive behaviour displayed, between children of different ages and in different contexts.

This section discusses some of the questions that can be asked about the generalisability of the findings of this study, and about the ethics of this type of research.

3.1 The behaviour that was observed

The behaviours that were modelled, and those that the children then later displayed in the third room, were all described as 'violent' or 'aggressive' acts. But were they really of the same nature or consequence as actual violent, aggressive acts where these are directed at other people? Perhaps children respond in one way to high-intensity, acted behaviour towards an inflatable doll, but in quite different ways if the violence is real and directed towards actual people. If children do behave in aggressive ways with inanimate objects in play-like situations, then does this mean they will also behave in similar ways with people? There is little evidence that this is so. It is possible that playing out violence with inanimate objects may actually reduce violence towards people.

A second point to note about the observation of the children's behaviour is that it took place only a short while after exposure to the aggressive behaviour of the model. Given that there was only a brief intervening period between the demonstration of violent behaviour and the observation phase, it is valid to ask the question: how long would the observed effects have lasted? The study by Bandura et al. (1963) did not address this question. It may well be that the increases in violent behaviour that were seen disappeared very quickly afterwards. They may even have been confined simply to the research sessions; perhaps the children thought that it was acceptable to behave in a violent way in this particular setting and would not behave in this way in other settings. Some subsequent research has suggested, however, that brief exposures to violent acts can have lasting consequences in some circumstances (Bandura, 1973).

It is also important to note that there was variation in the aggressive behaviour among the children within the different conditions, from one boy to another and from one girl to another. This is not so obvious when averages are compared for groups assigned to different conditions, but it does tell us that there are other factors at work, probably involving differences between children, either in their susceptibility to the influence, or in their willingness to show aggressive behaviour. This study was important in part because it led to other researchers asking these sorts of question. Bandura himself continued to explore the effects that he had demonstrated in this study, focusing on the differences in the characteristics of the models in particular. In later studies he showed that there were two important variables that affected the extent to which children would be influenced by the model. The apparent status of the model had an effect, as well as whether or not the model was seen to be rewarded for their aggressive behaviour (Bandura, 1973).

Finally, one can question whether the rather unusual, strange setting of the university laboratory, with adults doing strange and unfamiliar things, with the female researcher apparently being unmoved by the somewhat bizarre behaviour exhibited by the 'model', might have led to some rather situation-specific reactions from the children. In the journal article reporting this research, the authors say that 'In order to minimize any influence her presence might have on the subject's behaviour, the experimenter remained as inconspicuous as possible by busying herself with paper work at a desk in the far corner of the room and avoiding any interaction with the child' (Bandura et al., 1963, p. 5). (As explained in Chapter 2, 'participants' used to be referred to as 'subjects'.) However, this could have been seen by the children as suggesting that the observed acts were acceptable in this situation and with this adult.

They might have taken this to mean that showing this sort of behaviour was also acceptable and maybe even expected. It has even been argued that the children may have sensed that being aggressive was what was expected of them, and behaved accordingly (Borden, 1975).

Correlation
An association between two events, meaning that they tend to occur together more often than one might expect by chance.

Longitudinal studies
Studies that monitor and chart the development of psychological variables over long periods of time.

Direction of effect
Describes which of two variables is the initial cause and which is the resulting effect.

Box 3.2 Why do it this way?

An important aspect of Bandura et al.'s (1963) study is that it was one of the first *experimental* studies on media effects on behaviour. There is a very dangerous fallacy in everyday debates about media effects, and in how such effects are presented by the media. This is that correlation is often taken to indicate *cause*. The term **correlation** refers to an association between two events, meaning that they tend to occur together more often than one might expect by chance; for example, if individuals who commit violent acts are also found to have watched a violent video shortly beforehand. There are indeed many studies, in different countries, that have shown correlations between the amount of exposure to screen violence and aggressive behaviour, and some of these studies have been **longitudinal**, following children over several years (e.g. Gunter, 2008). Given such an association, it would be easy, but not necessarily correct, to jump to the conclusion that it was viewing the violent video that *caused* an individual to become violent (see Box 3.1).

There are two important reasons why simply observing a correlation between one thing and another is not adequate to show a cause–effect relationship. The first is that a correlation does not tell us what the **direction of effect** might be. In other words, if A and B usually occur together, does A cause B or B cause A? Does viewing violent media content necessarily make aggressive behaviour more likely? Could it be, instead, that children who are already more aggressive (for whatever reason) are also more likely to seek out and view violent media content? Second, a correlation does not tell us whether or not the observed relationship could in fact be the result of a third factor that affects both of the things that are being looked at. For example, some children might be more prone to violence than others because they are growing up in a violent household, in which violent videos are readily available. In this instance, the home environment could account both for the increased aggression and for the exposure to violent media content.

Conducting experiments is a way of overcoming the difficulties in interpreting observed correlations. The significance of an experimental study, if it is carefully designed, is that it can establish causality. Differences between the conditions are very likely to have been caused by the manipulation of the independent variable. This is because of the care taken to make sure that participants in the different conditions are as similar to each other as possible, either by matching for important other factors, such as prior levels of aggressive behaviour in the Bandura et al. (1963) experiment, or by randomly assigning participants to the different conditions. The other crucial characteristic of experimental studies is that the experimental conditions are very carefully controlled to be the same for each participant, and there is a control group. These essential elements of experimental research seek to isolate the influence of the variable of interest from the myriad of other variables that can affect behaviour.

The fact that an experiment can help establish causality does not mean that observing behaviour in the real world is unimportant, or unscientific. Indeed, real-world observations are crucial for developing explanations, but, unlike experiments, they cannot isolate the cause–effect links underlying what is observed.

3.2 Ethics

Although ethics issues do not affect the generalisability of the findings, it is nevertheless important to consider them when evaluating this study.

Activity 3.4

Think about the ethics of the Bandura et al. (1963) study in relation to the following three principles of research ethics:

- participants must be able to give informed consent
- participants must retain the right to withdraw
- the welfare of the participants must be protected.

For each one, make notes on how well you feel that these principles were followed by Bandura and colleagues in designing the experiment.

Bandura et al. (1963) do not mention any ethics review of their research, while it is now a requirement that such a review would be undertaken by a body such as an institutional research ethics committee. This is especially so when research is conducted on children, as additional issues have to be addressed. One of them concerns informed consent. When conducting research on children, it is not enough to obtain consent just from the child. The child's legal guardian (parent or caregiver) must also agree. In the case of the Bandura et al. (1963) study, the children attended the university nursery school, so it is likely that the relevant consent was obtained.

Perhaps the most significant ethics issue, however, concerns the effects of participation in the study on the children. They were exposed to events that they were very unlikely to experience in their everyday lives, and it is possible that there were effects other than simply the increase in aggressive acts towards the doll in the test phase. Also, it is easy to find video material of the original studies on the internet, so the identities of the children were not properly protected.

Finally, in the description of their study, the authors state that 'It was necessary for the experimenter to remain in the room during the experimental session; otherwise, a number of the children would either refuse to remain alone or would leave before the termination of the session' (Bandura et al., 1963, p. 5). This raises the issue of how well the children's right to withdraw was protected. Were the children freely consenting to their participation? Were some children coerced?

Summary

- The extent to which the findings of Bandura et al. (1963) are generalisable is questionable.
- Simply noticing that two elements are associated, for example viewing video games and behaving violently, is not good evidence that one causes the other.
- Experiments allow psychologists to examine cause–effect relationships.
- Where potentially harmful or distressing topics such as media violence are researched, ethics need to be especially carefully considered.

4   The mechanisms behind social learning

The Bandura et al. (1963) experiment stands as a 'classic' demonstration that children have a propensity to copy aggressive acts that they observe in visual media, either as filmed actuality or in a cartoon-like form. However, as I suggested in Section 3, the study also raised many important questions. This is often seen as the hallmark of a good piece of psychological research, indeed of scientific research more generally. Bandura et al. offered a clear answer to a specific question, but they also revealed new subtleties in human behaviour that were previously not identified, and suggested new questions to be addressed by future research.

Since 1963, there have been many studies and reviews of research into the effects of media violence on children and young people (e.g. Calvert and Wilson, 2008), and many psychologists have developed explanations about how and why such effects come about. Bandura's work, including his work subsequent to the 1963 study, pointed clearly to a process in which a model is more likely to be copied by children if the model is seen as being of high status, gaining rewards for their aggression and not receiving punishment. It also seems fairly well established that children are more likely to copy if the model is more like themselves (Bandura, 1973). Although these findings have not always been replicated in other people's research, in general other researchers have confirmed Bandura's findings (Ormrod, 1999). This gives us a starting point for thinking about how the process works, although it only tells us that the process is something to do with whether the individual identifies with the violent model. To say that someone identifies with some other person is to say that the other person assumes a particular significance, and that they are seen as an important 'reference point' – for example, as someone to look up to and to emulate. But it is important to explore further how a media portrayal operates within the person to raise the probability of subsequent copying. In psychology, these processes operating within the person are often called **mechanisms**.

4.1   Priming

One way in which it has been suggested that social learning operates is through **priming**. Viewing an aggressive model creates memories of

Mechanisms
The process or set of processes that underpin a particular psychological phenomenon, such as social learning.

Priming
Where exposure to a particular behaviour renders more likely the display of that behaviour in subsequent similar situations.

this behaviour, and associated emotions and responses. This then means that, when a similar setting or situation arises, a person is more likely to respond in accordance with the stored memory (Berkowitz, 1993). In other words, for a period after exposure these stored feelings and behaviours are more likely to come to mind than other sorts of feelings and behaviours.

The idea of priming suggests two things. First, the effect may be relatively short-lived, as later experiences are likely to prime other, different emotions and responses. Second, the expression of violence in the everyday world depends on cues — that is to say, stimuli in the environment — to trigger the primed behaviour. To have an effect, these cues need to have some similarity to elements of the media depiction. It is the association between the two that triggers the imitative behaviour. For example, imagine a movie scene showing a person purposely knocking a drink over someone, and that other person then punching the first person. In real life, an accidental spillage of drink over someone who had previously watched such a scene might prime that person to at least think about responding aggressively (and possibly punching the person who spilled the drink over them).

The idea of priming has been used primarily to explain the findings of experimental studies that focus on short-term effects of exposure to violence. However, some of Bandura's and others' later work showed that children can still reproduce specific violent behaviours up to at least eight months after they are shown them (Bandura, 1973). The relevance of priming to these longer term effects of exposure is less clear.

4.2   Attitudes and beliefs

Cognitive
To do with mental processes, such as perception, memory and thinking.

A mechanism by which longer-term effects might be explained is that exposure to violent content changes a person's attitudes and beliefs. This is an alternative **cognitive** mechanism that involves thinking processes. Here, a person's attitudes and beliefs towards specific aggressive behaviours, that is to say whether they view these behaviours in a positive or negative light, makes them more or less likely to produce such behaviours themselves.

Desensitise
A process whereby repeated exposure to a stimulus weakens an initially strong response.

One way in which this might happen is by repeated exposure to portrayals of violence. Although initially viewed negatively, the repeated exposure may **desensitise** a person and lead them to develop less negative attitudes towards aggressive behaviours. This in turn could make them less sensitive to viewing aggression and less inhibited about acting in an aggressive way. In addition, exposure to depictions of other people showing more positive attitudes towards violence might encourage a person to shift their attitudes, through a process of social influence.

There is some evidence for this mechanism, which has come mainly from studies of the effects of repeated viewing of sexual violence. These studies (e.g. Malamuth & Briere, 1986) have found changes in attitudes and beliefs that are highly persistent, although, as with the Bandura study, differences have been found between men and women in how they respond. For example, in one study (Weisz and Earls, 1995), men were found to become more accepting of interpersonal violence and more attracted to sexual aggression. These changes have also been found to depend very much on how the violence is portrayed, whether there are positive or negative outcomes for the perpetrator, and how the victim is shown to be affected by the violence.

4.3   Scripts

Since Bandura and colleagues conducted the Bobo doll studies, there has been increasing interest in psychology in the concept of **script** learning as a way in which children and adults acquire complex sequences of behaviour. Scripts are rich packages of sequences of behaviours, intentions, meanings and emotions, which offer scenarios to deal with situations that arise in everyday life. This explanation has drawn on observations of children in pretend play, when they often rehearse quite long and involved scenes, such as 'going to the doctor', where they are clearly building and rehearsing elaborate, routinised, stories of everyday life.

Script
An organised sequence of behaviours that is associated with a particular setting. A 'restaurant script', for example, would include a sequence of behaviours appropriate to eating in a restaurant.

Figure 3.6   'Going to the doctor': the role of scripts in pretend play

Clearly, having scripts available for everyday activities is an efficient approach, as one does not have to invent anew how to behave in every situation. How this plays out for the effects of violence in the media, according to script theory, is that children who regularly and frequently watch scenes of violence learn these sequences of behaviour as scripts. They come to see aggression as a means of solving problems, and hence these scripts become more likely to be used in real situations (Huesmann, 1998).

4.4   Multiple influences

One of the difficulties in the field of research into the effects of media violence is that there are some studies that seem to show no influence of watching violence on behaviour, while others show a large influence. Also, it is difficult for a single study to control adequately the many factors that affect how children and adults respond to screen violence. So, is it possible to bring together, in some way, the data from the different studies in this area and come up with an overall conclusion? One way in which this can be done is by conducting a **meta-analysis**. A meta-analysis involves combining the data from different studies and analysing it together, using complex statistical procedures.

There have been several such analyses in the area of research that you are reading about in this chapter. Some have focused on the effects of TV, some on those of film and others on those of computer games, but the largest and most comprehensive was carried out by Brad Bushman and Rowell Huesmann (2006). Included in the meta-analysis was data from studies of different media, including TV, film, computer games, comics and music. Overall, the results confirmed those of previous studies that looked at a smaller range of research and media types: exposure to media violence was found to be associated with subsequent violent or aggressive behaviour. However, this association was shown not to be particularly strong. Exposure to violence on screen, while of concern, is not the main cause of violent behaviour. It interacts with other factors such as personality, aspects of the environment, and so forth.

Anderson and Bushman (2002) attempted to draw together a diverse range of factors to provide a complex explanation of how repeated exposure to media violence might relate to aggressive behaviour. In addition to the mechanisms outlined in this section, such as those involving the influence of attitudes and beliefs, and of scripts, Anderson and Bushman also highlighted other factors. These included the role that the situation may play and the potential influence of the peer group, as well as other variables including personality. So, various processes might come together and affect the thoughts of the individual, their mood, and the behaviour they display, which, together with them selectively choosing environments in which aggression is more likely to be experienced and evoked, would then lead to more aggressive behaviour.

Meta-analysis
A technique for combining data from different studies on the same topic, and analysing it together, to derive an overall conclusion.

Figure 3.7   Violence between youths: the product of multiple influences

4.5   A note of caution

The meta-analysis by Bushman and Huesmann (2006) involved a range of different types of study, including experiments, surveys and longitudinal studies that followed people over varying lengths of time. An important point is that some of these looked at correlations between media use and aggressive behaviour. As I indicated in Box 3.2, finding associations, even if they are supported across more than one study, is not the same as clearly identifying that one factor causes another. In the case of screen violence, there is no unequivocal proof that serious acts of violence are directly caused by exposure to screen violence.

An example of a study that shows how cautious one must be when attributing violent behaviour to media influence is a study by Ann Hagell and Tim Newburn (1994). This study compared a group of seventy-eight teenagers who had committed violent offences with a group of teenagers who did not have a criminal record. The researchers interviewed these young people about their media habits and, among other things, asked them about their exposure to attitudes towards violent content. They found that the offenders did not seem to have any greater interest in screen violence. In fact, they appeared to have less access to such material and as a result viewed less of it than the comparison group. The offenders were less able to recall specific characters and violent scenarios, and seemed generally to be less identified with this sort of material. In other words, it did not seem as if media violence had much personal relevance to them. Evidently, it was other factors that contributed to their violent behaviour.

Summary

- There are several processes through which media portrayals may affect behaviour.

- Priming, desensitisation, attitude and belief change, and script learning have all been considered as important processes through which exposure to violent media may affect behaviour.

- Meta-analyses of a wide range of research findings have concluded that observing media portrayals of violence has a weak association with subsequent aggressive behaviour.

5 A call to action?

The question that all this research raises, even given the reservations that I have expressed, is: what could be done to reduce the potential impact on society of violent media? The authors of the major meta-analysis described in Section 4.4 commented on their results as follows:

> Although observing violence may increase aggression in the short term for adults and children, long-term effects are most likely to occur for children. Consequently, children need the most protection from repeated exposures to violence. Infrequent exposure is not likely to produce lasting consequences, but parents particularly need to be urged to protect their children against the kinds of repeated exposures that heavy play with violent video games or immersion in violent TV programs is likely to produce.
>
> (Bushman and Huesmann, 2006, p. 351)

This final section highlights that, as well furthering our understanding of human behaviour, psychological research has also made a contribution to government policies related to the media, and helped formulate guidance for parents. I shall look at two reports that have influenced policy on these matters. In fact, psychologists often find themselves giving evidence, preparing reports and sitting on working parties to develop advice based on reviews of research. The British Psychological Society has a Parliamentary Officer whose role is to keep up to date with government business and to help to ensure that the Society provides experts who can contribute to consultations and generally bring psychological knowledge to bear on social issues.

5.1 The Newson report

Following the murder of 2-year-old James Bulger in 1993, the Member of Parliament David Alton commissioned Elizabeth Newson, a developmental psychologist at Nottingham University, to produce a report on the issue of negative media effects on children. The report, 'Video violence and the protection of children' (Newson, 1994), was endorsed by a range of other professionals working in the area of children's health, and argued that there is evidence for a strong connection between watching violence on screen and carrying out violent acts.

The report also acknowledged the difficulty faced by psychologists seeking to establish a cause-and-effect relationship, highlighting that an experiment seeking to look at the effects of images of extreme violence on children would not be approved by an ethics committee. According to Newson, exposure to such images would traumatise children, and repeated exposure would lead to desensitisation, which means that the children would be adversely affected by taking part in research.

This report was influential in that it encouraged the notion of psychological harm to be included in government debates about video censorship. It provided support to those seeking to amend the Criminal Justice Bill to tighten video censorship. However, it was also very controversial, sparking critical comment from others who felt that evidence had been used selectively in the report. The debate raised by the report continues to the present day. As you have read in Box 3.1, it's fairly common for press reports of a murder or murders to make a link with the murderer having been found to have a collection of violent videos, and for this to be brought into evidence in court.

5.2   The Byron report

In 2007, there was increasing public debate in the UK about children and young people's unrestricted access to media. The debate was provoked by the rapidly growing access to the internet among children, and the launch of ever more violent computer games. *Grand Theft Auto*, in particular, was singled out as portraying extreme violence without consequences for the screen characters and also as being widely used by children younger than eighteen, the age rating for this game. The prime minister at the time, Gordon Brown, commissioned another psychologist, Tanya Byron, to carry out a review of the evidence on the risks to children's safety and well-being from exposure to material on the internet and in video games that might be harmful or inappropriate. The review was also to consider the effectiveness and adequacy of existing measures that are supposed to protect children from such exposure, and suggest any improvements or additional action. Another objective was to help parents understand the risks of access to inappropriate content and help them manage those risks.

Figure 3.8 Towards a greater protection of children in a digital world: the Byron Review

The report of the Byron Review, *Safer Children in a Digital World*, was published in March 2008 (Department for Children, Schools and Families (DCSF), 2008a).

With regard to the potential negative effects of violent content in video games, the author of the report reached the following conclusions, which for the most part concur with points made in this chapter:

- There is some evidence from laboratory-based research connecting playing violent video games with short-term aggression, but this may not generalise to the real world. Also, it has not been established that there are long-term effects.

- There is some evidence of a correlation between playing violent games and aggressive behaviour or attitudes in the real world, such as hostility or the tendency to get into fights. However, it is not possible to conclude from this evidence that one *causes* the other. So, playing violent video games may cause aggression, or alternatively more aggressive children may choose to play these games, or, indeed, there may be another, third variable that explains both choosing to play these games and behaving more aggressively.

As mentioned previously, the remit of the Byron Review was quite broad and, in addition to the risks associated with playing violent video games, it considered the risks associated with the internet.

Activity 3.5

Can you think of the different risks that exposure to the internet poses to children's safety? Start by thinking about the safety implications of different websites that children might access.

As regards the internet, the review used a grid similar to that in Table 3.1 to structure the wide range of factors that can form 'risk'. In your answer to the activity, you may have thought of some of these.

Table 3.1 Risk factors and internet use. The rows indicate three ways in which a child interacts with the internet (as 'recipient', 'participant' and 'actor') while columns differentiate between four types of content that might pose a risk to a child ('commercial', 'aggression', 'sexuality' and 'values/ideology')

	Commercial interests	Aggression	Sexuality	Values/Ideology
Content(What is found on the web?)Child as recipient	Advertisements Exploitation of personal information	Violent/hateful web content	Pornographic or unwelcome sexual content	Biased information Racism Misleading health advice
Contact(Someone making contact with child)Child as participant	Harvesting of personal information Children being tracked by advertising	Being bullied, harassed or stalked	Being groomed Arranging offline meetings	Being supplied with misleading information or advice
Conduct(Child contacts someone)Child as actor	Illegal downloading, hacking	Cyber-bullying or harassing other internet users	Creating and uploading inappropriate or illegal material	Providing misleading information or advice

Source: adapted from Hasebrink et al., 2008

What becomes clear from looking at Table 3.1 is that discussion regarding the potential negative influence of media has become considerably more complex since the Bandura et al. study. The digital world has increased the range of risks to which children might be exposed, including increased exposure to sexually inappropriate content, 'stranger danger' and cyber-bullying. The report draws attention to the fact that research cannot move at the pace of technological change, and the study of long-term implications is particularly difficult when both technology and its use are changing.

Importantly, the Byron Review highlights that children have the right to participate in new interactive technologies and should be able to do so in a safe and informed way. These technologies offer a range of opportunities for learning and development, as well as frequently being fun to engage with. The following point is made in the executive summary to the report:

> Having considered the evidence I believe we need to move from a discussion about the media 'causing' harm to one which focuses

on children and young people, what they bring to technology and how we can use our understanding of how they develop to empower them to manage risks and make the digital world safer.

(DCSF, 2008b, p. 2)

Figure 3.9   Introducing parental controls in software

The strategic objectives to emerge from the report therefore include reducing the availability of harmful and inappropriate material in the most popular areas of the internet, restricting children's access to harmful and inappropriate material and enhancing their resilience to the material to which they may be exposed. This will involve better regulation and better information and education.

5.3   Conclusion

This chapter has looked at the topic of aggressive behaviour and the influence of media portrayals of violence on children. The evidence related to this topic has led to much debate and discussion and identified multiple influences that relate to aggressive behaviour. In this final section you saw how the research conducted by psychologists has helped to shape new policies designed to reduce potential negative effects.

As you will see in subsequent chapters, social learning – that is, learning through observing the behaviour of other people – is not the only way in which children, and indeed adults, learn. But it is a potent form of learning, and understanding its mechanisms can be very helpful, not just in respect of our understanding of aggressive behaviour but also in relation to how people, and most importantly children, acquire new and useful skills and learn to engage in more positive aspects of behaviour.

Summary

- Psychological research on media and violence has made a contribution to government policy on media regulation.
- Studying the effects of media on children is made difficult by its changing nature and the ways in which children interact with it.

References

Anderson, C.A. and Bushman, B.J. (2002) 'Human aggression', *Annual Review of Psychology*, vol. 53, no. 1, pp. 27–51.

Bandura, A., Ross, D. and Ross, S.A. (1963) 'Imitation of film-mediated aggressive models', *Journal of Abnormal and Social Psychology*, vol. 66, no. 1, pp. 3–11.

Bandura, A. (1973) *Aggression: a social learning analysis*, Upper Saddle Place, NJ, Prentice Hall.

Berkowitz, L. (1993) *Aggression: Its Causes, Consequences, and Control*, New York, NY, McGraw Hill.

BBC News (2004) 'Game blamed for hammer murder', 29 July [online], http://news.bbc.co.uk/1/hi/england/leicestershire/3934277.stm (Accessed 15 February 2010).

Borden, R.J. (1975) 'Witnessed aggression: influence of an observer's sex and values on aggressive responding', *Journal of Personality and Social Psychology*, vol. 31, no. 3, pp. 567–73.

Bushman, B.J. and Huesmann, L.R. (2006) 'Short-term and long-term effects of violent media on aggression in children and adults', *Archives of Paediatrics and Adolescent Medicine*, vol. 160, no. 4, pp. 348–52.

Calvert, S.L. and Wilson, B.J. (eds) (2008) *The Handbook of Children, Media and Development*, Chichester, Wiley-Blackwell.

Dale, E. (1935) *The Content of Motion Pictures*, New York, NY, Macmillan.

Department for Children, Schools and Families (DCSF) (2008a) *Safer Children in a Digital World: The Report of the Byron Review*, Nottingham, DCSF Publications; also available online at http://publications.dcsf.gov.uk/default.aspx?PageFunction=productdetails&PageMode=publications&ProductId=DCSF-00334-2008& (Accessed 15 February 2010).

Department for Children, Schools and Families (DCSF) (2008b) *Safer Children in a Digital World: Executive Summary* [online], www.dcsf.gov.uk/byronreview/ (Accessed 15 February 2010).

Gunter, B. (2008) 'Media violence; is there a case for causality?', *American Behavioural Scientist*, vol. 51, no. 8, pp. 1061–1122.

Hagell, A. and Newburn, T. (1994) *Young Offenders and the Media: Viewing Habits and Preferences*, London, Policy Studies Institute.

Hasebrink, U., Livingstone, S. and Haddon, L. (2008) *Comparing Children's Online Opportunities and Risks across Europe: Cross national Comparisons for EU Kids Online*, London, EU Kids Online [online], www.lse.ac.uk/collections/EUKidsOnline/Reports/D3.2_ISBN.pdf (Accessed 15 February 2010).

Huesmann, L.R. (1998) 'The role of social information processing and cognitive schema in the acquisition and maintenance of habitual aggressive behavior' in Geen, R.G. and Donnerstein, E. (eds) *Human Aggression: Theories, Research, and Implications for Policy*, New York, NY, Academic Press.

Livingstone, S. and Bober, M. (2005) *UK Children Go Online: Final Report of Key Project Findings*, London, London School of Economics and Political Science.

Malamuth, N.M. and Briere, J. (1986) 'Sexual Violence in the Media: Indirect Effects on Aggression Against Women', *Journal of Social Issues*, vol. 42, no. 3, pp. 75–92.

Newson, E. (1994) 'Video violence and the protection of children', *Journal of Mental Health*, vol. 3, no. 2, pp. 221–7.

Ormrod, J.E. (1999) *Human Learning* (3rd ed.), Upper Saddle River, NJ, Prentice-Hall.

Weisz, M.G. and Earls, C.M. (1995) 'The Effects of Exposure to Filmed Sexual Violence on Attitudes Toward Rape', *Journal of Interpersonal Violence*, vol. 10, no. 1, pp. 71–84.

Conclusion

In the first three chapters of *Discovering Psychology* you read about the research of Theodor Adorno and colleagues on authoritarian personality, Stanley Milgram's obedience studies and the investigation by Albert Bandura and colleagues into social learning and aggression. All three chapters address a similar aim: understanding why people do harm to others.

An important point that emerges from the chapters is that psychological research is *historically situated*. The authors of the authoritarian personality study, some of whom fled Nazi Germany in the 1930s, were influenced by the events of the Second World War and the Holocaust. Milgram too was influenced by his Jewish heritage and he saw parallels between his findings and some of the issues that were emerging from the trial of Adolf Eichmann. Bandura worked at a time when television sets were introduced into American homes, and when access to violent media was of increasing public concern. However, the research of Adorno, Milgram and Bandura, although rooted in the period in which they worked, raised many questions which continue to intrigue psychologists today.

Another message that emerges from the chapters is that human behaviour is inherently *complex*. Adorno and others sought to identify aspects of *personality* that account for authoritarianism. Yet they were also aware that the situation plays an important role in authoritarianism and that, for the *potential for fascism* to be realised, the circumstances had to be right. Equally, although Stanley Milgram sought to isolate aspects of the situation that determine whether or not people will follow orders and cause harm to others, the research by Elms showed that the participants' authoritarian dispositions also played a part. Personality probably accounts, at least partly, for the fact that, while around two-thirds of participants in Milgram's study were prepared to administer lethal shocks to a fellow human being, there was a third who were not.

Similarly, Bandura's work on social learning provided evidence that observing a violent model, even one depicted on film, makes a child more likely to display aggressive behaviour. However, this observed link between media and violence has been shown to be complex, involving multiple mechanisms, which interact with a range of other factors influencing aggressive behaviour. What all of these findings suggest is that when we seek explanations for human behaviour – in this case for why people do harm to others – the answer is unlikely to be related only to personality, the situation or learning from others. These different factors (and indeed others) act together to produce particular and complex patterns of behaviour. It is down to psychologists to try to disentangle the contribution of each of the different factors.

The first three chapters also offered you a taster of different sub-disciplines of psychology. Chapter 1 introduced the *psychology of individual differences*, a term used to denote research that looks at personality, and at what make a person unique and different from others. Milgram's work is a classical study in *experimental social psychology*, in that it examines the way in which situational variables and the interaction with others affect human behaviour. The study by Bandura and colleagues is, on the other hand, a study in *developmental psychology*, in that it focuses on children's behaviour and their psychological development. However, a note of caution is necessary here. The boundaries between the sub-disciplines are not fixed. For example, Adorno's work was not just about personality, but also about its roots in childhood development. Also, authoritarianism research has had a far greater influence on social psychologists interested in explaining prejudice and political extremism than on researchers interested in personality. So, what Part 1 as a whole illustrates is that, while there may be differences between different sub-disciplines in psychology in respect of focus, emphasis or approach to a topic, they nevertheless overlap and interact in their study of human behaviour.

It is important to bear in mind that the chapters offered you a mere snapshot of three strands of psychological research that have investigated why people do harm to others. This was by no means a comprehensive or exhaustive review of the research in this area. There are many other ways of looking at issues of violence, aggression and obedience. Biological psychologists, for example, have explored what happens in the human brain when people engage in violent behaviour, and whether specific processes in different parts of the brain might differentiate people who have a tendency to engage in violence from those who do not. Forensic psychologists also seek to understand criminal and violent behaviour, with certain researchers focusing on developing more sophisticated ways of profiling offenders. Clinical psychologists too have been interested in the psychology of those who harm others, exploring, for example, the relationship between mental illness and criminal behaviour.

In reading Part 1, you also encountered a number of different *methods* used by psychologists to study the complexity of human behaviour. In Chapter 1 on the work of Adorno and colleagues, you learned about two different ways of studying personality: questionnaire-based personality scales and in-depth interviews. In Chapters 2 and 3 you read about the value of the controlled experiment as a method that allows researchers to manipulate specific variables and measure their effect on another. In the account of Bandura et al.'s work you also encountered observation as a specific technique for gathering data: the Bobo doll studies involved the systematic observation and coding of children's behaviour. In subsequent chapters you will learn more about these methods and encounter new ones as a more complex picture of psychology as a discipline begins to emerge.

When reflecting on method, it is important also to consider *ethics*. Chapters 2 and 3 highlighted the need for psychologists to protect the welfare of participants and to ensure that their integrity, and their status as a willing participant, is never jeopardised. Observing the rules and guidelines of ethics, however, protects the integrity not just of the participants, but also of psychology as a scientific discipline. Crucially, the fact that ethics has become embedded in the institutional framework of psychological research is in large part the consequence of the earlier debates about the limits of acceptable research. Milgram's study in particular pushed the boundaries of that debate. In Chapter 5 you will read about another example of ethically questionable research, concerning working with animals, which, while uncovering important things about psychology, also made psychologists re-examine their own practices.

Finally, the studies explored in Part 1 have highlighted that interacting with others is an important influence on human behaviour. Research on the authoritarian personality emphasised the role of interactions with parents, while Milgram explored interactions with an authority figure. Central to the notion of social learning are 'models', namely other people, observed and imitated by an individual. Chapters in Part 2 will examine an issue that is linked to this ever-present influence of others. If others have the capacity to influence what people do, how does this happen? Interestingly, as you will see in Chapters 4 and 5, some of the answers to these questions have come from research on animals, not humans.

Part 2

Introduction

Part 1 of *Discovering Psychology* highlighted the importance of interaction with others – harsh parents in Chapter 1, an authority figure in Chapter 2, and a violent 'model' in Chapter 3 – as a source of influence on human behaviour. That people are influenced by others might seem obvious. Many people cite family members or well-loved teachers as major influences in their lives, as individuals who 'made a difference'. Others blame harsh or neglectful parents, or poor schooling, for missed opportunities or adversity in life. Equally, few would challenge the idea that friends are a major influence on people throughout life, and that they affect, to some extent at least, what people do and how they do it. What is less obvious in each of these cases, however, is *how* others shape what people do.

This question is the key focus of Part 2 of *Discovering Psychology*. Let us look at the example of teachers, parents and friends again. Teachers exercise their influence because they are placed in charge of a child's education. They reward good behaviour and performance and occasionally punish transgression. In doing so they teach a child to differentiate appropriate from inappropriate behaviour and help them to acquire knowledge about the world around them. Do parents influence a child in the same way? While there is a clear overlap between the role of the teacher and the parent in a child's life, there is an obvious difference. Most children appear to form a powerful bond with their primary caregiver, usually a parent, very early on in life. This kind of attachment is not characteristic of relationships with teachers or other adults whom we encounter later in life. Similarly, unlike in the case of the relationship with parents or teachers, people have at least some choice of who their friends are. More importantly, they usually see them as equals, that is as being on the same level as themselves in respect of power relations. Not only does this make the pattern of influence different, but questions inevitably arise about what a 'friend' is and how friendships are formed and developed. Psychologists have explored these and other issues to do with the influence of others, and as you will see they have done so in quite different ways.

How behaviour is shaped is the specific focus of Chapter 4 by Frederick Toates. In this chapter you will learn how reinforcement makes a particular behaviour more likely to occur. Terms such as 'reinforcement' and 'punishment' have a common-sense meaning, but you will be introduced to their use within a particular field of psychology called *behaviourism*, which is concerned with how learning can occur through these processes. You will be introduced to the work of B. F. Skinner, who is one of the most influential psychologists of the twentieth century. Skinner argued that learning through reinforcement is common to all species, so much of his work involved studying animals, mainly rats and pigeons. Skinner developed a special device, the Skinner box, which provided a tightly controlled environment within which animal behaviour could be studied in a systematic way. The principles established by Skinner are used today in education, prison and therapeutic settings, as well as by many pet owners!

Chapter 4 describes a number of different studies conducted on rats and pigeons, and also cats and dogs, which were conducted to advance our understanding of learning. Non-human animals have been used in other psychological studies too. In Chapter 5, Deborah Custance explores the attachment between the young and their primary caregivers (researchers usually focus on the mother) and addresses the question of how this bond arises. The chapter focuses on the work of Harry Harlow, whose experiments on monkeys explored infant attachment. As you will see, while Harlow's findings led to profound changes to Western attitudes to child rearing, his experiments also underlined the need for ethics in psychological research with non-human animals. In fact, Harlow is today considered to be one of the most controversial figures in the history of psychological sciences, whose treatment of animals was often cruel. Chapter 5 also describes more recent research with human participants and looks at mothers' interactions with their infants and the different types of attachment that may be formed.

In the final chapter of Part 2, Chapter 6, Charlotte Brownlow explores the important role of friendship in the lives of children. As you will see, this is a relatively new area of research. One of the most influential studies in this particular area, by Bigelow and La Gaipa, was conducted in the 1980s. What makes this area especially interesting is that researching friendship in children poses a number of methodological questions. Building on what you already read in Part 1, this chapter will revisit the distinction between qualitative and quantitative data and explore the different ways in which qualitative data can be collected and analysed to shed light on the issue of children's friendship. The chapter also considers cultural differences in friendship and how the role of friends changes as children get older.

We hope that you will enjoy the chapters and gain not only a greater understanding of the different ways in which others may influence us, but also a sense of the different approaches and assumptions psychologists bring to their research.

Chapter 4
Changing behaviour

Frederick Toates

Brownlow
HarryHarlow
BF Skinner

Contents

Aims and objectives

After reading this chapter you should be able to:

- recognise changes that are attributable to learning
- assess the influences on and contribution of B.F. Skinner
- explain what is meant by 'behaviourist psychology'
- distinguish between classical and instrumental conditioning, and positive reinforcement, negative reinforcement and punishment
- consider the validity of extrapolating from the behaviour of animals in Skinner boxes to human society
- describe some contemporary developments that arise from Skinner's work.

1 Introduction

In Chapter 3, you met one form of influence on behaviour: imitation of 'models'. It described how, by means of imitation, behaviour can change. The chapter described this type of learning as 'social learning'. Children are said to *learn* to act violently, at least in part, by imitation. The implication would appear to be that children who exhibit violence might well have had a history of exposure to violent models. In this way, violent behaviour might arise and be maintained by such exposure. Conversely, it would seem to follow that non-violent children might owe their peaceful behaviour, in part, to a history of exposure to non-violent models.

The present chapter also concerns learning and tries to identify and characterise some other influences on behaviour. In doing so, it seeks to explain how certain behaviour arises and is maintained. Similarly, it is also concerned with how, under certain conditions, behaviour changes. This chapter will focus on an influence on behaviour that does not involve the learner observing a model. Rather, it concerns the fact that behaviour often appears to take its particular form because it has *consequences* that gave rise to it and that maintain it. When these consequences change, so also does the behaviour. This is best illustrated by an example.

Suppose that you visit a friend regularly over the years. Why did this behaviour start and why is it maintained? You might have started to visit for various reasons, such as a wish to establish a new friendship or out of sympathy for your friend. Whatever the reason for starting, it would appear that visiting regularly had the *consequence* that you received hospitality and good conversation. Suppose now that the friend stops showing any hospitality or good conversation and you come to terminate the visits. Common sense would suggest that this change in behaviour (stopping the visits) is because of the changed consequences of visiting. The purpose of this chapter is to put such common sense to the test of scientific scrutiny and to investigate when and how behaviour is initiated, maintained and changed as a result of its consequences. This chapter will say more about the reasons that behaviour continues once started, though it will not ignore the issue of how behaviour gets started.

The chapter also considers why sometimes behaviour fails to change in spite of good intentions to do so. Could it be that the consequences of the established behaviour are so strong as to resist efforts at change?

1.1   At the personal level

Everyone probably sooner or later encounters head-on the issue of changing their own behaviour. Many people have types of behaviour that they would rather lose and, conversely, good resolutions that prove very difficult to put into practice. This may apply to you. For example, you might wish to take more exercise and eat more healthily but good intentions get lost along the way.

Many people try to alter the behaviour of those with whom they come into contact: family, friends and work colleagues. People commonly attempt to persuade their loved ones to quit smoking by a mixture of emotional blackmail and the use of common-sense reasoning about the price of cigarettes. However, some people try (I think wisely, but don't let me sway you so soon) to alter the *consequences* that follow the target behaviour of the loved one: for example, putting money in a box for each cigarette resisted.

Activity 4.1

Try listing a number of things that you would like to alter about your own behaviour. Suppose that you have tried unsuccessfully to change something. Can you suggest why you failed? What consequences might have been maintaining the undesired behaviour?

Try to think of when you attempted to alter the behaviour of someone you know. If it was successful, note why you think that it was. If not, why do you think that you failed?

You will have arrived at a variety of examples. However, it is possible that, whatever the example, you might have identified a conflict for the control of behaviour. For example, if you have tried to quit smoking, you might well have accepted all of the arguments about health and expense. However, you have felt the urge to smoke that simply could not be resisted. It seems that smoking has had consequences in the past, for example, relaxation and a feel-good factor, which now stand in the way of quitting. Changing these consequences in some way, possibly by means of nicotine-free cigarettes, might help.

If you have tried to dedicate more time to study, you might have been hijacked by some competing activity that could not be resisted. Switching on a television has the consequence of producing instant relaxation and distraction from other problems. When you have tried to change the behaviour of someone else, they might well have reported just such a conflict. In addition, of course, they might have been resentful at what they saw as interference in their life.

1.2   At the professional level

It is the professional duty of some to try to change the behaviour of others for whom they have responsibilities. The consequences of behaviour can be manipulated to try to produce a desired change. For example, teachers try to alter the behaviour of their pupils to get them to learn and to avoid disturbances. Some schools make *rewards* the consequence of good behaviour, as in earning vouchers for conscientious attendance. The penal system tries to reform the behaviour of prisoners, to get them to abandon crime. Rewards, such as access to sports, television or days out, are offered for good behaviour.

Some people experience distress at their behaviour and request therapeutic interventions to change it. Such intervention sometimes takes the form of a therapist altering the consequences of the individual's behaviour.

Consider the following examples. A woman spends an excessive amount of time washing her hands in a fruitless effort to eliminate what she feels is their contamination. She is characterised as having an 'obsessional disorder'. It seems that the behaviour has the consequence of temporarily lowering the level of anxiety from where it was before washing. It would also appear that this consequence can have such a powerful effect that attempts to quit the behaviour are fruitless, even though she might acknowledge that her behaviour is irrational. Recognition that consequences could be maintaining certain behaviour suggests possible interventions. For example, the therapist might sit with the patient while urging her to refrain from washing, so as to prevent the normal consequences. In this way, the strength of the excessive behaviour may be weakened.

Suppose that a man cannot leave his home for fear of, say, coming into contact with the feathers of a pigeon. He would be characterised as having a 'phobia'. One might speculate that the relaxation of being at home is a consequence that helps to maintain this behaviour. Being at home might also have the consequence that, out of sympathy, friends start to visit him. The therapist might try accompanying him as he makes very brief excursions out of the house. The patient could earn the consequence of praise for each small increase in length of time outside the house. It might be arranged that visitors come only after he successfully leaves the house for a short period. Hence, positive consequences of going out are introduced.

Professionals have an idea concerning a desired form of behaviour and seek to bring actual behaviour nearer to that which is desired by altering the *consequences* of behaviour.

1.3   Identifying the role of learning

Learning usually occurs in parallel with other processes. Consider sports training. Suppose that you are increasing your endurance over days and weeks. It might be arranged that each increase in performance earns a reward of praise from your coach. This increases your motivation to strive harder. Your behaviour is observed to change. However, not all of the change in behaviour can necessarily be attributed to learning. Part of the improvement would most likely reflect adjustments by the body: for example, the increased strength of muscles and the increased efficiency with which the heart pumps blood around the body.

Alternatively, consider the example of the lowering in performance, such as walking distance and speed, which often accompanies increasing age. Again, this usually reflects such things as a weakening of muscles and a lowered efficiency of the heart. The term 'learning' would seem inappropriate in these cases and the changes would not form the object of study by psychologists. However, of course, psychological adjustments to such bodily changes are of concern to psychologists. For example, people find ways of adjusting to the changes of ageing, such as using a walking stick and taking on less strenuous challenges.

This section has identified an important psychological issue: it appears that a factor that causes behaviour to be maintained is the consequences that follow from it. Similarly, it appears that when behaviour changes, it can be because of a change in these consequences. But how can these assumptions be put on a firm scientific foundation? What characterises those consequences of behaviour that have such effects? What sort of experimentation would reveal the exact circumstances in which consequences have these effects? The focus of this chapter is the answers provided by the American psychologist B.F. Skinner.

Figure 4.1   B.F. Skinner (right) with the author of the present chapter (left)

Summary

- In addition to learning by imitation, it appears that behaviour arises, is maintained and changes because of the consequences that follow it.

- It appears that the consequences of behaviour can sometimes be such as to make it difficult to change behaviour, in spite of good intentions to do so.

- Not all changes in behaviour can be attributed to learning.

2   B.F. Skinner and the foundations of behaviourist psychology

2.1   Early life and scientific context

Burrhus Frederic Skinner was born in 1904, in the small Pennsylvania railroad town of Susquehanna. As a child, he showed great interest in exploring the natural environment and in devising mechanical gadgets. Family life was basic and puritanical. The possible significance of these events and interests for the adult Skinner are described later. On leaving school, he attended Hamilton College, where he mainly studied languages and literature, but with some psychology. Skinner later obtained a place at Harvard University to do research in psychology. There were several influences on the academic career of Skinner.

The first two influences deviate from the issue of the consequences of behaviour. However, they serve to illustrate again that there are several different forms of learning and they provide a historical context for Skinner's work.

Reflex
An automatic reaction to a stimulus.

Stimulus
A trigger to behaviour.

Ivan Pavlov was a Russian scientist who researched what is known as a **reflex**, an automatic reaction to a particular **stimulus**. The research concerned the reflex that underlies the production of saliva and digestive juices (in the stomach) by dogs when meat juice is dropped into their mouths. The meat juice is the stimulus to the reflex. This might not sound much like behaviour, but the study illustrated a very general principle of how change could be produced automatically.

All hungry dogs react to the stimulus of meat juice by the reflexes of producing salivation and digestive juices. Pavlov noticed that, after such experience of getting food, the dog reacted by salivating even before the food arrived in its mouth. For example, the sight of a colleague who had regularly brought the meat would be sufficient to trigger salivation. At first, this so-called 'psychic effect' was regarded as a nuisance, but later Pavlov studied it in its own right.

In his famous experiment, the stimulus of a tone was sounded just prior to the presentation of food. This combination of tone followed immediately by food was presented on a number of occasions. Then the effect of the tone, presented in the absence of food, was tested. The tone alone triggered salivation and the release of digestive juices (Pavlov, 1927). Here was a clear change in behaviour obtained under rigorously controlled conditions. It is as if the dog had learned that the tone meant food might follow.

John Watson, an American psychologist, brought Pavlov's research to the attention of American psychologists. He also conducted a famous experiment himself (Watson and Rayner, 1920), the ethics of which you might wish to question. An infant, called Little Albert, was presented with a tame rat. Watson observed Albert's reaction to the rat, this being one of warm acceptance and no fear. He then observed the reaction of Albert to a loud sound, banging a piece of metal behind Albert's head. Albert was observed to cry and to move away from the source of the sound. As the next stage, Watson presented the rat to Albert just prior to making the loud sound. Finally, Watson observed the reaction to the rat on its own. Albert now showed a defensive reaction of moving away from the rat, which exemplifies a change in behaviour as a result of experience. Albert might be said to have learned to show a defensive reaction to the stimulus of the rat.

The third influence on skinner takes us back to the consequences of behaviour. Edward Thorndike was an American psychologist who pioneered the study of animal behaviour, specifically the behaviour of cats in puzzle boxes (see Figure 4.2).

Figure 4.2   Thorndike's puzzle box

Thorndike (1898) was interested in the nature of learning in animals and whether this was fundamentally different from human learning. He placed a hungry cat in a cage (the puzzle box) and put some food outside it. By manipulating a latch, the cat could open the door and get to the food. Thorndike measured the length of time it took the cat to escape from the box over a number of attempts. Figure 4.3 shows how long it took an individual cat to escape across nine trials.

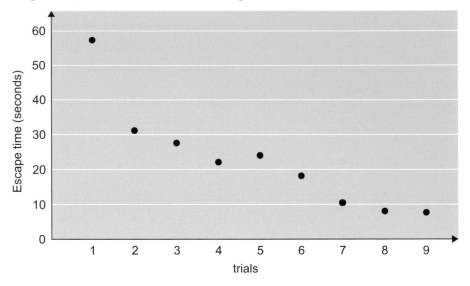

Figure 4.3   Measure of learning for one cat, showing the time needed to escape for each trial over nine trials

---

Activity 4.2

Have a look at Figure 4.3. The horizontal axis is numbered 1–9 representing each individual trial. The vertical axis shows escape time as measured in seconds (0–60 seconds). The dots represent the escape time for each trial. How would you describe the pattern of dots? Which trial shows the longest escape time and which the shortest? Which two trials differ most in respect of escape time?

As you can see, there is a lot of variation over the nine trials. The cat took longer to escape on the first trial than on the second or subsequent trials, and indeed the biggest difference is between the first trial, where the cat took about 58 seconds to escape, and the second trial, where the cat took just over 30 seconds. At the end of nine trials, the cat is rapidly escaping, taking less than 10 seconds. The pattern of dots in Figure 4.3 suggests that the cat gradually learned how to get out. There was a steep drop from first to second trial, and then a slower decline over the remaining trials, with a slight blip from fourth to fifth trial where the time to escape increased slightly.

Based on findings like this, Thorndike argued that learning in this situation consists of the formation of a link between the stimulus of the latch and the response of manipulation of the latch. The strength of this stimulus–response link is increased over trials because of the consequence of escape from the box: the satisfaction of eating. As the strength of this link increases, so the time needed to escape decreases gradually.

2.2   The emergence of a behaviourist psychology

Up to the time of Watson, psychology had been based largely upon the study of what happens *in the mind*, the so-called mental events. People reported what was 'on their minds' and these accounts were documented by psychologists (as in the case of Freud and his followers). What is on your mind is private to you and therefore described as subjective. I cannot observe it any more than you can observe what is on my mind. So, such psychology was based on *subjective* events. By contrast, behaviour is *objective* in that it can be observed by psychologists and measured.

Watson revolted against the way of doing psychology that involved subjective events (Watson, 1913). He argued that psychology should be based upon only observable data, with a focus on behaviour. It should be an objective science, rather as biology and chemistry are objective sciences dealing only with observable phenomena. The experiments of Pavlov and Watson fitted this way of doing science. Everything was 'public data' and measureable – in Pavlov's case it was the food, the tone and the salivation. In the study of Little Albert, the sound, the presentation of the rat and Albert's reaction were equally measurable. Watson argued that a science of psychology should concern itself only with such observable behaviour, and thereby this approach in psychology acquired the name **behaviourism**.

With Pavlov, new terminology entered the scientific vocabulary. The tone exemplified what became known as a 'conditional stimulus'. The meaning of 'conditional' is that there is a *condition* attached to the tone's power to trigger salivation; it has no intrinsic capacity to trigger such a response. The condition is its earlier pairing with food on a number of occasions. By contrast, meat is not a conditional stimulus since no such conditions pertain and it is therefore termed an 'unconditional stimulus'.

The process of changing behaviour in this way became known as 'conditioning'. Since Pavlov's was the first type of conditioning to be

Behaviourism
An approach in psychology, which argued that only observable behaviour should form the object of study.

Classical conditioning
Conditioning in which a stimulus acquires the capacity to trigger a response by virtue of its pairing with an unconditional stimulus.

Stimulus–response psychology
An approach to understanding behaviour that suggested that learning consists of the acquisition of new links between stimuli and responses.

Instrumental conditioning
A form of conditioning in which the outcome depends upon the action of the animal, as exemplified by obtaining food on turning a latch or negotiating a maze.

studied (and others were to follow), it became known as **classical conditioning** or Pavlovian conditioning. Note that the dog does not play a part in the sequence of when the external events occur. Both tone and food were under the control of Pavlov.

It was reasoned that links are formed between stimuli and responses and hence this approach to understanding behaviour was described as **stimulus–response psychology**.

2.3   The contribution of Skinner

Skinner subscribed to the principles of behaviourism and wanted a psychology based upon observable data. Though Skinner was aware of Pavlov's research, his own interest was more in the tradition of Thorndike. In the experimental arrangement of Thorndike, things were different from those of Pavlov and Watson, though the term 'conditional' could still be applied. Unlike Pavlov's dogs, the cat in Thorndike's study had control over the sequence of events: getting to food was *conditional upon* the cat's appropriate reaction, that is, turning the latch. The *consequence* of the cat's behaviour – access to food – altered the cat, making turning the latch more likely in the future. The cat was 'instrumental' in the sequence of events and hence this process of learning became known as **instrumental conditioning**.

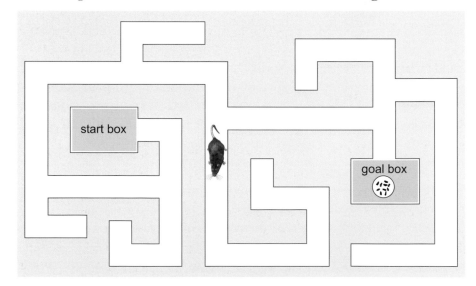

Figure 4.4   Maze

Skinner (1979) performed experiments on rats running in mazes (see Figure 4.4). The hungry rat is placed at the start box. On successfully negotiating the maze, it reaches the goal box, where it finds a small morsel of food. Finding food is the consequence of its behaviour. Behaviour (taking the correct turns) is said to be *instrumental* in the outcome (obtaining food). At first, the rat enters blind alleys. However, with experience, it gradually becomes more proficient. The rat is said to *learn* its way through the maze, learning being measured in two ways (see Figure 4.5): (a) the decrease in the length of time taken to get from start box to goal box or (b) the decline in the number of errors (blind alleys entered).

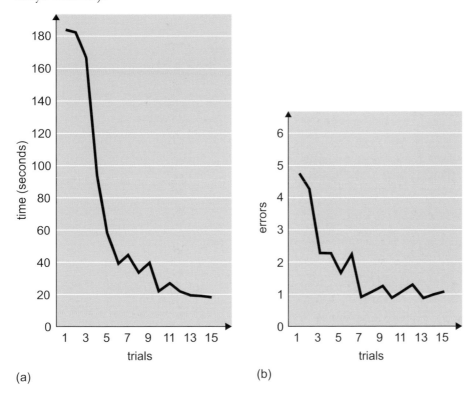

(a)

(b)

Figure 4.5 Learning a maze as measured by (a) time and (b) errors

Experimentation with mazes takes a lot of time and so Skinner invented a piece of apparatus that was later to earn the name 'the Skinner box'. Figure 4.6 shows the forms designed for the two favourite animal species used by Skinner and those working in his tradition (known as Skinnerians), namely rats and pigeons. When the rat presses the lever or the pigeon pecks the key, a small pellet of food drops into the food tray and can be eaten. If a hungry animal were simply to be left alone in the apparatus, it would probably learn to perform the response that earns food, but this would take a long time. Things can be speeded up enormously by a process known as **behaviour shaping**.

Behaviour shaping
The procedure of giving reinforcement for successive approximations to the desired response.

(a)

(b)

Figure 4.6   (a) The Skinner box designed for rats; (b) The Skinner box designed for pigeons

I will describe shaping rats, though an identical logic applies to pigeons. The desired response is lever pressing, and shaping consists of giving food for successive approximations to this response. When the experimenter presses a button, a pellet is given. On the first few occasions, the rat is given a free pellet to familiarise it with the apparatus and food delivery. Then the experimenter makes a demand by giving a pellet only when its front legs or nose are anywhere near the lever. This will normally persuade the rat to increase the amount of time that it spends with its front end near the lever. Then the experimenter makes the criterion for getting food harder: the rat must make physical contact with the lever. (As rats are naturally curious animals, they may well accidentally touch the lever.) After the rat makes contact, the criterion is made still more stringent: the rat must lower the lever. When it is reliably lowering the lever, the final stage of shaping occurs. The apparatus is now on automatic control. Only a full lowering of the lever such as to trigger the switch will deliver a pellet. If at any stage the rat regresses, the experimenter can take the remedial step of lowering the criterion and trying to 'lift the rat up' again.

Box 4.1 Why do it this way?

The Skinner box provides the extreme example of a *controlled environment*. The rat has very little to do and this increases the chances of its pressing the lever. The times of pressing are recorded. This was originally on paper (as you can see in Figure 4.6(a) and 4.7 below) but these days it would be on a computer. It is an efficient way of working as regards the psychologist's time, since, after the initial phase of shaping, the experiment runs itself. A number of rats can be run simultaneously.

The Skinner box minimises distractions from outside, so the effect of the consequence of behaviour (getting the pellet) can be studied in isolation from other influences such as imitation of another animal.

In the Skinner box, an experiment can be performed in that an independent variable can be manipulated and the effect on a dependent variable observed. For example, by depriving the rat of food for a period of time, its degree of hunger can be manipulated (independent variable) and the effect on lever pressing observed (dependent variable). Another possibility is to keep the level of hunger constant but to alter the amount of force that it takes to press the lever (independent variable) and to see what effect this has on lever pressing (dependent variable). Normally, the dependent variable is the frequency with which the rat presses the lever.

You might wonder what was so important about Skinner's findings. After all, circus trainers have known for centuries that behaviour can be changed with the help of food. With the invention of the Skinner box, however, behaviour was brought under rigorous scientific control and the rules governing reinforcement and behaviour were systematically studied. For behaviourists, the principles observed in the Skinner box are not just about animal training: they are applicable to real life situations, and underpin complex human behaviour.

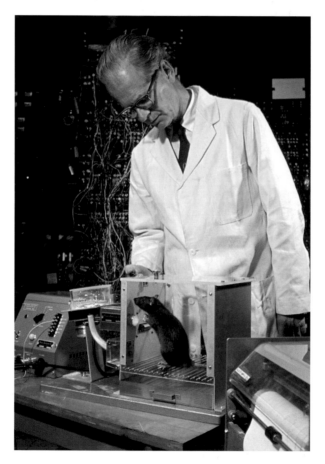

Figure 4.7   Skinner performing an experiment with a rat in the Skinner box

Since the food arrives as a result of the rat's response, this is a form of instrumental conditioning. However, it is a special form, since the timing of pellet delivery is in the hands of the rat. The rat sets its own pace. This is unlike the maze, where the experimenter picks the rat out of the goal box and places it back in the start box each time. The form of instrumental conditioning that is studied in the Skinner box is termed **operant conditioning**. This is because the animals *operate* on their environments to produce an effect. The rat is said to emit the operant of lever pressing.

2.4   The principle of reinforcement

Skinner suggested that this behaviour illustrates a very important general psychological principle, as follows. Behaviour changes as a result of its *consequences*: for example, lever pressing is followed by **positive reinforcement**, in this case, food. In other words, food 'reinforces' the behaviour that immediately precedes it. The word 'reinforce' means 'to strengthen' and that is the sense in which the word is used here. In Skinnerian language, the frequency of instrumental (including operant) behaviour increases as a result of reinforcement.

Here was an objective way of describing behaviour, in keeping with the principles of behaviourism. Behaviour that is reinforced will increase in frequency. To Skinner, there was no need to appeal to events in the head of the rat to explain behaviour. Psychologists needn't say that the rat *wanted* the food, that it *knew* that lever pressing would lead to food or that it *expected* lever pressing to lead to food or even that it *liked* the food. All such terms were avoided since they describe unobservables, which cannot be measured. Skinner also avoided speculating about events in the brain of the rat, though he accepted that learning involves the brain.

Food is not the only thing that can serve as positive reinforcement. If the animal has been deprived of water, then it can be trained to press a lever for the reward of small units of water. An animal might also be trained by the use of sexual reinforcement: a lever press could lead to brief access to a partner.

A reinforcer is defined simply by its capacity to reinforce. If the frequency of behaviour that is followed by the 'thing in question' increases, then the 'thing in question' is a reinforcer.

So far, I have described *positive* reinforcement. The adjective 'positive' refers to the fact that something that was not there before arrives as a result of the action: for example, food suddenly appears. There is another procedure that also strengthens behaviour, known as **negative reinforcement**, where something that is already present is removed. Suppose that a rat is placed in the Skinner box and a loud sound is

Operant conditioning
The form of instrumental conditioning that occurs in the Skinner box.

Positive reinforcement
The process of giving something as a consequence of a particular behaviour, which increases the frequency of showing that behaviour.

Negative reinforcement
The process of removing something as a consequence of a particular behaviour, which increases the frequency of showing that behaviour.

present. It might be trained to press the lever to switch the sound off and the loud sound would be said to act as a 'negative reinforcer'.

2.5   Some phenomena associated with reinforcement

It was noted that a reinforcer strengthens behaviour, as indexed by an increase in the frequency of the behaviour. Once the rat is trained in this way, what is the effect of the omission of reinforcement? The way to find out is to remove the food from the Skinner box. At first, the frequency of lever pressing increases and then gradually declines over days, until the rat finally quits. Removing food is termed applying **extinction**. After the rat has quit lever pressing, its response is said to 'have extinguished'.

Extinction
The removal of a reinforcer, e.g. taking the food pellets away from the Skinner box.

At one stage in his study, Skinner ran short of food pellets and needed a way to economise on them. He hit on the following solution. Once a rat or pigeon is trained, it is not necessary to reinforce *every* response in order to maintain behaviour. Rather, say, only every fifth lever press might be reinforced. Such a schedule of giving pellets is known as **partial reinforcement,** as opposed to 'continuous reinforcement' where every response earns a pellet.

Partial reinforcement
A schedule in which the rat gets reinforced only occasionally.

The shortage of food pellets had a very significant consequence. When they had been on partial reinforcement, as compared to continuous reinforcement, the animals persisted for much longer when applying extinction before they stopped pressing the lever (Skinner, 1939). This observation exemplifies the occasional role of chance in scientific discovery.

2.6   Punishment

Whereas positive or negative reinforcement strengthens the tendency to show the associated behaviour, there is also a technique, 'punishment', which lowers the probability of a given behaviour. The Skinnerian use of the term **punishment** has some similarities to its lay use, as in to *punish* a criminal offender.

Punishment
An event that follows a response and which leads to a decrease in the frequency of that response.

Suppose that a rat pokes its nose through a hole in its cage. First, the frequency with which it does this is recorded. Then, every time it does so, this triggers a loud sound and the frequency of nose poking is again measured. Suppose that, after introducing the sound, the frequency of nose poking *decreases*. It would be said that the sound is punishing nose poking. The sound is defined as *punishing* if there is a *decrease* in the frequency of behaviour. Hence, punishment is the mirror image of reinforcement and is similarly defined in terms of a change in behaviour.

Punishment again exemplifies the Skinnerian approach. The observation and measurement of behaviour is fundamental. Punishment is not defined in terms of its aversiveness as such but rather in respect of its effect on behaviour. The lay term 'punishment' refers to something that is merely *assumed* to have an effect on reducing undesirable behaviour, but the actual measurement is usually not made.

2.7 Stimulus–response psychology

How did Skinner's discoveries fit into the broader context of behaviourist psychology? Central to behaviourism would be how stimulus–response links change as a result of experience, as reflected in changes in behaviour.

So, how does Skinner's work fit the approach of stimulus–response psychology? The response seems clear: the lowering of the lever by the rat or key pecking by the pigeon. These can be measured objectively and their precise timing documented. Changes in behaviour over time can be measured, for example, increased frequency of lever pressing as the rat becomes more skilled at the task. So, everything seems neat and tidy for the application of stimulus–response psychology. Or does it?

A serious problem confronted Skinner: the response is clear but what is the *stimulus* to this response? You might speculate that the lever is the stimulus but the lever is present throughout.

Skinner resolved this issue along the following lines. He started by emphasising the distinction between the kind of conditioning that he studied and that studied by Pavlov. In Pavlov's case, there was indeed a discrete stimulus that triggered the response: for example, the tone triggered salivation. Behaviour of this kind was said to be controlled by stimuli that come before the response. Such behaviour was said to be elicited by stimuli, and the expression **elicited behaviour** came into use.

Elicited behaviour
Behaviour that is
triggered by a stimulus.

By contrast, the behaviour studied by Skinner was of a different kind and it was argued that it is not elicited by a stimulus that occurred prior to behaviour. Rather, behaviour was said to be freely emitted and it comes under the control of its *consequences*. As you have seen, sometimes these consequences are of a kind that strengthens the behaviour and they are said to be 'reinforcing'. At other times, the consequences of behaviour are punishing: that is, they lower the tendency to perform this behaviour. Behaviour that is freely emitted in this way and which comes under the control of its consequences was classified as **emitted behaviour**. Figure 4.8 summarises the distinction between elicited and emitted behaviour.

Emitted behaviour
Behaviour that is controlled by its consequences.

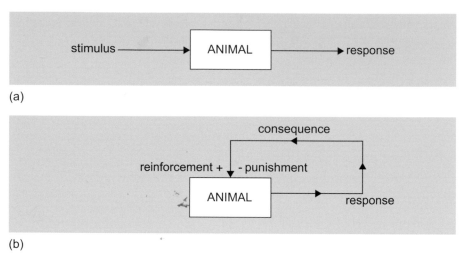

(a)

(b)

Figure 4.8   Two types of behaviour (a) elicited behaviour and (b) emitted behaviour. The plus and minus signs represent reinforcement and punishment, respectively

Of course animals did not evolve processes of learning in order to get by in psychology laboratories, so you might like to speculate on their significance for survival in the wild. Consider a hungry rat exploring and manipulating its natural environment. Certain actions will provide access to food: for example, tearing open a sack of grain. The reinforcement of these actions has a clear benefit for the rat.

So far, the focus of the chapter has been on rats and pigeons. However, Skinner was concerned that his ideas should be applied to humans and the discussion will turn to this in the next section.

Summary

- In instrumental conditioning, the sequence of events leading to reinforcement depends upon the behaviour of the animal.
- The Skinner box is a piece of apparatus in which operant conditioning (a form of instrumental conditioning) is studied.
- Whereas reinforcement increases the tendency to show a particular behaviour, punishment lowers it.
- Skinner drew a distinction between 'elicited behaviour', which is triggered by a stimulus, and 'emitted behaviour', which is controlled by its consequences.

3   From the Skinner box to human behaviour

Activity 4.3

Skinner argued that giving praise for desirable behaviour of a child in school reinforces that behaviour in the same way that a pellet reinforces lever-pressing in a Skinner box. Stop and think about this issue. Ask yourself whether things can really be that simple. Is there any fundamental difference in these situations?

Superficially, the two behaviours you reflected on in Activity 4.3 might well be very similar, but praise is surely more complex than a food pellet. For praise to serve as a positive reinforcer, it is necessary for the child to understand a spoken language and the meaning of praise (unlike the rat being reinforced with a food pellet). None of this undermines the power and efficacy of reinforcement, but it suggests that complex events going on in the mind of the child help to mediate the role of the reinforcer. Also, you might think that much human behaviour (e.g. visiting a friend) starts for reasons that are not accidental. There is often an *intention* involved: for example, to bring cheer to an individual.

3.1   The basic issue

Skinner (1953) argued that the principles of reinforcement and punishment that he so successfully studied in non-human animals in the laboratory could be extended to humans. He noted that any species confronts much the same set of problems in the wild: for example, how to find food and shelter and how to avoid excesses of heat and cold. Hence, a similar set of processes of learning might be expected when species are compared, and humans are just another species.

Skinner argued that human behaviour sometimes goes adrift as a result of faulty assumptions regarding its causes and a failure to make scientific observations of it. However, he asserted that behaviourist techniques can come to the rescue. Take, for example, a child who is misbehaving. The teacher stops the class at each instance and says 'Stop misbehaving or you will get into trouble'. The implicit assumption is that the threat will be punishing and hence the frequency of misbehaviour will come down. From a behaviourist perspective, a careful measurement of behaviour is needed. This might reveal that, far from decreasing the frequency of bad behaviour, when it was remarked upon the behaviour actually increased in frequency. Hence, what was believed to be punishment was actually positive reinforcement. It might be speculated that what constituted reinforcement was the attention that the teacher was giving to the child.

Skinner (1971) suggests that punishment is relatively ineffective as a control of behaviour. To illustrate this general assumption, consider again the misbehaving schoolchild. Suppose that punishment had been used to decrease bad behaviour. Can you see a problem with such a solution? Punishment, even if effective, teaches only what *not to do* rather than what *to do*. A vacuum can be left within the child's life. The child might rebel against the school by playing truant.

If the misbehaving schoolchild's disruptions are being reinforced by their teacher's attention, then omission of reinforcement should be associated with a decline in the undesirable behaviour. In addition to imposing extinction conditions, the teacher could try to positively reinforce behaviour that is incompatible with the undesirable behaviour. For example, when a child is paying attention or at least not being disruptive, praise might be offered. These techniques have been tried in classrooms with success (e.g. Swinson and Harrop, 2005).

3.2 Extrapolation to humans: its validity and implications

So long as Skinner studied rats and pigeons, few psychologists raised serious concerns. The notion that animal behaviour is controlled by its consequences triggered stimulating discussion among psychologists concerning the limits of this approach. Even some extrapolation from non-humans to humans might have been tolerable to most, as in employing techniques of reinforcement in schools, mental hospitals and prisons. However, Skinner went much further than simply presenting a toolbox of techniques for altering problematic behaviour.

Skinner made a fundamental and highly controversial assumption: *there is a universal principle of reinforcement that applies to human behaviour and which can account for most of this behaviour.*

This Skinnerian faith in reinforcement is based on the principle of **determinism** and the rejection of 'free will'. Determinism is the

Determinism
The belief that everything that happens, including human behaviour, is determined by past events.

assertion that everything that happens in the world, including human behaviour, is determined by what went before. So, if only psychologists knew enough about the events in the life of a person, they would be able to predict the future behaviour of this person. The counter-argument to Skinner (the free-will position) is perhaps that which appeals most broadly to people: humans have the capacity to make free and spontaneous choices, for which they can be held responsible and accountable. Their behaviour is not simply at the mercy of their history of reinforcement.

Skinner's assumption produced a passionate intellectual battle. His critics countered with the argument that there are fundamental differences between humans and other species. Non-humans might be rigidly determined in their behaviour but humans are different. Humans speak a sophisticated language and have complex cultures. They have insight into their behaviour and can make conscious choices. Humans are capable of articulating the determinants of their behaviour and reporting them to others, or of remaining inscrutable as to why they did something. Their behaviour, it was claimed, is characterised by long-term planning, purpose and intention. The possession of conscious awareness, language and culture means that humans can consciously work through plans of action (e.g. to get a university degree by means of study over years) and then freely execute them. Such a vocabulary sounds decidedly not 'rat-like' or behaviourist in its assertions.

Activity 4.4

Stop and consider the relevance of Skinner's argument for some of your behaviour. Could you better use positive reinforcement in dealing with friends and family? Do you feel that you function better when positively reinforced for desirable behaviour rather than being negatively reinforced or punished for wrongdoing? Do you feel that you have free will or that your behaviour is determined by what happened in the past?

Most people would surely agree that past experiences have a strong determining influence. For example, someone growing up in a violent family might be expected to be more prone to exhibit violence, in part because violent behaviour has been reinforced and in part modelled. However, it is important to note that not all people exposed to violent behaviour go on to become violent, and so such an explanation cannot be the whole story. This is why most psychologists would not go so far as Skinner and assume total determinism.

3.3 The social, political and ethical issue

Skinner argued that psychology needed to be used to change the world into a better place. Indeed, he had a utopian vision of a world that functioned on the basis of positive reinforcement, while avoiding aversive forms of control such as punishment. He became a missionary in the cause of changing the world and felt this would happen only if human behaviour were changed. This required meeting two closely related requirements:

1 A science of human behaviour is accepted, based upon *behaviour*, avoiding references to what goes on inside the head, such as intentions, motives, and so on.

2 Societies are designed according to the principles of a scientific understanding of behaviour, with positive reinforcement at centre stage.

Therefore, Skinner (1953, 1971) argued that rather than target people's minds, social change would occur if it were based upon insights gained from studying rats and pigeons.

Let us first briefly consider the old way of explaining behaviour. Traditionally, behaviour is explained in terms of mental events as reported by introspection. For example, consider a person who puts money in a charity box to help the poor. It might be said that they did so with the *intention* of alleviating suffering. They *thought* about the plight of poor people, they *felt* bad about this and they made a *free decision* to give. As free beings, they might equally well have walked by on the other side of the street, ignoring the poor. To persuade people to give to charity, one might need to change their hearts and *minds*.

This type of explanation, of course, appeals to mental events and these were to be avoided in a behaviourist psychology. Rather, Skinner (1953, 1971) argued that the charitable person had a history of being reinforced for performing similar behaviour. Each time in the past that they showed giving behaviour, they received reinforcement in the form of, for example, thanks and social acceptance. Hence, their present behaviour is to be explained *historically* in terms of the consequences of similar behaviour in the past.

Consider a judge sentencing a criminal to life in jail for murder. The summing-up would usually involve something along the lines of 'You are an *evil* person with little in the way of a *conscience*, who *willingly* opted for a career in crime and finally took the life of another. You chose a path of evil and now society requires that you pay the price and feel remorse.' It would sound very odd indeed if a Skinnerian judge were to say, 'You had a long history of being positively reinforced for violent behaviour. Now you will receive positive reinforcement only for socially acceptable actions, while your anti-social actions will undergo extinction.'

Skinner's best-known book was entitled *Beyond Freedom and Dignity* (Skinner, 1971) and it reached number one in the American bestseller charts. In 1975, Skinner became the most famous scientist in America (Guttman, 1977). The title of his book might seem to be a deliberate provocation and it needs some unpacking. Skinner urged society to reject the assumption that free will is the main determinant of behaviour. The 'dignity' that society was being asked to move beyond referred only to a particular kind of dignity: that which derives from achievement. That is to say, people like to take credit (acquire 'dignity') for those actions of which they are proud, whereas they tend to avoid responsibility for those of which they are not proud. Extenuating circumstances can invariably be brought to bear in the latter case. According to Skinner, rather than accept determinism for bad actions and free choice for good ones, people need to reject the double standard. Behaviour is deserving of neither praise nor condemnation; rather, it needs dispassionate analysis in relation to its determinants.

The book earned criticism like few books before it. Even United States Vice-President Spiro Agnew (in the presidency of Richard Nixon) described Skinner as 'most dangerous'. It is not hard to see why an American politician would take this stance. The political foundations of the United States are based on the individualistic assumption that people are responsible for their actions. They are responsible for the good and bad that happens to them and can blame no one but themselves. To take away personal responsibility was seen as basically anti-American. Skinner was also criticised by those on the left too. He saw the root cause of social problems as coming from a particular history of reinforcement of individual behaviour. This was incompatible with the left-wing view that wrongs are caused by broader social forces, such as the capitalist economic system, which operate beyond the individual.

Summary

- Skinner argued that the principle of reinforcement can be applied very widely to human behaviour.

- According to Skinner, determinism applies to all behaviour and the notion of free will is not compatible with scientific thinking.

- Skinner believed that a science of behaviour with positive reinforcement at centre stage and avoiding aversive controls could solve the world's problems.

4 Behaviourism after Skinner

Only a few psychologists these days would describe themselves as behaviourists. The revolutionary zeal of Watson and Skinner to build a new science of psychology based upon observable behaviour might appear, then, to have failed.

Although psychology has not adopted behaviourism as its fundamental framework, it nonetheless owes much to the early behaviourists. The systematic observation of behaviour and its measurement is implicitly used by a range of psychologists and it might be argued that this derives from behaviourism's early emphasis upon objectivity. The techniques of reinforcement are widely in use in hospitals, prisons and schools.

The whole behaviourist enterprise was based upon the assumption of determinism and the rejection of free will. This argument still rages back and forth, with passionate advocates of each position. However, it is unlikely that one side will score a victory. Instead, this is an issue that cannot be resolved.

In surveying the Skinnerian argument, some have been led to conclude that what is termed a 'pragmatic position' might need to be adopted. At times psychologists might choose to act as if people have free will, whereas at other times psychologists might feel that determinism offers the most insight.

4.1 Different types of learning

You read about Albert Bandura's research in Chapter 3.

Skinner's emphasis was on the importance of operant conditioning. However, over the years, there has been an increasing recognition that there are several different types of learning. For example, learning by imitating role models has been demonstrated by Albert Bandura. There is also an increasing recognition that classical conditioning occurs much more widely than was earlier appreciated. It tended to be thought at one time that it was applicable mainly to reflexes such as salivation. Now it is realised that more complex behaviour can reflect such learning. For example, in drug addicts, an urge to seek and take drugs can be triggered by being in an environment (e.g. one in which pushers or other addicts are present) that has been associated in the past with drug taking (Siegel, 2005).

Figure 4.9   Environment acting as a trigger for behaviour

4.2   The value of the Skinner box

The Skinner box is a favourite piece of equipment in a wide range of laboratories among researchers of many orientations. It is a simple, well-controlled and very efficient way of observing behaviour in non-human animals. Consider, for example, a researcher who is studying vision in birds. He or she can exploit what Skinner termed **discrimination learning**. Typically, a bird is first trained to work for food. Then pellets are available only when a red light in the box is on but not when a green light is on. After a time the bird will come to discriminate, so that it pecks the key when the red light is on but not when the green light is on. It has shown thereby that it can discriminate between these colours.

Suppose that a new species of bird is discovered and the researcher wishes to know whether it has colour vision. One way of doing this is to perform a discrimination test. A member of this species is trained in the Skinner box to earn food. Food is then made available only if the bird pecks a disc of a particular colour. If the bird proceeds to peck only when presented with a disc of a particular colour, then it can be inferred that it has colour vision.

Research on drugs designed to counter anxiety also uses rats in Skinner boxes. How could you measure anxiety in a rat? How could you measure a reduction in anxiety as a result of taking a drug? First, a

Discrimination learning
Learning to respond in the presence of one event (e.g. a green light) but not in the presence of another (e.g. a red light).

hungry rat is trained to earn food pellets. Then a tone is followed by a mild shock to the feet. Rats come to fear the tone, in that it is followed by a brief lowering of their lever pressing. Then they can be injected with the drug to see whether this reduces the disruption to lever pressing that is caused by the tone. When drugs that are used to lower human anxiety were given to the rats, they reduced the disruptive effect of the tone (Lane, 1992).

Without doubt, the Skinner box is useful and the *procedure* of reinforcement is a highly effective way of studying and changing the behaviour of an animal. However, disagreement concerns the *interpretation* placed upon the results obtained in the Skinner box. Skinner urged psychologists not to apply mental terms to behaviour but that has not stopped many psychologists from doing exactly that. For example, some (e.g. Bolles, 1972) argue that, in the Skinner box, the animal learns to *expect* food (it forms an **expectancy**). It learns an association between its behaviour and the arrival of food. There is some evidence to support this position, which fits with common sense. When extinction terms are applied, rats are said to show an emotion that is termed 'frustration' (Gray, 1987). Why is it called this? The logic is as follows. In response to stress, particular hormones are released into the blood stream. These same hormones are released when extinction is applied, suggesting that the experience is stressful. Frustration is the term used to describe the human emotion experienced under comparable conditions and so psychologists apply this also to rats.

Expectancy
The formation of mental state where an animal comes to expect something to happen after something else has happened.

Activity 4.5

If you have a pet, reflect on its behaviour and whether you can recall any signs of expectancies.

Most cat and dog owners can probably find examples. The prospect of a walk or food seems to trigger anticipation of good things to follow shortly. The sound of a can-opener triggers more than just salivation (e.g. running from a distant room to the site of the food).

4.3 Therapeutic procedures

Contemporary therapy for psychological distress owes much to insights derived from behaviourism. For example, children who are displaying self-harm, such as head-banging, have been treated with techniques of reinforcement for non-harming behaviours (Flora, 2004). Adult patients in mental hospitals who are uncommunicative and uncooperative have been taught communication and social skills by reinforcing appropriate behaviours and ignoring inappropriate behaviour (Flora, 2004). One of the most powerful techniques for treating people with obsessional and phobic disorders (see Section 1) involves identifying and removing reinforcement for the behaviour that is excessive. At the same time, any reductions in the target behaviour can be reinforced with praise.

There are two important qualifications to add and these serve to frame behaviourist approaches in modern terms:

First, the efficacy of reinforcement can depend upon the patient's understanding of what is going on, as mediated by means of a spoken language. Indeed, reinforcement is likely to be only one aspect of the therapeutic procedure. Another aspect is likely to focus on the patient's thought processes.

Second, closely connected with the notion of behavioural interventions for change is the explicit recognition that interventions also target processes of learning that are not based on reinforcement. For example, consider again the patient with a phobia about going outdoors. The therapist who escorts the patient on his excursions outdoors is actually presenting a model of behaviour that can be imitated by the patient.

Summary

- There are relatively few psychologists these days who would describe themselves as 'behaviourists'.

- Despite most psychologists rejecting the full Skinnerian message, the techniques devised by Skinner are in wide use.

- Some researchers speculate that animals learn expectancies.

- There are various types of learning, of which operant conditioning is only one. The range of therapeutic techniques reflects this diversity.

5   The relevance of Skinner to today's world

By carefully examining behaviour and its consequences, it is possible to identify common features of a number of social problems. Some forms of behaviour that are problematic have an immediate consequence of positive reinforcement. However, the aversive effects of these same forms of behaviour arise long after the behaviour. This section will provide examples of the conflicting nature of the immediate and long-term consequences.

5.1   Addictions

The original meaning of the word 'addiction' was extreme dedication to something (to 'give over') (Alexander and Schweighofer, 1988). Thus, one could equally well be addicted to, say, praying, love or drugs. For a period starting in the nineteenth century, the use became confined largely to drugs, and addiction was seen as essentially a medical problem needing a medical solution. Recently, there has been a swing back to something nearer to the original meaning, with awareness that people can be addicted to a whole range of things including gambling, shopping, sex, exercise or junk foods, as well as to drugs (Alexander and Schweighofer, 1988; Alexander, 2008). In the extreme, non-drug-related addictions can be as destructive as the drug-related ones, leading to bankruptcy and loss of job, health and family.

In each addiction, it appears that there is a strong and immediate positively-reinforcing consequence of behaviour, whereas the unpleasant consequences are long delayed. In order to try to treat addictions, it is essential to understand how it is that people become addicted.

Let's consider the example of smoking. Inhaling nicotine is instantly reinforcing in the sense of encouraging the smoker to repeat the behaviour. Nicotine arrives in the bloodstream within a second or so of puffing the cigarette and exerts its effects on the brain. By contrast, the negative consequences, such as coughing and breathing difficulties, might arise long after the smoking habit is well established and might not be linked closely to the act of smoking. Other consequences, such as lung cancer and heart disease, might occur years into the future and, at the moment, there is only the threat of them to deter smoking. Such threats are often ineffective.

Gambling is another particularly interesting example from the point of view of a Skinnerian analysis, since it fits very well with an interpretation in terms of a special form of partial reinforcement. The gambler keeps going even when there are only very occasional reinforcements, which come at unpredictable times. By analogy, the rat pressing a lever for food on such a schedule takes a long time to quit when extinction is applied. The person addicted to junk food is under the control of a reinforcement process that was highly effective in our early evolution, when food was scarce and much effort needed to be spent in obtaining it. These days, food is relatively easy to obtain.

Figure 4.10   A form of partial reinforcement?

5.2   Global survival

Today it is often argued that, for human life on earth to survive, people need to change their ways. This means shifting from our reliance on oil and implies changing the behaviour of much of the world's population. The affluent countries need to consume and pollute much less. How can people be persuaded to do this? The present chapter describes a possible contribution arising from psychology. In the context of global survival, people can *learn* to change their behaviour.

Skinner was one of the world's first 'greens', if not *the* first. In 1948, he published what amounted to a green manifesto, outlining how a society could be organised without waste or competition to provide for all. His green manifesto (Skinner, 1948) was extraordinarily prescient. In its 1976 edition (p. xvi), he argued: 'Not only can we not face the rest of the world while consuming and polluting as we do, we cannot for long face ourselves while acknowledging the violence and chaos in which we live.'

Consider the nature of the problem in terms of short-term consequences, reinforcement and long-term consequences. For example, cars are quick, comfortable and offer privacy and status ('positive reinforcement'). The benefits from car use are personal and immediate. The costs in terms of climate change and loss of public transport ('punishment') are long-term and diffuse rather than immediate and personal. By contrast, the use of energy-efficient means of transport such as walking, bicycles, trains and buses involves immediate exposure to the elements ('punishment'). The costs in terms of discomfort are immediate and personal, whereas the benefits to the environment are diffuse and long-term. A look at today's problems suggests the value of considering the Skinnerian position. For example, regular appeals are made to change our ways. They usually involve the assumption that first people's minds need to be changed and then they will change their behaviour appropriately. People are urged to think of the future and therefore to consume less energy. Money is spent on promotion campaigns urging us to consume less. However, evidence shows that simply appealing to people to change their ways is relatively ineffective (Katzev and Johnson, 1987).

Someone adopting a Skinnerian perspective would urge that the solution is to change the nature of the reinforcers in use. Some of the behaviours that need to be reduced are inherently positively reinforcing and so they need to be made less so. According to a Skinnerian perspective, the situation is analogous to that of the rat in the Skinner box. In this case, the government, local council or supermarket chain decides what behaviour will be reinforced and what will be the reinforcer. For example, the local council might decide that people will be offered tokens for recycling rubbish. The assumption is that this will increase the amount of recycling. Some supermarkets already offer a small discount for reusing bags. This is analogous to the experimenter deciding the nature of the reinforcer in the Skinner box (for example, the size of the pellet or whether to use a partial reinforcement schedule).

Box 4.2   A problem with the Skinnerian solution

Skinner's solution to environmental problems involved extrapolating findings from the Skinner box and applying them to the complex issue of environmental change. However, there is a problem with this extrapolation when it comes to changing behaviour on a global scale. For the rat in the Skinner box or the prisoner who earns tokens for good behaviour, it is clear who holds the power to give or withhold reinforcements and what their intentions are. Similarly, when consumers are encouraged to recycle more, it is the local council, the supermarkets or the government that have the power to reinforce the desired behaviour. In the case of global issues, however, things are less straightforward. While there is no doubt that the world as a whole needs to pollute less, or that affluent countries need to reduce their energy consumption, it is far less clear who holds the necessary power to offer adequate reinforcements and shape behaviour to achieve the desired effect. In other words, if the world is a Skinner box and we are all rats, who is Skinner? One might argue, therefore, that Skinner's global green project does not take adequate account of the power relations required for global behaviour shaping.

Figure 4.11   Rewards for recycling: reinforcement of environmentally responsible behaviour

5.3   Concluding remark

A general consensus is that behaviour is under a range of controls and operant conditioning is just one form of learning. In Chapter 3 you were introduced to social learning and the role of observation and imitation. You are not expected to decide which is the correct way of explaining behaviour – in terms of observation *or* because of behaviour's consequences. Both processes exist side by side. Indeed, behaviour might sometimes occur as a result of imitation *and* be strengthened still more by its consequences. Furthermore, many psychologists would argue that it is not sensible to put operant conditioning at centre stage. However, it is a control that might well have been underestimated, and a consideration of Skinner's approach could very usefully inform our day-to-day lives as well as public policy making.

Summary

- Much behaviour that is problematic can be characterised by immediate reinforcement followed by long-delayed aversive consequences.
- Addictions, overconsumption and ecologically undesirable behaviours fit this pattern.
- Skinner urged a reform of society so as to introduce reinforcement for environmentally responsible behaviour.

References

Alexander, B.K. (2008) *The Globalization of Addiction: A Study in Poverty of the Spirit*, Oxford, Oxford University Press.

Alexander, B.K. and Schweighofer, A.R.F. (1988) 'Defining "addiction"', *Canadian Psychology*, vol. 29, no. 2, pp. 151–62.

Bolles, R.C. (1972) 'Reinforcement, expectancy, and learning', *Psychological Review*, vol. 79, no. 5, pp. 394–409.

Flora, S.R. (2004) *The Power of Reinforcement*, Albany, NY, State University of New York Press.

Gray, J.A. (1987) *The Psychology of Fear and Stress*, Cambridge, Cambridge University Press.

Guttman, N. (1977) 'On Skinner and Hull: a reminiscence and projection', *American Psychologist*, vol. 32, no. 5, pp. 321–8.

Katzev, R.D. and Johnson, T.R. (1987) *Promoting Energy Conservation: An Analysis of Behavioral Research*, Boulder, CO, Westview Press.

Lane, J.D. (1992) 'Neurochemical changes associated with the action of acute administration of diazepam in reversing the behavioural paradigm conditioned emotional responses (CER)' *Neurochemical Research*, vol. 17, no. 5, pp. 497–507

Pavlov, I.P. (1927) Conditioned reflexes: An Investigation of the Physiological Activity of the Cerebral Cortex, Oxford, Oxford University Press.

Siegel, S. (2005) 'Drug tolerance, drug addiction, and drug anticipation', *Current Directions in Psychological Science*, vol. 14, no. 6, pp. 296–300.

Skinner, B.F. (1939) *The Behavior of Organisms: An Experimental Analysis*, New York, NY, Appleton-Century-Crofts.

Skinner, B.F. (1953) *Science and Human Behavior*, New York, NY, The Free Press.

Skinner, B.F. (1976 [1948]) *Walden Two*, New York, NY, Macmillan Publishing.

Skinner, B.F. (1979) *The Shaping of a Behaviorist*, New York, NY, Alfred A. Knopf.

Skinner, B.F. (1971) *Beyond Freedom and Dignity*, New York, NY, Knopf.

Swinson, J. and Harrop, A. (2005) 'An examination of the effects of a short course aimed at enabling teachers in infant, junior and secondary schools to alter the verbal feedback given to their pupils', *Educational Studies*, vol. 31, no. 2, pp. 115–29.

Thorndike, E.L. (1898) *Animal Intelligence: An Experimental Study of the Associative Processes in Animals*, New York, NY, Columbia University Press.

Watson, J.B. (1913) 'Psychology as the behaviourist views it', *Psychological Review*, vol. 20, no. 2, pp. 158–77.

Watson, J.B. and Rayner, R. (1920) 'Conditioned emotional reactions', *Journal of Experimental Psychology*, vol. 3, no. 1, pp. 1–14.

Chapter 5
Determined to love?

Deborah Custance

Contents

Aims and objectives

After studying this chapter you should be able to:

- summarise some of the most influential findings of psychological research on attachment in humans and other species

- describe Harlow's maternal deprivation experiments with rhesus macaques and explain their importance with respect to attachment theory

- outline some of the ethical implications and the scientific value of using non-human animals in psychological research

- describe Mary Ainsworth's observational research on children's attachment

- recognise that behaviour based upon a biologically inherited system is not necessarily rigid and determined.

1   Introduction

The 1989 United Nations' Convention on the Rights of the Child declared that: '[T]he child, for the full and harmonious development of his or her personality, should grow up in a family environment, in an atmosphere of happiness, love and understanding' (UN, 1989).

The 1959 United Nations Declaration of the Rights of the Child also stated that, 'a child of tender years shall not, save in exceptional circumstances, be separated from his mother' (UN, 1959).

Is love a basic human right? Can we really dictate love? Is mother-love especially important for the healthy development of young children? What is this thing called 'love' anyway? It is certainly an extremely powerful emotion. It is an emotion that draws and bonds us to another person. We yearn for the presence of a loved one, they preoccupy our thoughts and we turn to them in times of joy and sorrow. Yet, why do we love? Is it for the benefit of the other person or is it driven by selfish motivations? Where does love come from? Do we learn it or are we born with the capacity to love?

In this chapter, I will explore the nature of love, in particular the love between a child and its mother. The bond that develops between the child and the mother, or other primary caregiver, has been called **attachment**. I will consider the major scientific theories of attachment and some of the most influential studies that have been conducted on the subject.

1.1   What is attachment and where does it come from?

It seems obvious that all children and their parents should love each other. They should both derive pleasure and satisfaction from cuddling and playing together. For a parent, the sometimes overwhelming feelings of protective love may either come almost instantaneously with the birth of their child or grow over the first few months of the child's life.

Most human infants begin to show a preference for one person over and above everyone else at approximately 7 months of age. If they are separated from that special person (who is usually, but not always, their mother) they tend to become very distressed and will do all they can to be reunited with them. Soon after establishing this primary attachment, children begin to extend their affections to an inner circle of special

Attachment
A relatively long-term, emotionally important relationship in which one individual seeks proximity to and derives security and comfort from the presence of another.

people, which usually includes other family members, close family friends, nannies or child minders.

This chapter focuses mostly upon the close emotional bond that develops between mothers and infants. This is because much research has focused upon mother–infant attachment. Yet you should bear in mind that there are lots of different types of attachment: father to child, grandparent to grandchild, romantic relationships, the dog–human bond, and even the strong emotional ties that some children form in response to certain objects such as soft toys or cloths have all been discussed in terms of attachment. Thus, even though I will focus primarily on the mother–infant bond, attachment refers to any relatively long-term emotionally important relationship in which one individual seeks proximity to and derives security and comfort from the presence of another.

John Bowlby was the first scientist to use the term 'attachment' to refer to the mutually affectionate bond that develops between a child and his or her caregivers. In the 1950s Bowlby proposed a theory to explain how and why attachment relationships develop. In order to appreciate how radical Bowlby's ideas were when he first proposed them, it is necessary to consider the alternative theories that existed at the time.

Activity 5.1

Without reading ahead, spend a couple of minutes considering the following questions:

- Why do you think children and their caregivers form close, mutually affectionate relationships?
- Why does a mother or father love their child?
- Why does the child form such strong feelings for his or her parents?

Initially, the questions in Activity 5.1 seem obvious, even easy, don't they? However, don't be surprised if your mind went completely blank and you couldn't think of any reasons for why children and parents love each other. Obvious questions are often devilishly difficult to answer. Most people take it for granted that parents and infants love each other and they rarely stop to question why.

Figure 5.1   Different types of attachment

1.2   Cupboard love or love in the blood?

Before Bowlby published his work on attachment, there were two main theories that purported to explain the bond that develops between infants and their parents: the psychoanalytic theory, and the behaviourist or learning theory.

You read about psychoanalysis in Chapter 1, Section 1.

Psychoanalytical theorists, such as Sigmund Freud, suggested that we love our parents because they satisfy our basic biological needs. Thus, as babies, we learn to love whoever feeds us, provides warmth by holding or cuddling us and alleviates discomfort by changing our nappies and burping us. According to Freud, infants become distressed when they are separated from their primary attachment figure because they are frightened that their basic needs will no longer be satisfied. Bowlby labelled accounts such as this 'cupboard-love theories' (Holmes, 1993).

You learnt about behaviourism in Chapter 4.

The behaviourist approach to parent–infant bonding is also based upon cupboard love. Babies love their parents because they have learned to associate them with positively rewarding experiences such as being fed and cuddled. Food, warmth and the alleviation of discomfort are unconditional stimuli in the sense that children find these things immediately or intrinsically rewarding. In contrast, infants do not immediately value their caregivers. Instead, they learn to value them, especially their mother if they are being breastfed, because she is habitually associated with the primary reinforcers of food and comfort. Thus, the infant's mother constitutes a conditional stimulus.

In many ways psychoanalytic and behaviourist accounts of infant attachment seem intuitively correct. It seems obvious that a child learns to love its parents because they satisfy its basic biological needs. Yet, according to Bowlby's account, cupboard love does not form the basis of attachment.

Ethology
The study of animal behaviour under natural conditions.

Bowlby's work on attachment was influenced by Konrad Lorenz and Niko Tinbergen, two scientists who are widely acknowledged as the founding fathers of **ethology**, namely the study of animal behaviour under natural conditions. In the first half of the twentieth century, Lorenz and Tinbergen studied wild birds and noticed that the chicks of some species seemed to possess certain behavioural responses right from the very moment of hatching rather than having to learn them. For instance, Tinbergen observed that newly hatched herring gull chicks would peck at a red spot on the lower mandible of their parents' beaks.

In response to this pecking, gull parents regurgitate partially digested fish for their chick to eat. Tinbergen suspected that the chick's pecking response was inborn or **innate**. To explore the phenomenon further, Tinbergen collected newly hatched chicks that had never had the opportunity to peck at their parents' beaks and waved various objects in front of them, counting how many times they pecked. He discovered that they would peck not only at naturalistic adult gull beaks, but also at objects that moved gently up and down and contrasted with foreground and background colours. Thus, herring gull chicks seem to be born with a crude, but nonetheless effective programme for pecking at certain types of stimuli. Based upon these observations, Tinbergen argued that the pecking reflex was an **evolved predisposition**. To understand what Tinbergen meant by this, we need to know a little bit about Charles Darwin's theory of evolution by natural selection.

Darwin argued that biological organisms have evolved or changed over time. He proposed a mechanism called natural selection by which this change might take place. The individual members of all species differ from one another in various ways. They may be slightly different sizes or heights, they may be different colours, some may possess slightly better eyesight or hearing … and so on. Some of these variations may increase an individual's chances of survival or their chances of finding a mate and producing lots of healthy offspring. If an advantageous trait can be biologically passed on to an organism's offspring, then more individuals in the next generation will possess that particular trait and they will then pass it on to their offspring. Some inherited traits may be primarily physiological, yet research suggests that a number of them involve behavioural tendencies that are also capable of increasing an organism's chances of survival and reproductive success. Presumably, possessing from the moment of hatching the tendency to peck at stimuli with certain features greatly increases a herring gull chick's chances of survival.

Influenced by evolutionary theory and ethological research, Bowlby put forward the radical proposition that human infants possess inbuilt or innate tendencies that lead them to forge emotionally powerful ties to stimuli with certain properties (Bowlby, 1979). He argued that these tendencies are the product of the evolutionary pressure for survival. For the infant, the need to bond with a caregiver is a matter of personal survival. The young of many species, including humans, are born weak and helpless. Without the protection of a diligent caregiver, they would starve, freeze or be eaten by a predator. It is therefore vital that they

Innate
Relating to a behaviour, disposition or characteristic that is present from birth.

Evolved predisposition
A behavioural tendency that increases an organism's chances of survival and reproductive success.

elicit loving care from and maintain proximity to an adult who can provide them with food, warmth and protection. Thus Bowlby argued that infants possess certain inbuilt mechanisms for encouraging care-giving responses from their parents. Infants cry, particularly if they are separated from their parents, and smile to indicate pleasure during an interaction. Bowlby (1979, p. 37) observed: 'Babies' smiles are powerful things, leaving mothers spellbound and enslaved. Who can doubt that the baby who most readily rewards his mother with a smile is the one who is best loved and best cared for?'

But what is in it for the parents? Obviously, infants do not provide food and safety. So why should the parents be primed to be psychologically manipulated by their children in this way? From an evolutionary perspective, children constitute the tickets to the parents' biological immortality or, to put it less romantically, long-term genetic survival. Individuals can cheat death to a certain extent by leaving a biological legacy in the form of copies of their genes that are passed on through the generations. This has led them to develop an innate predisposition to care for the young.

Although both parents and infants are likely to possess inbuilt predispositions to bond to one another, Bowlby mostly focused on attachment from the point of view of the child. He proposed that infant attachment is based upon three main factors: (a) an inbuilt predisposition to enjoy social interaction; (b) an innate bias to become attached to things with certain properties, and (c) an inbuilt fear of the unknown and unfamiliar. Notice that none of these factors involve food: this is not cupboard love.

1.3   Love at first sight: imprinting

One of the major influences upon Bowlby's ideas was, perhaps rather surprisingly, the behaviour of geese. The Austrian ethologist Konrad Lorenz was fascinated by the tendency of newly hatched goslings to follow their mother wherever she went. In order to test the phenomenon further, he raised a clutch of goose eggs. Practically the first thing the goslings saw upon hatching was Lorenz, or, to be more precise, his wellington boots. As you can see in the delightful photograph (see Figure 5.2), the young birds would follow Lorenz in his wellington boots wherever he went.

Figure 5.2   Konrad Lorenz followed by a small flock of imprinted goslings

Lorenz called this process of bonding **imprinting** (Lorenz and Kickert, 1981; Hess, 1958). Several species of bird and even one species of mammal, the shrew, imprint. As soon as the babies are mobile, they tend to follow anything that moves. Under natural conditions, the thing that is most likely to be moving about in the vicinity of the youngster is its parent. However, in laboratory tests with baby birds, they have become imprinted upon a toy duck on wheels, yellow rubber gloves and even a geometrical shape moving back and forth behind a plate-glass window. If newly hatched ducklings follow a moving object for about ten minutes, imprinting occurs. They will then follow it wherever it goes and cry piteously if they become separated from the object of their affection. Early laboratory studies have shown that imprinting occurs during a specific period in a young bird's life. Eckhard Hess (1958) found that if ducklings do not become exposed to a moving object within the first three days of their life, after that point instead of imprinting they become frightened and avoid all unfamiliar stimuli.

It would seem clear that imprinting is an innate or evolved system. Yet ducks and geese are very different from humans. When Bowlby first suggested that humans might also possess similar inbuilt tendencies to bond, the scientific community was highly sceptical. He needed more convincing evidence. That evidence would come from a species closely related to humans – monkeys.

Imprinting
An innate system that allows rapid learning to occur in animals immediately after birth. It involves developing attachment to a specific individual or object.

Summary

- Psychologists have been interested in attachment, in particular the bond between a baby and its primary carer.
- Important insight into the study of attachment came from ethological studies of animal behaviour.
- Drawing on ethological research and evolutionary theory, John Bowlby challenged the behaviourist and psychoanalytic theories of attachment, arguing that infants possess innate tendencies that lead them to forge emotionally powerful relationships with primary caregivers.

2 Key study: Harlow's monkeys

Harry Harlow was an American psychologist who investigated whether infants bond with their mother because of cupboard love (i.e. the fact that their mother provides them with food) or, as Bowlby suggested, an inbuilt tendency to become attached to stimuli that possess certain properties (such as being warm and soft to the touch). The problem is that, under normal circumstances, mothers simultaneously provide food and tactile comfort for their babies. An observational study alone could not separate out the influence of these two factors. To test it experimentally, one group of mothers would have to be prevented from feeding their babies, while another group would have to be prevented from holding and cuddling them. Although, for reasons of ethics, such an experiment is impossible with humans, he could conduct it with monkeys.

You read about ethics in Section 3 of Chapter 2 and Section 3.2 of Chapter 3.

Some of the most influential work on attachment was conducted by Harlow on a group of rhesus macaques (*Macaca mulatta*), a medium-sized monkey with light brown fur and a pink face. In the wild, they are found throughout mainland Asia. They are reasonably easy to keep and breed in captivity and are often used in research.

It is interesting that Harlow came to study attachment in rhesus monkeys almost by accident. He had hoped to study intelligence in rats, but when he took up employment at the University of Wisconsin he discovered, to his great consternation, that the rat laboratory had been dismantled. However, when he started observing monkeys at the local zoo, he quickly realised that their intellectual abilities outstripped those of rats. Harlow secured funding for a primate laboratory at the university and set out to study intelligence in monkeys.

One of the problems with the wild-caught monkeys that were used in the laboratory was that they often carried disease. As a result the baby monkeys were separated from their mothers and housed in separate cages on their own. During daily cage cleaning Harlow noticed that the babies would protest as the sanitary pads that lined their cages were removed. This serendipitous observation intrigued Harlow. Why does the baby form an attachment to a sanitary pad? To answer this question Harlow embarked on the famous (some would say infamous) research into monkey attachment.

Figure 5.3   Harry Harlow (1905–1981)

Harlow suspected that the infants' affection for the pads was primarily based upon 'contact comfort'. Despite the fact that the baby monkeys had all their physical needs catered for in terms of food, water and shelter, they seemed to be bonding with the only soft object in their otherwise hard and harsh environment. In fact, Harlow observed that, 'a baby monkey raised on a bare wire-mesh cage floor survives with difficulty, if at all, during the first five days of life' (Harlow 1958, p. 675). Harlow hypothesised that the tactile qualities of stimuli were more important for infant monkey bonding than the provision of food. He designed a series of experiments to test this idea further, which will be described later in Section 2.2.

202

Figure 5.4   Contact comfort

2.1   Researching animals

Activity 5.2

Take a couple of minutes to think about the advantages of using monkeys to study attachment. Draw up a list of pros and cons for studying monkeys rather than humans. What can we do and learn by studying monkeys that would not be possible by studying humans alone?

One advantage of studying monkeys rather than humans is that scientists can conduct experiments with non-human subjects that for ethical reasons would not be permitted with human participants.

A possible disadvantage of using non-human animals in place of humans is that you can never be completely sure of the degree to which the findings are applicable to humans. Humans and monkeys are genetically very similar to one another (rhesus macaques and humans share 94 per cent of their DNA). But just because monkeys exhibit a certain pattern of behaviour, it does necessarily mean that humans do so as well. You can read more about the issue of cross-species comparisons in Box 5.1.

You read about experiments in Chapters 2 and 3.

leading onto
Ainsworth

Box 5.1   Why do it this way?

Why do psychologists study monkeys or other animals, if they are ultimately interested in human psychology?

Non-human animals are often used in psychological research as a substitute for humans. In Harlow's case, ethical considerations prohibited him from conducting his experiments on human infants. Had he somehow been able to conduct his experiments on humans, he would no doubt later have been prosecuted for his actions. However, he enjoyed a career in which he spent over 20 years socially isolating monkeys in various different ways. As you will see later, since Harlow completed his research, psychologists have become increasingly aware of the importance of ethics in animal research and guidelines have been put in place to protect animal welfare.

Another advantage of using non-human animals in research is that they are often thought to provide a simpler model of behaviour than that found in human beings. Humans are extremely complex creatures and it can be very difficult to disentangle all the different factors that influence our behaviour. Non-human animals are often less sophisticated and their behavioural responses can be easier to interpret.

Monkeys and apes are often preferred in psychological research on animals. Human beings are genetically very similar to other species of primate. We share approximately 98.8 per cent of our DNA with chimpanzees and 94 per cent with rhesus macaques. Yet one must be very careful how one interprets this genetic similarity. We share 50 per cent of our DNA with a banana. A small difference in DNA can make a huge difference in a species' anatomy and behaviour. For one thing, despite a 1.2 per cent difference in our DNA, humans have a brain three times the size of a chimpanzee's.

So, rather than making simple comparisons between species, animal researchers look for general behavioural principles that can then be used to draw inferences about human behaviour. For example, the fact that birds show imprinting does not provide very convincing evidence that human bonding is based on similar mechanisms. However, if one looks across many species – from those genetically distant from humans up to our closest non-human relatives – and finds bonding processes similar to those exhibited by humans, the idea of common underlying mechanisms becomes more convincing.

2.2   Wire versus terry-cloth mothers

To test the idea of 'contact comfort', Harlow (1958) constructed two types of surrogate monkey mother (See Figures 5.3 and 5.5). The first was called the terry-cloth mother. It was made from a block of wood covered in a layer of sponge rubber and sheathed in a layer of towelling (or terry-cloth as it is called in America). A light bulb behind the terry-cloth mother provided a source of gentle heat. A bottle could be inserted through the cloth mother's body, from which the baby could feed. The second type of mother was made of a cylinder of wire mesh that was adequate for clinging on to, but lacked any contact comfort. It too could have a feeding bottle inserted into it. Harlow placed these mothers in separate cubicles attached to the babies' living quarters. He tested eight newborn monkeys. For four of the monkeys the terry-cloth mother provided milk, while the wire mother did not, and for the remaining four monkeys the wire mother provided milk while the cloth mother did not. In this way, Harlow could directly compare the variables of contact comfort and food provision.

To describe Harlow's experiment in more formal scientific terms, the independent variable (i.e. the aspect of the experiment that was manipulated) was the type of mother presented to the babies (i.e. wire or terry-cloth). The dependent variable (i.e. the aspect that Harlow measured and expected to be affected by the independent variable) was the degree of bonding as revealed by how much time the monkeys spent clinging to each of the surrogate mothers and the amount they cried when either of them was removed.

You were introduced to independent and dependent variables in Section 2.3 of Chapter 3.

The results of Harlow's experiment were unequivocal. The babies showed a clear preference for the terry-cloth mother over the wire mother regardless of which of them produced milk. If the wire mother provided milk, the babies would cling to the terry-cloth mother and only approach the wire mother to feed, returning to the terry-cloth mother immediately afterwards. If the wire mother was removed from the cage, the babies hardly reacted. If the terry-cloth mother was removed, they became highly distressed.

Figure 5.5   A baby monkey clings to its terry-cloth mother. The wire mother with its feeding bottle can be seen in the background

Harlow's findings appeared to confirm John Bowlby's contention that the infant–parent bond is based on innate tendencies rather than cupboard love. Harlow's systematic and controlled experiment showed that contact comfort was more important than food in the formation of attachment. The fact that the babies became upset only when the terry-cloth mother was removed and showed little concern in response to the removal of the wire mother provides strong evidence that they were bonded to the former, but not the latter.

Harlow confirmed these results by running three more experiments. Conducting just one experiment in which the babies were presented with a wire mother who provided food and a warm soft terry-cloth mother who provided comfort would probably not have been sufficient in and of itself to convince people. Since both of the artificial mothers were placed adjacent to each other in each baby's cage, it would not be very surprising if they chose to enjoy the best of both worlds – clinging to the terry-cloth mother for comfort and popping over to the wire mother when they were hungry. One becomes more convinced with the subsequent experimental manipulations.

In one experiment, Harlow separated the babies from their mothers and placed them into a cubicle where they could lift a hatch to look at either their terry-cloth mother, the wire mother, or a bare cage. The babies lifted the hatch most to look at the terry-cloth mother and looked at the wire mother no more often than the bare cage.

In another experiment, he showed that the babies treated the terry-cloth mother as a 'safe base'. The concept of a safe base is important in infant–mother attachment. Mothers (or other important caregivers) are thought to provide a safe base, allowing infants to go off and explore or play, but also to rush back to if they feel threatened. Harlow found that when the babies were placed in a large room full of toys they would curl up in a terrified ball if there was no mother or just the wire mother present (Figure 5.6). However, if the terry-cloth mother were present they would run and cling on to her and eventually pluck up the courage to explore, returning to her on a regular basis (Harlow, 1958).

Harlow's experiments made it absolutely clear that a baby monkey's bond with its mother was not based on cupboard love. Even when the cloth mother provided no food, the babies showed a clear preference for her over a lactating wire mother. Baby monkeys seem to possess a predisposition to bond to objects with certain tactile qualities regardless of their ability to provide food.

Figure 5.6 The response of a baby monkey placed in an unfamiliar playroom without the terry-cloth mother

2.3 Monkey maternal deprivation and abuse

Harlow continued studying attachment in monkeys for the next 20 years. The experiments became increasingly dark and disturbing. He became interested in what it would take to break the bond. Do infants remain attached even when their caregiver is abusive? Certainly, observations of abused human children suggest that they will often continue to cry for and seek proximity to an abusive parent. Harlow decided to study the phenomenon by constructing a truly vicious surrogate mother which he called 'The Iron Maiden' (Blum, 1994). The Iron Maiden blew pressurised cold air out of its body so violently that it would throw the baby monkey against the bars of its cage. In addition, at random intervals a prod would eject to push the baby monkey away from the Maiden's body. Despite this abuse, the baby monkeys continued to cling and maintain proximity to their monstrously abusive surrogate mother.

Harlow also began to raise baby monkeys under conditions of partial and total social isolation (Harlow, 1962; Harlow et al., 1965). Partially isolated monkeys were kept in separate cages, but could see, hear and smell one another. Totally isolated monkeys were raised in permanently lit, solid-walled chambers where they had no visual or physical access to the outside world or to any other living being (either monkey or human). The monkeys were placed in the chamber a few hours after birth and kept under these conditions for three, six, twelve or twenty-four months.

Both partially and totally isolated monkeys exhibited severely disturbed behaviour. They would compulsively suck their inner cheeks and tongue, perform repetitive stereotyped behaviour (such as rocking or pacing back and forth), stare blankly into space as if detached from their environment, and they would violently attack and bite their own bodies. When they were eventually allowed access to other monkeys, they were often overly aggressive and proved unable to form normal social relationships.

When the isolation-reared monkeys grew up, they developed into highly socially disturbed adults. The males were often unable to initiate mating and the females aggressively rebutted the sexual attention of males. If forced to mate, and if the females became pregnant and gave birth, they were most often neglectful mothers, but some proved to be horribly abusive.

Significantly, some of these damaging effects of isolation were shown to be at least partially reversible. For example, when 6-month-old totally isolated monkeys were placed with 3-month-old mother-reared infants, over time they exhibited a marked improvement in their behaviour. So much so that Harlow described the 3-month-old companions as 'monkey psychiatrists' (Suomi et al., 1972). Also, although 75 per cent of isolation-reared monkeys proved to be inadequate mothers upon producing their first baby (compared to only 5 per cent of females raised by their biological mother), they tended to exhibit improved mothering skills with the production of each subsequent infant (Suomi, 1978).

Summary

- Psychologists conduct research on animals to study patterns of behaviour that are thought to have developed through evolution.

- Because of the evolutionary proximity between humans and non-human primates, psychologists have used monkeys to study the evolutionary basis of human behaviour.

- Harry Harlow's experiments on monkeys provided important evidence for Bowlby's claim that infants tend to bond with soft and warm objects that provide tactile comfort, rather than with those that provide food.

3 Evaluating Harlow's work

Many people are shocked by Harlow's research. Indeed, he is one of the most controversial figures in the history of psychological science. His experiments on monkeys seem cruel, even sadistic. Nowadays, the worst excesses of Harlow's research would not be permitted. As discussed in Box 5.2, modern psychological research, on both humans and other animals, is subject to rigorous ethical scrutiny.

Box 5.2 Ethics of animal research

Often the *scientifically* best way to study something is far from the most ethical. For instance, the best way to study attachment in humans is not to test monkeys, but to experiment on children. However, it would be entirely unethical to conduct Harlow's maternal deprivation or abuse experiments using humans. This raises the question: is it ethical to use non-human animals in such research?

Animals are used in a wide array of psychological research, from observing species under wild conditions to conducting vivisection upon animals in laboratories. When testing humans the welfare of participants is paramount and no research should be allowed if it is at all likely to cause long-term discomfort or distress. The same high standards of protection are not applied to non-human animals. Nevertheless, there are strict guidelines.

The British Psychological Society has published guidelines for psychologists working with animals, according to which psychologists must be able to demonstrate that the benefits of a study justify the costs to the animals in terms of suffering. Also, researchers must do all they can to minimise the likely suffering caused. Ethics committees, comprised of scientific experts, university officials and responsible members of the general non-academic community, evaluate written proposals and decide whether or not a piece of research can proceed.

When Harlow embarked upon his research, none of these ethical guidelines or procedures were in place. Harlow's first experiments with wire and terry-cloth mothers involved only eight monkeys. The benefits of his findings in terms of improving our understanding of attachment were profound. Thus, one could argue that although those eight baby monkeys suffered, the suffering was justifiable because human society benefited greatly from the knowledge gained. The problem was that Harlow did not stop there and

---

eventually dozens if not hundreds of monkeys were subjected to extreme levels of distress and physical harm.

Harlow's experiments have been strongly criticised. Modern ethical procedures would no doubt prohibit such research. Indeed, one of Harlow's colleagues, William Mason, commented that Harlow 'kept this going to the point where it was clear to many people that the work was really violating ordinary sensibilities, that anybody with respect for life or people would find this offensive' (Blum, 1994, p. 96). In some ways, the ethics guidelines are there to protect animals from psychologists who don't like animals. Harlow was one such psychologist. He once said that the only thing he cared about was 'whether a monkey will turn out a property I can publish. I don't have any love for them. I never have. I don't really like animals. I despise cats. I hate dogs. How could you love monkeys?' (Slater, 2004, p. 137).

Whatever one thinks of the ethics of Harlow's research, it is undeniable that the findings from his initial experiments added weight and impetus to the implementation of some of the most profound changes in Western child-rearing attitudes and practice. Before Harlow, the main emphasis in human childcare was placed on providing for bodily needs. Highly influential theorists, such as Freud and Watson, thought that children should be treated with a rather cold unemotional detachment. Freud claimed that maternal over-gratification of an infant's needs could be harmful. Similarly, in a book on child rearing, the founder of behaviourism, J.B. Watson, advised: 'Never hug and kiss [your children], never let them sit in your lap. If you must, kiss them once on the forehead when they say good night'. (Watson, 1928, p. 81–82).

He went on to say:

> [W]on't you then remember when you are tempted to pet your
> child that mother love is a dangerous instrument – an instrument
> which may inflict a never-healing wound, a wound which will make
> infancy unhappy, adolescence a nightmare, an instrument which
> may wreck your adult son and daughter's vocational future and
> their chances for marital happiness.
>
> (Watson, 1928, p. 87)

Many child-rearing policies and practices reflected a philosophy of
emotional detachment. Just after birth, babies were briefly held up for
mothers to see and then whisked away from the maternity ward to be
placed straight into cribs or incubators. Mothers were encouraged not to
overindulge their babies and to establish strict feeding and sleep
routines. Mothers were also advised that it was a very bad idea to pick
their babies up on demand, that in fact they would 'spoil' them if they
picked them up too often. Breastfeeding was portrayed as inferior to
bottle-feeding. If a baby or older infant had to be admitted into
hospital, parental access was limited to restricted visiting hours. A strict
and unemotional upbringing was thought to toughen children up and
prepare them for the rigours of adult life.

All of these attitudes and practices have been challenged and to a great
extent overturned since the 1950s when Harlow first embarked on his
attachment research. At the time, John Bowlby was at the forefront of
the campaign to change public policy on child-rearing practices. Bowlby
penned the United Nation's Declaration on the Rights of the Child in
1959 (see the quotes at the start of this chapter). However, when he
insisted that children had the right to love and that they should not be
removed from their mother other than in exceptional circumstances,
many people remained unconvinced. At that stage, Bowlby had very
little scientific evidence to back up his claims. Harlow's studies are
important because they provided Bowlby with some much-needed
experimental support.

Summary

- Harlow's work on the effects of maternal deprivation on behaviour in monkeys proved controversial as it violated the welfare of animals.

- Psychological work on animals is today regulated by strict guidelines issued by professional bodies such as the British Psychological Society.

- Harlow's original studies on attachment in monkeys contributed to important changes in the way society views the relationship between infants and their primary carer.

4   Since Harlow

Although Harlow's experiments provided compelling evidence that
bonding in monkeys was based on contact comfort rather than
cupboard love, it does not necessarily follow that the same is true of
humans. One must always bear in mind that, despite the similarities,
monkeys are not humans. Scientific evidence on attachment in humans
was sorely needed. Bowlby and other child researchers set about
designing studies that could reveal the nature of human attachment.
Unlike Harlow, they could not remove human babies and rear them
under different conditions in ways that might damage their emotional
and psychological well-being. Thus, attachment research in humans has,
to a great extent, relied on less intrusive observational studies and
questionnaires.

4.1   Sensitive responsiveness in Glasgow

Rudolph Schaffer and Peggy Emerson (1964) conducted a classic
observational study on the development of attachment in Glaswegian
babies. They visited the homes of sixty working-class Glaswegian
mothers every month for the first year of their babies' lives and once
more at 18 months. They measured the strength of the attachment by
(a) how upset the babies became when they were temporarily separated
from their mother or other family members, and (b) how nervous they
seemed to be around strangers. Schaffer and Emerson found that
between birth and 3 months of age, the babies did not discriminate
between people. At 4 months of age, they began to show preferences
for certain people. At 7 months, they developed a clear preference for a
single attachment figure (who was often but not always their mother)
and many of them had developed a fear of strangers. Soon afterwards,
at about 9 months, the babies formed multiple attachments with a small
inner social circle, which often included the father, grandparents and
siblings.

Notably, Schaffer and Emerson found that human infant attachment did
not seem to be based upon cupboard love. Just over a third of the
babies (39 per cent) formed their first attachment with someone other
than the person who fed or changed them, such as a grandparent. The
most important factor in determining their primary attachment figure
was not who looked after their basic biological needs, but who
responded most sensitively to their signals. Thus, in support of

ethological theory, human infant attachment seemed to be based upon what Schaffer and Emerson (1964) referred to as **sensitive responsiveness**.

4.2   Ainsworth and the Strange Situation

No discussion of attachment theory would be complete without including the work of Mary Ainsworth. Ainsworth joined John Bowlby's research group at the Tavistock Clinic in London in 1950. Initially, Ainsworth was far from convinced about the validity of Bowlby's ethological account of attachment. 'It seemed obvious to her ... that a baby loves his mother because she satisfies his needs' (Ainsworth, personal communication in Bretherton, 1992). Yet, when she started observing the interaction between mothers and babies in detail, the relevance of Bowlby's ideas became immediately apparent.

Ainsworth conducted her first observational study of attachment in 1953. She had moved to Uganda with her husband and they lived there for two years. During that time, she was able to raise a small amount of money which allowed her to collect observational data from twenty-six Ugandan families with unweaned babies between the ages of 1 and 24 months. She observed the families for two hours every fortnight over a period of nine months.

Despite Freud and Watson's insistence that 'mollycoddling' children is detrimental to their development, Ainsworth found that the more responsive the Ugandan mothers were to their babies' signals, the less the babies cried and the more confident and explorative they seemed to be. If the mothers were unresponsive and emotionally detached, in the way Watson had advocated, their infants tended to cry a lot more and often seemed clingy and insecure. Thus Ainsworth was able to show that, just as with Harlow's terry-cloth mothers, human mothers seem to act like a 'safe base', promoting independent exploration in their infants.

It might strike you as somewhat paradoxical that providing more attention and affection would encourage a child to be independent. Yet the idea is that if a child knows that they always have a safe base to return to, this will give them the confidence to go off and explore. It is a bit like bungee-jumping from a tall platform. If you are sure that your bungee cord is dependable and securely attached, you are much more likely to possess the confidence to jump.

Sensitive responsiveness
Tendency in children to bond with persons who respond most sensitively to their signals.

Ainsworth conducted a similar study in the US and found that, just as with the Ugandan families, maternal sensitivity appeared to promote confidence and independence in children. For example, she found that the infants of mothers who had provided extensive tender holding during the first three months of life sought contact less often from 9 to 12 months of age. Moreover, when contact did occur, it seemed to be more satisfying and affectionate. She concluded that, 'an infant whose mother's responsiveness helps him to achieve his ends develops confidence in his own ability to control what happens to him' (Bell and Ainsworth, 1972, p. 1188).

Ainsworth's first two observational studies were extremely work-intensive and time-consuming. However, based on this work, Ainsworth developed a highly influential and much-used observational procedure called the **Strange Situation**. This involves a simple, albeit somewhat artificial situation which allows psychologists to study attachment in a controlled environment and in a more 'efficient' (i.e. much less time-consuming) manner.

Strange Situation
A way of assessing attachment security in a laboratory setting. It consists of a standardised set of episodes involving a child, their mother and a stranger in a sequence of separations and reunions.

The Strange Situation has most often been used to assess infants between the ages of 12 and 24 months. The procedure consists of a series of seven consecutive three-minute-long episodes.

Episode 1. The mother and infant enter an unfamiliar room that contains two chairs and a selection of toys. The infant is allowed to explore the room while the mother sits and reads.

Episode 2. A stranger enters the room, chats briefly with the mother and then attempts to interact with the child.

Episode 3. The mother leaves the room and the stranger attempts to comfort or play with the child. This episode is cut short if the child becomes very upset.

Episode 4. Reunion occurs. The mother re-enters the room, pauses for a few seconds by the door to allow the child to initiate approach, and then interacts with the child as normal. The stranger leaves the room.

Episode 5. The mother leaves the child alone in the room. This episode is cut short if the child becomes very upset.

Episode 6. The stranger re-enters the room, pauses by the door and then attempts to comfort and play with the child.

Episode 7. Reunion with the mother occurs and the stranger leaves.

Figure 5.7   Episodes 2–4 of the Strange Situation. A stranger enters the room and engages with the child (2); the mother then leaves the child alone with the stranger (3); before returning to be reunited with the child (4).

As you can imagine, some children became very upset when they were separated from their mother in Episode 5. It would be completely irresponsible to leave a young distressed child unsupervised in a room that was unfamiliar to them. The Strange Situation procedure takes this ethical issue into account. The children are constantly monitored either through a one-way mirror or via a wall-mounted video camera that is linked to a monitor in an adjacent room. Both the experimenter and mother watch the children during the separation episodes. If the child becomes too upset the episodes are cut short and the mother returns before the three minutes are up.

Ainsworth proposed that the Strange Situation reveals different types of attachment in children. Ainsworth and Bell (1970) classified the majority of children (70 per cent) as *secure*. Secure children happily explored the environment in the presence of their mother. They were upset by their mother's absence but they were quickly comforted upon reunion and would often return to play. Fifteen per cent were classified as *anxious-resistant*. These children would not explore even in the mother's presence. They were very upset on separation, but they acted in an ambivalent manner upon reunion. They would often approach, but as soon as their mother tried to hug them or pick them up, they would pull away or struggle to be put down. They sometimes seemed angry with their mother, even striking out at her. Neither mother nor child appeared to derive much comfort or satisfaction from the reunion. The final 15 per cent were categorised as *anxious-avoidant*. These children seemed rather distant and aloof from the outset. They were not particularly upset during separation and would snub their mother upon her return by looking or moving away from her. Since Ainsworth's initial observations, a fourth category, *disorganised*, has been added. Disorganised infants show signs of indecisiveness and confusion. They often exhibit rather bizarre responses to separation, such as freezing,

Ainsworth revealed different kinds of attachment

- Secure
- Anxious resistant
- Anxious avoidant
- disorganised

rocking or hair-pulling. Disorganised attachment has been associated with parental neglect or abuse.

Activity 5.3

Having read about the different categories of attachment, reflect on how it might feel to be a parent with an infant who has just been observed in this Strange Situation. How would you respond to your child's attachment being put into one of the four categories? Can you think of reasons why a parent might object to this?

One problem with the Strange Situation research is that inferences are often made about a child's attachment style on the basis of a single observation. In doing so, it may underestimate the importance of other factors, such as the child's mood, how well they had slept that day and the extent to which they are used to situations similar to that to which they were exposed in the study. The latter proved to be especially relevant when the Strange Situation was used to test infants from different countries and cultures. Although the majority tended to follow a pattern similar to that found in the United States (i.e. 70 per cent secure, 15 per cent anxious-resistant and 15 per cent anxious-avoidant), there were some notable exceptions. These exceptions highlight why some might object to the use of the Strange Situation to classify their child's attachment.

Criticism

Israeli children raised in a residential community or settlement called a kibbutz showed a much higher incidence (33 per cent) of what Ainsworth called the anxious-resistant response (Fox, 1977). The kibbutz children were raised together in large peer groups. They spent long periods away from their parents under the care of a kibbutzim nurse called a *metapelet*. The children were very used to being separated from their mother, but very unused to seeing strangers.

Data from a study in Japan (Takahashi, 1986) showed an absence of anxious-avoidant attachments and just as with the kibbutz children about one-third were categorised as anxious-resistant. However, the researchers pointed out that in normal circumstances the Japanese babies were hardly ever left alone in a room by their mother. Most of the babies became very upset during separation and on reunion. Despite being instructed to stand motionless for ten seconds by the door, when the mothers returned nearly all of them went straight over and picked their baby up. Thus the Japanese babies had no opportunity to be anxious-avoidant.

Perhaps the most surprising results came from Germany. Only 40 per cent of the children were categorised as securely attached, while 49 per cent of them showed an anxious-avoidant response (Grossman et al., 1981). The high incidence of avoidant behaviour in German children was explained in terms of the fact that German children are encouraged to be independent from a very early age.

Ecological validity
The extent to which a study reflects naturally occurring or everyday situations.

The Israeli and Japanese data bring into question the **ecological validity** of the Strange Situation study for these cultures. Ecological validity refers to the degree to which an experiment or controlled observational procedure reflects the everyday normal behavioural tendencies of participants outside of testing conditions. Scientific studies with low ecological validity are often uninformative or even misleading. The Strange Situation seemed an inappropriate procedure to use in the Japanese study since those mothers never left their babies in a room alone or with a stranger. Thus the babies' and mothers' reactions were to a set of circumstances that never occurred in their everyday lives. Similarly, in their everyday lives the kibbutzim children were very unused to seeing strangers; hence this aspect of the Strange Situation also lacked ecological validity for them. Ainsworth developed the Strange Situation to test American children from whom she had already collected many, many hours of naturalistic observations. Thus it has high ecological validity for Americans, but when it is applied to other cultures one must be very careful when interpreting the results.

4.3 Evaluating the use of attachment categories

Ainsworth believed that the differences in human infant attachment types were entirely due to the mother. Secure infants have mothers who are responsive to their signals. The children within the so-called anxious-resistant or anxious-avoidant attachment categories have less responsive mothers and have developed coping strategies to deal with the fact that their mother will not always sensitively respond to their needs. Yet Ainsworth has been criticised for placing a culturally specific value system on the data. She assumed that being more independent and explorative is a desirable outcome of responsive mothering. This might be true in American society, with its emphasis on autonomy and individualism, but it might not be true in other cultures.

In addition, the labels Ainsworth applied to the different attachment categories (i.e. 'secure' and 'anxious') are value-laden. The secure pattern is assumed to be optimal in all situations, but this might not be the case. There is evidence from baboons to suggest that no particular mothering style or attachment category is necessarily better or worse than others. Rather, they are flexible and adaptive responses to different sets of social circumstances.

Altmann (1980) observed that the wild baboons tend to adopt two contrasting mothering styles. Some are restrictive, preventing their babies from wandering away and limiting their access to other baboons. Other mothers are laissez-faire, allowing their babies to wander where they like and interact with whom they like. In general, low-ranking mothers are restrictive, while high-ranking mothers are laissez-faire. Baboon troops can be dangerous places. There is a strict social hierarchy and baboons can be very aggressive. If you are low-ranking, it is dangerous to let your baby interact too much with other baboons because, should they get into trouble, you will almost certainly lack the social clout to be able to help them out. In contrast, high-ranking mothers can much more easily run to their baby's aid. It is not that one mothering style is inherently preferable to the other; each is an appropriate response to a particular context. Human mothering is likely to be just as flexible and adaptive. Thus, rather than a particular mothering style or attachment type in humans being inherently preferable to all others in all circumstances, different styles might suit different situations.

4.4   Strange Situation research on other animals

You might be surprised to discover that the Strange Situation has also been used to investigate different species. The attachments of the chimpanzees who were raised in a nursery by human caregivers appeared surprisingly similar to those found in human infants (van Ijzendoorn et al., 2009). The main difference was a high incidence of disorganised attachment. In this respect, the chimpanzee data seemed similar to that obtained from children raised in Romanian orphanages where adults interacted very little with the children beyond tending to their physical needs. (You can read more about the Romanian orphans later in this chapter.)

Along with colleagues, I have conducted studies on the dog–human bond using the Strange Situation (Palmer and Custance, 2008; Prato-

Previde et al., 2003). We were amazed to see how similar the dogs' responses were to those of human children. Most of the dogs were adult, but just like human children, they only liked to play and explore when their attachment figure (i.e. their owner) was present. When their owners left the room, the majority of dogs sat by the door, whining, barking and howling. On reunion, nearly all the dogs approached their owner, ecstatically greeted him or her and then after a short while most of them were happy to start playing or exploring again. In other words, the majority of dogs appeared to be securely attached.

Summary

- Observational studies on human infants have shown that attachment behaviour in children is not based on cupboard love.
- Mary Ainsworth's Strange Situation study provided researchers with a convenient and expedient way of assessing attachment in children.
- Cross-cultural research suggests that attachment should be viewed as flexible and adaptive. Different attachment styles develop under different conditions and in response to different situations. There is no such thing as a universally preferred attachment style.

5   The flexibility of attachment

Despite the findings of researchers such as Harlow, Bowlby and Ainsworth, many people continued to vehemently resist the suggestion that any aspect of human behaviour, including attachment, is inbuilt or innate. As soon as one suggests that behaviour has evolved, there is a tendency for people to assume that it is somehow 'set in stone' or 'determined by our genes'. There is the fear that if our behaviour is shown to be the product of a genetically inherited trait, it means that we have no free will or control over it. Indeed, when Bowlby was first developing attachment theory, he promoted the view that human attachment is based on a rather rigid system that determines the course of all our future relationships. In this final section, I hope to show that innate predispositions might not be as fixed as one might think.

Earlier in the chapter I mentioned two innate predispositions: herring-gull-chick beak pecking and imprinting. Early research suggested that these inherited behavioural patterns are rigid and irreversible. Thus, it was thought that whatever object a newly hatched bird first imprinted on, however unsuitable, the process would be irreversible; there would be no way to replace it with another object. Researchers also thought that it was impossible for birds to imprint after their critical period, mainly because after that time they develop a fear of all unfamiliar stimuli. Finally, it was also thought that imprinting had long-term consequences in terms of forming a template for all subsequent relationships.

As ethologists studied these innate behaviour patterns in more detail, it became clear that they are not as rigid as was first presumed. Hoffman (1978) exposed 5-day-old ducklings to a moving rectangle. Initially, the ducklings all attempted to flee, terrified of this unfamiliar stimulus. Since they were in an enclosed area and could not escape, they huddled in a corner until eventually their fear subsided. Soon afterwards, they started to follow the rectangle and emitted distress calls when they were separated from it. They had imprinted more than two days after their species' usual critical period had elapsed. Modern ethologists have adopted the term 'sensitive' rather than 'critical period' to reflect the fact that imprinting, and indeed all innate behaviour patterns, tend to show some degree of flexibility.

Even after imprinting has occurred, the effects are not necessarily irreversible. Guiton (1966) exposed baby chickens to yellow rubber gloves so that they became imprinted upon them. When they reached adulthood, they did indeed try to mate with similar gloves. However, when they were given the opportunity to interact for some time with members of their own species, they shifted the focus of their amorous attention to these biologically more appropriate targets.

5.1   Is there a critical period in human attachment?

How does one test whether there is a similarly critical period in human attachment? It would be unethical to deliberately prevent or hinder young children from forming an attachment in the first few years of their life just to see if they would be able to form such a bond after this period. Tragically, there have been unintentional incidences in which children have been prevented from bonding during their early years. Jill Hodges and Barbara Tizard (1989) studied children from a care home in which there was a huge and constant turnover of staff. By the age of 2, the children had experienced an average of twenty-four carers each. Thus none of the children had been able to establish a long-term, meaningful attachment. When the children reached the age of 4, the care home was disbanded. Twenty-five of the children were returned to their biological parents, thirty-three were adopted and seven remained institutionalised with occasional fostering. When the children reached the age of 16, Hodges and Tizard interviewed and administered questionnaires to the children, their biological or adoptive mothers and their teachers. They found that, in comparison to children who had not experienced institutional care, all the children in the sample tended to have problems with siblings, poor peer relationships, and teachers found them more quarrelsome. Despite the fact that their early institutionalisation seemed to have some long-term detrimental consequences, the children were still clearly able to make attachments after the age of 4. Seventeen out of twenty-one adoptive mothers felt that their child was deeply attached to them. However, only half of the children restored to their biological families described themselves as deeply attached. Maybe this was because many of them went back to conditions of poverty and privation or because some of the parents indicated that owing to their difficult circumstances they had mixed feelings about the return of their child. It appears, therefore, that the quality of attachment depends not so much on the child's age (in terms of a critical period) as on the adults, their relationship with the child, and the broader social context.

5.2 The maternal deprivation hypothesis

A key feature of Bowlby's work during the 1940s and 1950s is the emphasis on the importance of the mother. Although Bowlby sometimes argued that he used the term 'mother' to refer to any primary caregiver, he has been heavily criticised for placing so much responsibility and pressure on mothers. In the aftermath of the Second World War, the role of women in society was changing dramatically, as they increasingly sought to escape their traditional gender roles. It was felt that Bowlby was preaching that mothers should stay at home and raise their babies.

Figure 5.8   Escaping the traditional role of woman as homemaker

One of the most controversial of Bowlby's ideas is the so-called **maternal deprivation hypothesis** (Bowlby, 1944). He proposed that any separation of a week or more between a child under the age of 5 and its primary attachment figure, usually the mother, would have a long-term detrimental effect. He derived this hypothesis from his observations of young offenders.

Bowlby had been treating a young offender at the Tavistock Clinic in London and he came to suspect that the boy's problems were related to his disrupted relationship with his mother. He recruited forty-four

Maternal deprivation hypothesis
The idea developed by John Bowlby that any separation of a child from its mother of a week or more before the age of 5 will have negative long-term effects for the child.

young men who had been arrested for thieving and compared them with forty-four non-offending adolescents (Bowlby, 1944). A third of the offenders were diagnosed with 'affectionless psychopathology', which means they lacked a sense of moral conscience. Bowlby discovered that, in contrast with non-offenders, most of the young offenders had been separated from their mother for at least one week before the age of 5. He suggested that breaking the bonds of attachment in early life will lead to intellectual, social and emotional problems in later life that will be permanent and irreversible.

You learned about correlation in Chapter 3, Box 3.2.

One of the main problems with the data from the 'forty-four thieves' study was that it was correlational. A correlation indicates that as one factor increases, another factor is likely to increase or decrease in tandem with it. However, correlations cannot definitively indicate that two factors are *causally* linked. There might be one or a number of other underlying factors that are the true causal agents. The juvenile offenders that Bowlby studied all came from poor homes. It might be that poverty leads to a higher incidence of separation between young children and their parents. For instance, poorer people tend to experience lower levels of health and are more likely to be hospitalised, which would involve children and parents being separated. Equally, poverty alienates people from society and is therefore also likely to cause higher incidences of anti-social behaviour. Rather than maternal separation causing delinquency, poverty might independently affect both whether or not children are separated from their family *and* the levels of theft and delinquency.

Michael Rutter (1981) conducted a study into the roots of delinquency among young people and found evidence to suggest that maternal separation was in fact not the most important factor. He conducted a survey of 2000 9–12-year-old boys from the Isle of Wight. He also studied a group of boys from London whose parents had suffered mental illness. Rutter found that if parental separation was due to physical illness or the death of the mother, the boy was unlikely to turn to crime. However, if separation was due to the mental problems of one or both parents or to stress and conflict within the family, then the boys were four times more likely to turn to crime. Rutter concluded that the cause of anti-social behaviour was the familial stress and conflict that occurred before separation, rather than separation itself.

Also, Schaffer and Emerson (1964) pointed out that, by 9 months of age, infants have normally established a small network of attachment relationships. Thus, even if they are separated from their primary attachment figure, such as their mother, they often have other emotionally significant people they can turn to. Hence, separation should be less detrimental than Bowlby proposed.

5.3   Does early attachment have a long-term effect?

Bowlby argued that a person's attachment in childhood lays the foundation upon which all future relationships are built. If someone's first attachment relationship is faulty or unhealthy in any way, then this will adversely colour their relationships for the rest of their life. Thus, if the primary attachment relationship was loving and secure, the person would grow up to be emotionally open, confident and able to establish healthy adult relationships. In contrast, if the primary attachment bond was unhealthy and insecure, they are likely to grow up being either overly clingy or emotionally cold toward others.

Actually, there is rather mixed evidence as to whether early attachments really do have long-term consequences. A positive association has been found between a secure attachment and curiosity and problem solving at age 2, social confidence at 3, empathy and independence at 6 and, in the case of boys, a lack of behavioural problems at age 6 (Lewis et al., 1984). Yet, when Peter Zimmermann and colleagues interviewed a group of 16-year-olds, they found that early attachment patterns at 12–18 months of age (reported in retrospect) were not a good predictor of later relationships (Zimmermann et al., 1997). Later events, such as parental divorce, had a much bigger impact on the nature of the 16-year-olds' current attachments.

Michael Rutter and colleagues have also provided evidence to suggest that early unsuitable attachment experiences can be overcome to a certain extent (Rutter et al., 2007). After the downfall of the Romanian Communist regime in 1989, hundreds of orphans were found living in deprived and squalid conditions within state institutions. The children had received very little attention or affection within these deplorably understaffed orphanages.

Figure 5.9   Children in a Romanian orphanage

Rutter and his colleagues followed the progress of 111 of these orphans who were adopted in the UK. Thankfully, the children were all adopted into loving families. At age 6, most of the children had made good recoveries. However, those children adopted after the age of 2 showed high levels of *disinhibited attachment*. Disinhibited attachment is a rather strange phenomenon in which children behave in an overly familiar and clingy manner with people they hardly know. Having been starved of love and attention for the first two years of life, the children seemed desperate to establish attachments even with complete strangers. In 2007, when the children were 11 years of age, only half of them had recovered from their earlier disinhibited attachment style. It seems that children exposed to physical privation and emotional deprivation can make a full recovery if they are adopted into a loving family, but that this is more likely to occur if they are adopted at an earlier age.

As the Romanian orphans show, love is an extremely powerful thing. Once the orphans had been placed in loving families, they showed a remarkable ability to overcome extreme physical and emotional deprivation. When they first arrived in Britain, over half of the orphans exhibited learning difficulties. By their fourth birthday, the majority of them had an IQ that fell within the normal range. Quite understandably, some orphans continued to experience problems, particularly if they were adopted late. However, this does not diminish the huge strides forward that nearly all of them achieved. So, although absent or severely inadequate early attachments are clearly harmful, children seem to be remarkably resilient and, given the opportunity and a great deal of love, they can prevail.

5.4   Conclusion

The care of a loving adult is so important for an infant's survival that it is not surprising that the tendency to form attachments has evolved. Different sources of evidence from birds, monkeys and humans suggest that attachment is not based upon cupboard love. Instead, humans and other animals possess inbuilt tendencies to form attachments with stimuli that possess certain features. However, human attachment is not rigidly fixed in early infancy. The past sixty years of attachment research have shown that, although it may operate according to certain inbuilt parameters, it is a complex and flexible system that still allows organisms to adapt to changing circumstances.

Summary

- According to Bowlby's maternal deprivation hypothesis, even temporary separation from the mother or primary caregiver early in life can have negative consequences for subsequent behaviour.

- Subsequent evidence – some of which comes from studies of children who grew up in conditions of considerable deprivation – suggests that in the right circumstances, difficulties encountered in early childhood, including the lack of an attachment, can be overcome.

- Human attachment is partly determined by innate behavioural tendencies (such as the tendency to form attachments to soft objects or primary carers who tend to be most responsive), but it is also influenced by changing circumstances.

References

Ainsworth, M.D. and Bell, S.M. (1970) 'Attachment, exploration, and separation: illustrated by the behavior of one-year-olds in a strange situation', *Child Development*, vol. 41, no. 1, pp. 49–67.

Altmann, J. (1980) *Baboon Mothers and Infants*, Cambridge, MA, Harvard University Press.

Bell, S.M. and Ainsworth, M.D.S. (1972). Infant crying and maternal responsiveness, *Child Development,* vol. 43, no. 4, pp. 1171–90.

Blum, D. (1994) *The Monkey Wars*, Oxford, Oxford University Press.

Bowlby, J. (1944) 'Forty-four juvenile thieves: their characters and home-life' (Parts I and II), *International Journal of Psychoanalysis*, vol. 25, pp. 19–53 and pp. 107–28.

Bowlby, J. (1979) *The Making and Breaking of Affectional Bonds*, London, Tavistock Publications.

Bretherton, I. (1992) 'The origins of attachment theory: John Bowlby and Mary Ainsworth', *Developmental Psychology,* vol. 28, no. 5, pp. 759–75.

Fox, N.A. (1977) 'Attachment of kibbutz infants to mother and *metapelet*', *Child Development*, vol. 48, no. 4, pp. 1228–39.

Grossman, K.E., Grossman, K., Huber, F. and Wartner, U. (1981) 'German children's behavior toward their mothers at 12 months and their fathers at 18 months in Ainsworth's Strange Situation', *International Journal of Behavioral Development*, vol. 4, no. 2, pp. 157–81.

Guiton, P. (1966) 'Early experience and sexual object choice in the Brown Leghorn', *Animal Behaviour,* vol. 14, no. 4, pp. 534–8.

Harlow, H.F. (1958) 'The nature of love', *American Psychologist,* vol. 13, pp. 673–85.

Harlow, H.F. (1962) 'Development of affection in primates' in E.L. Bliss (ed.) *Roots of Behavior,* pp. 157–66, New York, NY, Harper.

Harlow, H.F., Dodsworth, R.O. and Harlow, M.K. (1965) 'Total social isolation in monkeys', *Proceedings of the National Academy of Sciences of the United States of America,* vol. 54, no. 1, pp. 90–7.

Hess, E.H. (1958) '"Imprinting" in animals', *Scientific American*, vol. 198, no. 3, pp. 81–90.

Hodges, J. and Tizard, B. (1989) 'Social and family relationships of ex-institutional adolescents', *Journal of Child Psychology and Psychiatry,* vol. 30, no. 1, pp. 77–97.

Hoffman, H.S. (1978) 'Experimental analysis of imprinting and its behavioral effects' in Bower, G. (ed.) *The Psychology of Learning and Motivation*, vol. 12, pp. 1–37, New York, NY, Academic Press.

Holmes, J. (1993) *John Bowlby and Attachment Theory,* New York, NY, Routledge.

Lewis, M.L., Feiring, C., McGuffog, C. and Jaskir, J. (1984) 'Prediction psychopathology in six-year-olds from early social relations', *Child Development,* vol. 55, no. 1, pp. 123–36.

Lorenz, K.Z. and Kickert, R.W. (1981) *The Foundations of Ethology,* New York, NY, Springer-Verlag.

Palmer, R. and Custance, D.M. (2008) 'A counterbalanced version of Ainsworth's Strange Situation Procedure reveals secure-base effects in dog–human relationships', *Applied Animal Behaviour Science,* vol. 109, no. 2, pp. 306–19.

Prato-Previde, E., Custance, D.M., Spiezio, C. and Sabatini, F. (2003) 'Is the dog–human relationship an attachment bond? An observational study using Ainsworth's Strange Situation', *Behaviour,* vol. 140, no. 2, pp. 225–54.

Rutter, M. (1981) *Maternal Deprivation Reassessed,* New York, NY, Penguin.

Schaffer, H.R. and Emerson, P.F. (1964) 'The development of social attachments in infancy', *Monographs of the Society for Research in Child Development,* vol. 29, no. 3, pp. 1–70.

Slater, L. (2004) *Opening Skinner's Box: Great Psychological Experiments of the Twentieth Century,* London, Bloomsbury.

Suomi, S.J., Harlow, H.F. and McKinney, W.T. (1972) 'Monkey psychiatrists', *American Journal of Psychiatry,* vol. 128, no. 8, pp. 927–32.

Suomi, S.J. (1978) 'Maternal behavior by socially incompetent monkeys: neglect and abuse of offspring', *Journal of Pediatric Psychology,* vol. 3, no. 1, pp. 28–34.

Rutter, M., Colvert, E., Kreppner, J., Beckett, C., Castle, J., Groothues, C., et al. (2007) 'Early adolescent outcomes for institutionally-deprived and non-deprived adoptees: I. Disinhibited attachment', *Journal of Child Psychology and Psychiatry,* vol. 48, no. 1, pp. 17–30.

Takahashi, K. (1986) 'Examining the Strange Situation procedure with Japanese mothers and 12-month-old infants', *Developmental Psychology,* vol. 22, no. 2, pp. 265–70.

United Nations (UN) (1959) 'Declaration of the Rights of the Child', General Assembly resolution 1386 (XIV), New York, NY, UN; also available online at www.un.org/cyberschoolbus/humanrights/resources/child.asp (Accessed 13 April 2010).

United Nations (UN) (1989) 'Convention on the Rights of the Child', General Assembly resolution 44/24, New York, NY, UN; also available online at www.un.org/documents/ga/res/44/a44r025.htm (Accessed 13 April 2010).

van Ijzendoorn, M.H., Bard, K.A., Bakermans-Kravenburg, M.J. and Ivan, K. (2009) 'Enhancement of attachment and cognitive development of young nursery-reared chimpanzees in responsive versus standard care', *Developmental Psychobiology,* vol. 51, no. 2, pp. 173–85.

Watson, J.B. (1928). *Psychological Care of Infant and Child*, New York, NY, Harper and Bros.

Zimmermann, P., Fremmer-Bombik, E., Spangler, G. and Grossman, K.E. (1997) 'Attachment in adolescence: a longitudinal perspective' in Koops, W., Hoeksma, J.B. and van den Boom, D.C. (eds) *Development of Interaction and Attachment: Traditional and Non-traditional Approaches*, pp. 281–91, Amsterdam, North-Holland.

Chapter 6
Making friends

Charlotte Brownlow

Contents

Aims and objectives

After studying this chapter you should be able to:

- outline the complexities surrounding the understandings and definitions of friendships
- reflect on some of the key methodological approaches that have been used to research friendship
- consider the influences that peers may have on an individual's behaviour
- describe the role that cultural experiences may play in our understandings and experiences of friendship
- outline the possible changing nature of friendships in the light of new technologies and the possibilities that these may offer for 'global friendships'.

1   Introduction

In the previous chapter you were introduced to the work of Harry Harlow and the way in which psychological research has looked extensively at children's relationship with, and attachment to, their parents and caregivers. There is another important set of relationships in a child's life, and that is with their friends. For a long time, however, the role of friends and the potential influences of friends on the behaviour of children had been neglected in the literature. This may seem quite surprising given the frequent references that are made in everyday exchanges to the influence of friends on an individual. For example, people may make generalisations regarding a young person 'being in with the wrong crowd' or talk about the 'good influence' that a particular new friend has become.

Given the importance of friendship in everyday life, it is worthwhile looking more closely into psychological research in this area. Friendship is different from many other relationships that individuals are involved in. For children in particular, friendship takes on a very different meaning from other relationships such as those with parents, other adults and siblings: friendship is usually characterised by both parties having equal power. This is unlike many other relationships children have. In a relationship with an adult, the adult is usually the dominant party. This makes friendship between children an interesting relationship to focus on. In particular, psychologists have asked questions concerning the best way to measure and study friendship, the role of peer influence on behaviour, cultural differences in expressing and understanding friendship, and the possible changing nature of friendship given the rising importance of modern technologies in our lives. These are issues that will be explored in this chapter.

1.1   What is friendship?

Friendship may have different meanings to different people and I would like to start by thinking about what friendship is and how we can define it. Before I go on to consider how friendship has been defined by psychologists, I would like you to pause and think about what friendship means to you and how you would define the concept of 'friendship'.

Activity 6.1

Spend a few minutes considering the term 'friendship'. Think about what this term means to you, and what sort of things you expect from a friendship. It may be helpful to think about one specific friend and your relationship with them. Write down some of the features of this relationship that you think are important.

Now think about what the term 'friendship' may mean to children. Do you think that this will differ depending on what age the children are? Write down some of the features of friendship that you think may be important to children.

Now compare your two lists. Have you identified similar features on both lists or are they different? Which features of friendship are similar and which are different?

The questions raised in Activity 6.1 concerning the definitions of friendship and the possible changes as individuals progress through childhood, adolescence and adulthood will be a theme that I will be returning to in the chapter. You may want to reflect back on your thoughts from this activity again once you have completed your reading of the whole chapter.

Figure 6.1 Early friendships

The concept of friendship can be difficult to define and may mean different things to different people at different times. As William Bukowski and colleagues point out, our language does not necessarily differentiate between the friendships of infants and toddlers and those of adolescents and adults despite the differences between these two types of relationship in respect of qualities and expectations (Bukowski et al., 1996). Bukowski et al. therefore question whether a single definition of friendship is possible, one that can adequately describe close relationships between people in a range of different populations. In addition to the potential age-related differences in understanding friendship, the influence of culture should also be considered. This is a question that I will be returning to later on in this chapter.

A further question for consideration when researching friendship is how the boundaries of friendship are determined. An important researcher of friendship, Willard Hartup, notes that researchers have tended to define friendship in a simplistic way that focuses on the differences between 'friend' and 'non-friend'. Hartup (1996) argues that friendship is far more complex than this, and a whole spectrum of relationships is possible on a continuous scale from best friend to good friend to occasional friend to non-friend. In addition to the complexities associated with types of friend, it is also important to remember that children are involved in a whole range of relationships, including those with family members and other adults such as teachers, as well as peers. In any investigation into the understanding of friendship, other social networks must be borne in mind and friendship should be considered within the context of the other relationships.

So, researchers investigating this topic need to have an understanding of what they mean when they talk about friendship. Generally, researchers agree on three elements as being important in the friendships of children and adolescents (Bukowski et al., 1996). Each person in the friendship should:

- gain equal benefits from the relationship – the relationship should draw on the importance of cooperation and the satisfactory resolution of potential conflicts
- have a liking for the other(s) and a desire to spend time with them
- have fun and express affection for the other(s).

1.2   The role of friendships and the influence of peers

One of the main issues in friendship research is how peers may exert an influence on a child or an adolescent. This will be a key consideration of this chapter too. As you read on, you need to keep in mind questions concerning the meaning of friendships at various stages in life and the possible influence of peers, both positive and negative, on an individual's behaviour. Friends, for example, may have a strong impact on the type of music that a person listens to or the clothes that they wear. In Section 4, I will return to this question and consider the influence that friends may have on the uptake of smoking. However, it is also important to consider the potential positive effects that friends may have on behaviour. Friends can sometime have a beneficial effect on academic achievement in school, on participation in out-of-school activities and on avoiding risky behaviours. However, what is the mechanism by which peers exercise this influence? And is this influence consistent throughout life?

Figure 6.2   Growing importance of peer influence in adolescence

Phil Erwin (1998) notes that the significance of peer relationships increases and changes with age. For young children, parents are the main source of support and guidance. As children mature into adolescence, the influence of peers becomes more important. However, despite occasional disagreements with parents over issues such as curfews and clothing (common sources of dispute within families), the values of parents and peer groups are not necessarily opposed (Erwin, 1998). Indeed, Erwin argues that the peer group can often act as a powerful force of support for many of the values held by parents, owing to friendships typically being formed between people of similar backgrounds. Therefore, even though some groups can be thought to promote anti-social behaviour, their significance for most adolescents has frequently been overestimated (Erwin, 1998). The general influence of peers is typically seen to decline after the early teens, owing to the increasing focus on romantic relationships, which may serve to move an individual's attention outside the friendship circle.

Before moving on to look at the subject of peer influence, however, it is important to explore in more detail the changing understanding of friendship in childhood, a topic that was investigated in a key study by Brian Bigelow and John La Gaipa.

Summary

- Defining friendship is a complex endeavour, as 'friendship' can mean different things to different people at different times.
- The role of friendships and the influence of peers change with age as parents and carers are increasingly replaced by peers as the main source of support.
- While there are examples of peers influencing behaviours in a negative way, the significance of peers in reinforcing positive behaviours may well be underestimated.

2   The changing nature of friendship in childhood

A pioneering study on children's friendship was carried out by Brian Bigelow and John La Gaipa (1975). In the 1970s, at the time when they began their research, very little was known about children's friendships. The focus of relationship research at the time was mainly on emotional relationships and on understanding what attracts one person to another. In a bid to explore the under-researched area of children's friendship, Bigelow and La Gaipa looked at the differences in children's understanding of friendship at various stages of development. They devised a novel means of investigating the gradual changes in the interpretation of friendship as children grow older. In doing so they helped to shed new light on the important role that friends play in children's lives.

In order to investigate children's understanding of friendship, Bigelow and La Gaipa asked children to think about their best friend of the same sex and write an essay about what they expected of their best friend and how this might be different from their expectations of other friends and acquaintances. Bigelow and La Gaipa compiled a large sample of 480 essays written by children aged between six and fourteen years who came from upper-working-class and lower-middle-class homes in Windsor, Ontario, Canada. Children who took part in the study were recruited from eight schools – thirty girls and thirty boys from each.

The research approach adopted by Bigelow and La Gaipa was very different from those that you have previously encountered in this book. Rather than conducting observations of children's behaviour, carrying out a well-designed experiment or administering a questionnaire, Bigelow and La Gaipa collected data in the form of written essays. This meant that all the data that they collected was in a written, text format. Their decision to use essays as a source of data raises a number of questions that I would like you to think about as I go on to consider Bigelow and La Gaipa's work.

Before the study began, the researchers came up with a list of different characteristics of a best friend that they anticipated the children might include in their essays. Particular expectations are made of best friends that are not necessarily true for other friends and acquaintances, including notions such as sharing common activities, engaging in organised play, admiration, loyalty and commitment, genuineness, and similarity in attitudes and values. Bigelow and La Gaipa arrived at twenty-one different categories of friendship expectations, which were then used to analyse the children's written accounts of their best friend.

Bigelow and La Gaipa used an approach called **content analysis**: they took all of the 480 children's essays and compared them against their list of twenty-one friendship expectations in order to count how many times each particular expectation was mentioned (which is usually referred to as a 'frequency count'). Once the occurrences of the different expectations had been highlighted in the essays, Bigelow and La Gaipa were able to use the frequency counts to look for any patterns in the data that would provide information about the changing nature of children's friendships. They carried out comparisons, for example between younger and older children in their sample, and also looked for differences in the understanding of friendship between boys and girls.

Content analysis
An approach to the analysis of written, audio and visual material that involves identifying and counting pre-selected features relevant to the research question.

Figure 6.3   Sharing common activities as a basis for friendship

Bigelow and La Gaipa found some important differences in the expectations that children have of a best friend at different ages. Sixteen of the original twenty-one friendship expectations were more frequent in the older children's descriptions of their best friend compared to the younger children's. This suggests that expectations of a best friend become increasingly complex and sophisticated as children get older. There was a clear progression from a focus on shared activities to prioritising intimacy and the importance of similarity in attitudes and values.

Bigelow and La Gaipa also looked at gender differences. Recall that each child was asked to write about a friend of the same sex, so the comparison was made between boy–boy and girl–girl friendships. They found that generally the differences between boys and girls were relatively minor. However, interestingly, there were differences regarding expectations of activities concerned with organised play, with boys being more likely to cite this as an expectation. Bigelow and La Gaipa explained that this was largely owing to competitive group sport being more of a male activity in their particular sample.

Bigelow and La Gaipa proposed that the findings of the study could be considered in terms of a three-stage model of the development of friendship expectations. In the first stage there is an emphasis placed on shared activities and concrete expectations such as the ability to see each other and the importance of geographical closeness. At this age, parents are also likely to be important in facilitating the meeting of children and hence the development of friendships. The second stage sees a transition from the focus on individual needs to an emphasis on sharing, loyalty and commitment. In the final stage, expectations draw upon the importance of similarity in attitudes, values and interests and the potential for the development of an intimate and confiding relationship. Friendship expectations therefore become more complex as children develop.

Activity 6.2

The method used to collect data about children's friendship is an important area for consideration. Pause for a few minutes and think about the method used by Bigelow and La Gaipa. The researchers asked children aged between six and fourteen years to write essays about what they would expect from a best friend of the same sex.

What do you think about Bigelow and La Gaipa's method? Do you think that it is a good way of tapping into children's friendship expectations? What might be some of the problems with this approach?

Remember that this research was undertaken at a time when there was not a strong research focus on children's friendships, and its importance lies in the fact that it drew attention to what was at the time an under-researched area. However, you may want to consider how easy it is, particularly for young children, to express themselves in written form. Bigelow and La Gaipa comment in their research paper that this may be an important issue for consideration, in that children, especially younger ones, may lack the verbal and written skills necessary to effectively discuss expectations in this form.

2.1 Quantitative or qualitative data?

Let's now consider in a little more detail Bigelow and La Gaipa's approach. Children were asked to write an essay about what they felt were important expectations of their best friend. This novel method enabled the children to write whatever they felt was individually important to them, and the data that was collected is in the format of written text. Therefore it was *qualitative* in nature.

However, Bigelow and La Gaipa then compared each of the children's essays with a list of expectations that they had created before collecting the data and made a frequency count of how many times each of the expectations appeared in the children's essays. They therefore transformed qualitative data (written text) into quantitative data (frequency counts). In doing this, it could be argued, they lost the individual and personal dimension of the children's accounts. On the other hand, the numerical summary enabled them to draw inferences about the differences between the age groups and make more systematic comparisons between boys and girls. This decision to convert the written descriptions into numerical summaries is further examined in Box 6.1.

You read about the distinction between qualitative and quantitative data in Box 1.1, Chapter 1.

Box 6.1   Why do it this way?

Bigelow and La Gaipa's approach allowed each child to write their own individual account of friendship expectations. However, these individual accounts were then compared and scored in relation to a predetermined set of friendship expectations, ultimately changing the nature of the research data from descriptions to frequency counts. Bigelow and La Gaipa, therefore, ultimately transformed written, textual data into the kind of data that could be quantified. Several issues are raised by this decision.

First, given the total number of children participating in the study, the decision to code essays according to an agreed set of categories enabled the researchers to analyse the large number of essays in a consistent manner. It would be extremely difficult and

---

time-consuming to preserve the individual voices and opinions within such a large sample. Working with a large sample was, however, crucial to the study because Bigelow and La Gaipa wanted to make generalisations about children's friendships, and develop a model of the developing nature of friendship that could be applied to a wider population.

Remember also that Bigelow and La Gaipa came up with a number of different expectations that they looked for in all the essays. This means that they were looking for aspects of friendship that are common across the essays, rather than at individual features of each child's friendship experience. Had they been interested in individual accounts, a much smaller sample of essays would have been collected and studied in more detail.

Finally, the fact that the essays were explored in relation to categories generated by the researchers is important. Children's expectations of friendship may not be the same as those that Bigelow and La Gaipa expected to find. It is possible that there were expectations other than those that the researchers looked for in the essays, which would have been overlooked by the content analysis.

The work of Bigelow and La Gaipa is important for our understanding of friendship for several reasons. First, it placed the concept of children's friendship on the research agenda. Second, it provided some interesting findings concerning the changing nature of friendship and how expectations of friends develop as children get older. The latter issue is linked to the question that I posed in Section 1 concerning the difficulties with defining friendship, and the differences that may exist between friendships of young children and those of adolescents and adults. Finally, Bigelow and La Gaipa introduced an interesting and novel research method for studying relationships, namely using written accounts and descriptions as data.

Summary

- The work of Bigelow and La Gaipa is important as one of the first studies of children's friendship.

- Bigelow and La Gaipa (1975) provided evidence of the changing nature of friendship expectations between the ages of six and fourteen.

- Their work illustrates how qualitative data can be transformed into quantitative data, through content analysis.

3 Researching children's friendships

In this section I would like to focus more closely on the subject of method, and contrast the approach taken by Bigelow and La Gaipa with some other ways of researching friendship. I would particularly like to focus on the use of more qualitative research approaches, which are frequently used in this area.

3.1 Qualitative research methods: interviews

One way of researching children's friendships would be to interview children about them. This involves the researcher having a list of questions that they want to ask children, although these questions are used flexibly so that the interviewer can follow up on any interesting comments that the children make. This approach ensures that all those taking part in the study are asked more or less the same questions, while at the same time allowing each child being interviewed to bring up issues that the researcher may not have otherwise considered.

You were introduced to interviews as a way of collecting data in Chapter 1, section 2.3.

However, when using interviews in research on children, it is important to consider the language skills of the children and how well they would be able to verbalise their thoughts and feelings to an (often unfamiliar) adult researcher. Interviews may therefore be more suited for research involving older children and teenagers.

An example of using interviews for researching friendship can be found in the work of William Damon. Here is an extract from his interview with Jack, an American thirteen-year-old, about his friendship with Jimmy:

Interviewer: Why is Jimmy your best friend?

Jack: I don't know, I guess it's because we talk a lot and stuff.

Interviewer: What do you talk about?

Jack: Secret stuff, you know, what we think of him or her or whoever. And sports, things we both like to do.

Interviewer: How did you meet Jimmy?

Jack: I don't know; hanging around, I guess. We just sort of got friendly after a while.

Interviewer: When did you get friendly?

Jack: After we found out we didn't have to worry about the other guy blabbing and spreading stuff around.

Interviewer: Why would you worry about that?

Jack: Well, you need someone you can tell anything to, all kinds of things that you don't want to spread around. That's why you're someone's friend.

Interviewer: Is that why Jimmy is your friend? …

Jack: Yes, and we like the same kinds of things. We speak the same language. My mother says we're two peas in a pod.

Interviewer: What would you say you like best about Jimmy?

Jack: Well, you know, we can say what we want to around each other, you don't have to act cool around him or anything. Some of the older kids are always pretending to be big shots, acting real tough. That kind of stuff, it … turns me off.

Interviewer: How do you know who to become friends with and who not to?

Jack: Well, you don't really pick your friends, it just grows on you. You find out that you can talk to someone, you can tell them your problems, when you understand each other.

(Damon, 1977, pp. 163–4)

Thinking back to the work of Bigelow and La Gaipa, we can see many similarities between Jack's account and what they identified as children's expectations in a best friend, especially in relation to loyalty, closeness and trustworthiness. Note for instance that Jack mentions 'not blabbing and spreading stuff around', 'saying what we want around each other' and talking about 'Secret stuff' as key aspects of friendship. So, although Damon (1977) was using a very different method from Bigelow and La Gaipa, he was touching on similar issues. A key difference that remains, however, is that Damon's work is focused at an *individual* level. Damon did not compare Jack's responses to predetermined categories or try to make generalisations with regard to developmental age.

Figure 6.4   Loyalty, closeness and trustworthiness: the basis of friendship among teenage boys

3.2   Qualitative research methods: ethnography

William Corsaro argues for yet another approach to studying children's friendships, one that is very different from those introduced previously. Corsaro is interested in how children talk to *each other* and believes that research on children's friendships should focus on children's individual understandings of the word 'friend'. Corsaro's approach is therefore different from that of Bigelow and La Gaipa in that he is not interested in translating the children's words into numbers and looking for general patterns. Rather, like Damon (1977), he is interested in an individual child's understanding of friendship. Also, Corsaro seeks to explore what friendship means in particular places at particular times, and how it is described in communication between children, rather than in a formal interview with an adult researcher.

Ethnography
A research approach where the researcher carries out extensive observations of a group through being involved in their activities over a period of time.

In his work on children's friendships, Corsaro makes detailed notes of children's activities and their interactions with others, and also video-records them. This is an example of an **ethnographic** approach to research. In order to carry out this work, the researcher needs to become a member of a particular group and carry out observations from within the group for months or sometimes even years. Because the researcher is also a member of the group that they are studying, they will become familiar with important cultural influences and values that are commonly shared by the group, thus enabling them to develop a very complex picture of what is happening within the group. If the researcher chose to adopt experimental methods (e.g. Bandura's Bobo Doll study), or conduct observations from outside the group (for instance Ainsworth's Strange Situation study), some of these often complicated and subtle influences might be missed.

You read about Bandura's research in Chapter 3 and Ainsworth's research in Chapter 5.

Activity 6.3

What are some of the issues that may be raised by such an approach? Think particularly about the advantages and disadvantages of using ethnographic methods.

Consider the use of this type of research method when studying children's friendships. Can a researcher become an active participant in a child's social world?

The questions raised in Activity 6.3 are important when deciding whether to conduct an ethnographic study. First, one of the strong benefits of using this method is the rich and complex data that can be generated. Rather than asking a child to verbalise their thoughts and feelings on the topic of friendship, which, depending on the child's age, may be quite a challenging task in itself and something they have never done before, the approach enables the researcher to observe a first-hand account of the child's experiences.

However, there remains an important question concerning how the researcher can become part of the social grouping, particularly when researching with children and adolescents, where the researcher's typically adult status will be all too conspicuous. Corsaro (2006) notes that it can be especially hard to 'blend in', given that physically adults are larger than children and are perceived by children as being 'in charge'. In order to achieve the status of the child's friend, the researcher would need to overcome such problems. From experience of using ethnography in his own research, Corsaro suggests an approach in which the researcher initially watches and observes from a distance for a while and then waits for the children to approach him and invite him into their social world. He has found that this has worked well in the research that he has carried out.

Figure 6.5   William Corsaro with a group of children

Using this ethnographic approach, Corsaro has highlighted many interesting aspects of children's understandings of friendship and how they may be developed and maintained. The following is an example of the kind of data that was collected during Corsaro's observation of a group of children aged three playing in a box. Martin and Dwight are in a box and Denny runs by:

Martin to Denny: Denny!

Denny to Martin: Martin!

[Denny climbs in box next to Martin.]

Martin to Denny: Dwight is here.

Denny to Martin: Can I come?

Martin to Denny: Yeah, you can come.

Denny to Martin: Yeah, 'cause I'm your friend, right?

Martin to Denny: 'Cause I'm your friend.

(Corsaro, 1985, p. 163)

In the example above you can see how children are using the concept of friendship in order to gain access to play activities. Corsaro also found that children referred to themselves as friends because they were playing together.

Using such methods to investigate children's friendships has provided examples that show that children can talk about friendship in quite abstract and complicated terms, at a younger age than previous research suggested. For example, Jenny and Betty are playing in a large wooden box. Betty has just come back to Jenny having played with another child, Linda:

Betty to Jenny: I do like you, Jenny … I do.

Jenny to Betty: I know it

Betty to Jenny: Yeah. But I just ran away from you. You know why?

Jenny to Betty: Why?

Betty to Jenny: Because I –

Jenny to Betty: You wanted to play with Linda?

Betty to Jenny: Yeah.

Jenny to Betty: I ranned away *with* you. Wasn't that funny?

Betty to Jenny: Yes.

Jenny to Betty: Cause I wanted to know what happened.

Betty to Jenny: I know you wanted – all the time – you wanna know because you're my best friend.

Jenny to Betty: Right.

(Corsaro, 1985, p. 166)

Jenny and Betty are only three years old, yet are clearly showing that they are concerned about how the other felt when they played with someone else. Betty reassures Jenny that she knew why Jenny wanted to know where she was and that they are still best friends. This showing of concern and regard for others is something that Bigelow and La Gaipa argued becomes an important aspect of friendship much later in a child's life, not at the age of three.

In order to explain the discrepancy between Corsaro's finding and that of Bigelow and La Gaipa, we need to consider the issue of method, that is *how* researchers explored children's understandings of friendships. It may be that subtleties such as the ones apparent in the examples above can be tapped into by engaging with children in *their* environment on *their* level. By contrast, a complex task such as writing about expectations of friendships, or explaining experiences to an adult interviewer, might yield an incomplete picture of a child's understanding of the social world. What Corsaro did was to engage with children on their own terms. Then, by reflecting on his notes and video recordings, and by analysing the conversations between children, he explored and illuminated the world of children's friendship.

Box 6.2 Working with textual data

A researcher who adopts a more qualitative approach in their research needs to think about the ways in which interview or ethnographic data can be analysed. Recall that Bigelow and La Gaipa transformed their qualitative data into quantitative data. They looked for the occurrence of previously decided-upon categories, and created numerical summaries in the form of frequency counts. However, it is possible to analyse textual data without transforming it into numbers. One way of doing so would be to look for themes across the transcripts or written accounts (without having a predetermined set of categories against which the accounts would be compared) and then summarise these themes using the children's actual words and utterances as illustrative examples.

Analysing qualitative data in a way that retains the individual view of the participants is an important challenge for qualitative researchers. Generally, qualitative approaches have moved away from collecting data from lots of participants, with the view of generalising findings to the population as whole. Instead, research involves collecting data from fewer participants, which is then analysed in more detail. Examples from personal accounts are used to illustrate broader ideas and conclusions, which are rooted in the data, namely the experiences and opinions voiced by participants.

There are different ways of analysing textual data, but a common starting point is to read and reread transcripts of interviews, recorded conversations or written accounts and look for common and recurring themes. Unlike in the case of Bigelow and La Gaipa, the aim is not to look for categories that have been chosen in advance by researchers, but to pull out, from what participants have actually said, the main themes.

> Because analysis of textual data aims to preserve the individual perspective, it allows a more detailed and rich picture of a person's understanding and expectation of friendship to emerge.

Summary

- There are different approaches to studying friendships and these will generate different data, which can be analysed in different ways. Each approach has distinct advantages and disadvantages.

- Qualitative approaches seek to understand friendship from an individual's perspective. These approaches draw on personal accounts of friendship formation and friendship experiences.

4 Contemporary explorations of friendships

In recent years, psychologists have built on the early research on friendship in childhood and adolescence and have explored a number of more specific aspects of this type of relationship. Among them are positive and negative social influences exerted in the context of friendship, and the effects of culture on interaction between peers.

4.1 The social influences of friendships

Friendships have been cited as being an important influence, both positive and negative, on a range of behaviours. For example, friendships influence how children experience starting school, which means that as well as being a source of companionship, friends are also important in giving support to a child's learning. The importance of peer relationships continues across the lifespan. Researching friendships in adults has the advantage that participants can better articulate and reflect upon their experiences, and talk about how peers have influenced them.

Activity 6.4

Let's pause briefly to consider the question of influence by our peers. Think about whether you have ever been influenced by or have influenced your peers and in what way – for example with regard to fashion, activities, hobbies, etc. Was this influence positive or negative?

Are we inevitably influenced by our friends? Can we actively choose to follow or resist peer influence?

Working in Australia, Kim McLeod and her colleagues focused on the influence of friends on the uptake of smoking among adolescents. McLeod et al. (2008) used telephone interviews to collect qualitative data, which enabled them to explore the social context of smoking behaviour, with a particular focus on the role of friends. McLeod et al. argue that early work on the influence of friendships tends to view adolescents as passive recipients of peer influences. So, for example, they may go along with and behave in a similar way to their peers without much reflection. An alternative view is that adolescents in fact play an active role in selecting the peers that they associate with and that peer influence involves a more complex dynamic.

In order to investigate the influence of friends on smoking behaviour, McLeod et al. studied identical twins, of whom one smoked and the other didn't, and explored whether this difference was related to the friendship groups of the twins. McLeod et al. argued that qualitative methods are more appropriate when studying the often-complicated relationships between friends because they enable an in-depth understanding of the issue of peer influence from the perspective of the individual. McLeod et al. interviewed fourteen pairs of identical twins, nine female and five male pairs, who differed in their smoking status. Their ages ranged from 27 to 33 years.

In their analysis McLeod et al. found that the different friendship groups of the twin pairs reflected the twins' decision to be a smoker or not. While some of the twins reported sharing friends at secondary school, after this all the participants reported having their own friendship circles that were different from their twin's. The participants reported that having friends who smoked, or didn't smoke, had an effect on their smoking status. Smokers in this study accounted for their behaviour in terms of social mobility, for example using smoking as a way of adopting a rebellious image, or gaining access to a particular group or scene. It also enabled a sense of group acceptance to be nurtured. Similarly, the non-smoking twins reported the dominance of a non-smoking image within their chosen social circles. McLeod et al. therefore concluded that both smokers and non-smokers are aware of the role that smoking can play in creating a social image and developing and maintaining a sense of collective identity.

However, it is important to note that, of the participants in this study, few smokers discussed their smoking uptake as a direct outcome of peer influence. They were not encouraged or made to smoke by their peers. Rather, they reported that they became smokers because the people that they wanted to associate with happened to be smokers. The participants described their friendship circle as consisting of people whom they wanted to spend time with, and smoking was just one of the many things that members of this social circle engaged in. The findings of McLeod et al. therefore point towards a complex influence of friends on an individual's behaviour, which can depend on wider issues of fitting in and social approval.

Figure 6.6   Growing importance of image, group acceptance and perhaps rebellion: friendships among young adults

4.2   Cultural influences on the concept of friendship

So far I have considered friendship in very broad terms and have not examined any potential differences between different groups of people with regard to how they perceive and interact with friends. Indeed, this is reflected in early studies of children's friendships, which were primarily conducted within North American and UK contexts. What I would like to do now is consider issues of culture and how they may influence friendship formation and expectations.

The need for a focus on the influence of culture has become increasingly important in psychological research. In Chapter 5 you read about Mary Ainsworth's Strange Situation study and how the descriptions of attachment behaviours put forward by Ainsworth reflected Western assumptions about what constitutes appropriate attachment style, without taking into account cultural differences in child-rearing practices. This is also the case when researching friendship. Being aware of the many similarities and differences between cultural understandings of friendship may lead us to a different understanding of what the term 'friendship' means.

Yorkys González, Digno Moreno and Barry Schneider (2004) – researchers working at two universities, one in Cuba and one in Canada

– sought to explore the influence of culture through the comparison of friendships within **collectivist** and **individualistic** societies. The authors proposed that individualistic cultures are characterised by the valuing of individual goals and achievements, and this could therefore be considered to be inconsistent with the responsibilities of a close friendship. In contrast, the authors characterised collectivist cultures as those that focus on values such as concern for others and the maintenance of harmonious relationships. These are features that are conducive to the development of close friendships. In order to explore the potential differences between friendships in two different cultures, González et al. compared the friendships of adolescents in Canada, which they drew on as an example of a culture of individualism, and Cuba, which they drew on as an example of a collectivist culture.

González et al. used the method developed by Bigelow and La Gaipa. They asked 300 Cuban and 294 Canadian adolescents to write an essay about their best friend of the same gender and consider what they expected of their best friend. Specifically, the adolescents were asked to consider their best friend rather than other friends and think about the features that made a best friend different from other schoolmates. González et al. also analysed the essays by looking for and counting the occurrences of a set of categories that were very similar to those used by Bigelow and La Gaipa.

González et al. found that there were some important differences as well as similarities between the two groups of participants. Authenticity, loyalty and acceptance featured in essays that were collected in both countries. However, the authors found that essays by the Cuban adolescents were more likely to also discuss issues concerning giving and receiving help. The Cuban essays were also more likely to focus on character admiration as a criterion for a close relationship. In contrast, Canadian essays were more likely to focus on issues concerning the sharing of common interests and a shared history of social interaction.

Collectivist cultures
Cultures characterised by a focus on values such as concern for others and harmonious relationships.

Individualistic cultures
Cultures characterised by a focus on valuing individual goals and achievements.

Figure 6.7   Friendship in Cuba

From their study, González et al. concluded that the essays from the Cuban and Canadian adolescents reflected many aspects of the cultural values of the society within which the adolescents grew up. The authors proposed that the Canadian responses, with their focus on common interests, reflected the values of a society that prioritises individual preferences and choices. In contrast, the Cuban essays frequently mentioned mutual assistance, which again reflected dominant ideals within the society, where the welfare and interests of other group members are considered to be especially important. González et al.

were, however, keen to point out that there were important similarities between the two cultures, and, more importantly, that no judgement should be made about whether individualist or collectivist cultures foster 'better' styles of friendship.

While González et al.'s study provides some important insights into the importance of considering culture when investigating friendship, other studies have shown that the categorisation of cultures as individualist or collectivist may be too broad. A subsequent project led by Doran French examined the proposition that friendships in collectivist cultures are less extensive but more intimate than those found in cultures shaped by individualism. French et al. (2006) compared the friendships of Indonesian, South Korean and US college students. They used a research approach that required participants to keep a record, over a two-week period, of social interactions with friends. Participants were also asked to rate the quality of their relationship with their two best friends. The responses from students in the US, Indonesia and South Korea were then compared using eight different criteria, such as 'intimate disclosure' (the extent to which they confided in the friend) or 'exclusivity' (the extent to which they would rather spend time alone with the friend). French et al. proposed that if the concepts of collectivism and individualism are useful for understanding friendship, then the friendship patterns of Indonesian and South Korean college students should be similar, as both South Korea and Indonesia are characterised as collectivist cultures. In turn, these should be different from friendship patterns among American college students owing to the cultural focus on individualism in the United States.

Their findings, however, suggested something different. Indonesian and South Korean students differed from each other on seven of the eight criteria that were used for comparison. Moreover, both were more similar to the American students than to each other. This suggests that categories such as 'collectivist' and 'individualist' may be too general to adequately capture the subtle and varied ways in which culture influences friendships. French et al. therefore concluded that friendship research needs to be more sensitive to the complex ways in which cultures differ from each other and how these differences may affect expectations of friendship.

Summary

- Findings from studies on friendship suggest that the influence of peers is both subtle and complex.
- Cultural influences may have an important role in shaping our understandings of friendship.
- Concepts such as individualism and collectivism that are sometimes used when exploring cultural differences may be too general to capture the subtle influence of culture on human behaviour and social interaction.

5   A new direction for friendship research?

In this chapter I have considered the concept of friendship, and have paid close attention to the methods used by researchers in investigating people's experiences and expectations of friendships. While keeping methods in mind, I would now like to broaden our focus and look at the different ways that people may experience interactions and friendships, paying particularly close attention to the role of new technologies.

5.1   The changing nature of friendships: the role of new technologies

The development of new technologies has had a significant impact on the way that people choose to interact with each other. The availability of mobile phones with texting facilities, for example, makes it easier to send short messages to other people without the need for what could be a lengthy telephone conversation. Similarly, the development of internet technologies has meant that people can communicate online through a range of tools such as email, web forums, real-time chat and webcam video conferencing. Such developments mean that it has become easier to maintain and possibly develop relationships over long distances. The use of such tools therefore questions some early assumptions regarding the nature of friendship and a requirement for geographical closeness in the development and maintenance of a relationship. Given the increasingly important role that the internet has come to play over recent years, I would like to pay particular attention to the role of the internet in the development and maintenance of online friendships.

Figure 6.8   Interacting with friends, online

Activity 6.5

Spend a couple of minutes considering the following questions. Have you used internet technologies for either friendship formation or friendship maintenance? Do you feel that people can be as intimate in online relationships as they can be in face-to-face relationships? Do you feel that certain types of people would be drawn to this type of friendship? What are some of the positives and drawbacks offered by the use of such new technologies?

I will explore these issues in the rest of this section.

Following the rapid uptake of internet technologies and the dominant role that they play in some people's lives, there have been debates concerning whether the use of the internet will isolate individuals or act as a way of connecting them to others. If such technologies do act as ways of developing and confirming social ties, then will online relationships be as intimate and close as those offline? Major questions have been raised concerning the quality of online friendships owing to the lack of non-verbal social cues that many of us rely on in the development and maintenance of relationships. For example, common sources of confusion for online interactions are messages employing humour or sarcasm. However, while it could be argued that the absence of non-verbal cues such as nodding in agreement, smiling and so on could be a problem for online friendships, there is a whole system of contextual cues that have been developed in order to help facilitate online relationships and overcome the potential difficulties that may be caused by the lack of face-to-face non-verbal cues. These cues are referred to as emoticons and serve to provide further clues about the intended meaning of the message. For example, any potential misunderstanding about the meaning of a message can be avoided with the use of a smiley :-) or a winking smiley ;-). These symbols appear to be an important resource for internet users in the absence of non-verbal cues and voice tones that guide interactions in face-to-face settings. Other resources include a common pool of acronyms, such as LOL (laugh out loud), which also compensate for the lack of non-verbal cues.

5.2 A new kind of friendship?

The first decade of the twenty-first century saw the emergence of a new form of online communication: social networking websites. These sites have created new ways of developing and maintaining friendships over the internet. Social networking sites facilitate contact between people who share interests, and enable them to interact with each other and exchange information and images. They have a whole host of features that enable users to communicate with each other. For example, users can post information about themselves, upload photographs, and receive and send messages to friends. They can also locate other users of the site with whom they may have been friends in the past but have lost touch. Such sites therefore make it possible for people to develop, rekindle and maintain friendships without the need for geographical closeness.

Social networking sites have seen a rapid growth in use since their emergence in the early 2000s. According to a press release issued by Facebook (one of the more popular social networking sites), in September 2009 there were an estimated 300 million active users of Facebook, with more than 150 million users logging on to their account every day (Facebook, 2009).

In a study that examined the uses of social networking sites, John Raacke and Jennifer Bonds-Raacke (2008) found that US college students reported spending a significant amount of their time on these sites, leading the authors to conclude that the sites must therefore be meeting the personal and social needs of users. Participants in Raacke and Bonds-Raacke's study reported that online social networking is especially important for keeping in touch with both current and old friends, and making new friends, indicating that the users of such technologies considered such online relationships to fit within the category of 'friendship'. The increase in the use of new technologies may therefore lead us to question our earlier understandings of friendship, in that geographical proximity and face-to-face interaction are clearly no longer as important a factor in friendship as they once were.

Users of online social networking may report having several hundred 'friends' with whom they interact. However, can we really be friends with so many people in the same way that we can be with a smaller social group? Maybe our language cannot differentiate between online social networking friends and other friends? This leads to a potential problem for the social networking sites. What do they call people who interact online? One possibility is for sites to grade friendships, whereby users can opt for a certain type of communication and higher level of disclosure with close friends while having a different, more 'shallow', interaction with people who are more likely to be referred to in face-to-face interactions as 'acquaintances'. In any case, the possibilities that online networking provides for forming and maintaining relationships require us to think very carefully about what the terms 'friend' and 'friendship' mean.

There have also been several questions posed, particularly in the media, concerning the potentially damaging consequences of excessive engagement with social networking sites. Does the increased communication with friends online lead to a loss of the ability to communicate in face-to-face situations? Recent research by Raacke and Bonds-Raacke (2008) suggests that users of social networking sites consider their online relationships as an important form of friendship. At the same time, these do not preclude or impair the development and maintenance of offline relationships. In fact, individuals use new technologies in very different ways. Some may choose to tap into the benefits of online developments as a way of maintaining a current relationship over geographical distance, while others may initially meet online and then, as their friendship develops, meet in the 'offline world' as well.

5.3   A new kind of method?

Online friendships also lead us to return to two other important themes that I have focused on in this chapter: those of method and the importance of culture in our understandings of friendship. New ways of expressing and experiencing friendships may require new methods through which to investigate friendships. Researching on the internet has many advantages, including the opportunity to interact with and gather data from people from a wider range of geographical locations than would be possible with more traditional data collection methods. This means, for example, that researchers could extend the work of Bigelow and La Gaipa or González et al. and ask lots of people from very different places around the world to write an essay about their best friend and email it to them. Researchers could also use a more qualitative ethnographic method inspired by, for example, the work of Corsaro, and become members of online groups and chat to people online about their friendships. However, any work online raises the difficulty that researchers cannot always be certain about who their participants are, given that people can adopt whatever online identity they choose.

It is also necessary to consider the important cultural variations in understanding friendship and how online friendships reflect these. Much of the communication on the internet is still conducted in English, and research in this area tends to be limited to the English-speaking world. What about the parts of the world that do not communicate in English or which currently do not have widespread access to the internet? If research were limited to online methods, these populations would be excluded.

These issues cannot be easily resolved, but should nevertheless be acknowledged and borne in mind by researchers. Nevertheless, given the increasingly important role that the internet plays in the lives of many individuals, the development of global online friendship networks remains a possible exciting new avenue for future friendship research.

5.4   Conclusion

In order to understand the complexities involved in the formation and maintenance of friendships in children and adolescents, psychologists need to adopt a sophisticated research approach. They need to take into account the limits to children's abilities to express themselves through written language or interviews, and pay greater consideration to the way culture can influence what is expected of friends. Also, when considering the influence of peers on behaviour, it is important to view children and adolescents as active parties in the friendship rather than as passive recipients, easily influenced by others.

The pioneering work of Bigelow and La Gaipa has played a central role in highlighting the developmental shifts in friendship expectations and the changing understandings of friendship as children mature. However, at the time when Bigelow and La Gaipa conducted their research, they could not have anticipated that three decades later children would be as likely to interact with friends online as they are in the playground and that the meaning of the word 'friend' would be extended to cover these online relationships. This is yet another example of the way in which technological advancement and the changing nature of human interaction constantly throws up new challenges for psychologists to address.

Summary

- New technologies have become more widely available in recent times, and may necessitate a revision of the concept of friendship.
- The popularity of online networking opens up the possibility that some of the traditional aspects of friendship, such as geographical closeness, may become less important.
- These new ways of interacting with friends may mean that new methods for investigating friendship will need to be developed.

References

Bigelow, B.J. and La Gaipa, J. (1975) 'Children's written descriptions of friendship: a multidimensional analysis', *Developmental Psychology*, vol. 11, no. 6, pp. 857–8.

Bukowski, W.M., Newcomb, A.F. and Hartup, W.W. (1996) 'Friendship and its significance in childhood and adolescence: introduction and comment' in Bukowski, W.M., Newcomb, A.F. and Hartup, W.W. (eds) *The Company They Keep. Friendship in Childhood and Adolescence*, New York, NY, Cambridge University Press.

Corsaro, W.A. (1985) *Friendship and Peer Culture in the Early Years*, New Jersey, NJ, Ablex Publishing Corporation.

Corsaro, W.A. (2006) 'Qualitative research on children's peer relations in cultural context' in Chen, X., French, D.C. and Schneider, B.H. (eds), *Peer Relationships in Cultural Context*, New York, NY, Cambridge University Press.

Damon, W. (1977) *The Social World of the Child*, San Francisco, CA, Jossey-Bass.

Erwin, P. (1998) *Friendship in Childhood and Adolescence*, Psychology Focus Series, London, Routledge.

Facebook (2009) *Pressroom* [online], http://www.facebook.com/press/info.php?statistics (Accessed 25 September 2009).

French, D.C., Bae, A., Pidada, S. and Lee, O. (2006) 'Friendships of Indonesian, South Korean and US college students', *Personal Relationships*, vol. 13, no. 1, pp. 69–81.

González, Y.S., Moreno, D.S. and Schneider, B.H. (2004) 'Friendship expectations of early adolescents in Cuba and Canada', *Journal of Cross-Cultural Psychology*, vol. 35, no. 4, pp. 436–45.

Hartup, W.W. (1996) 'The company they keep: friendships and their developmental significance', *Child Development*, vol. 67, no. 1, pp. 1–13.

McLeod, K., White, V., Mullins, R., Davey, C., Wakefield, M. and Hill, D. (2008) 'How do friends influence smoking uptake? Findings from qualitative interviews with identical twins', *The Journal of Genetic Psychology*, vol. 169, no. 2, pp. 117–31.

Raacke, J. and Bonds-Raacke, J. (2008) 'MySpace and Facebook: applying the uses and gratifications theory to exploring friend-networking sites', *CyberPsychology and Behaviour*, vol. 11, no. 2, pp. 169–74.

Conclusion

In Part 2 of *Discovering Psychology* you read about the work of B.F. Skinner on learning, about Harry Harlow's experiments on attachment in monkeys and about Brian Bigelow and John La Gaipa's study on children's friendships. All three chapters addressed a similar aim: understanding various influences on human behaviour. The chapters examined how behaviour is shaped through specific reinforcement schedules, how it is influenced by innate factors that determine the relationship with – and attachment to – caregivers in infancy, and how our lives are shaped through the experience of a different kind of attachment which is formed in and throughout childhood.

An important point to emerge from Part 2 is that research conducted by psychologists does not just involve human participants but may also centre on non-human animals. Psychologists study animals for different reasons. The research described in Chapter 4 investigated a very basic form of learning which is thought to apply to most species. The principles of behaviour shaping, uncovered in the Skinner box using rats and pigeons, are thought to apply beyond the laboratory and to humans too. Primary attachment investigated by Harlow was also believed to constitute an evolved behavioural pattern, which meant that inferences about human attachment could be drawn from animal research.

It is worth noting, however, that psychologists sometimes study animals also for practical reasons. Harry Harlow's experiments described in Chapter 5 could not have been conducted on human infants for reasons of ethics. Although even today psychologists sometimes use animals as substitutes for humans, animal research is regulated by strict ethical guidelines that take into account issues of animal welfare. So, many of Harlow's experiments would be deemed unethical today, just as it is now no longer possible to replicate the work of Stanley Milgram described in Chapter 2.

Like Part 1 of *Discovering Psychology*, Part 2 underlines the fact that researchers are often influenced by the broader social and intellectual context. Skinner's work was influenced by the findings of Ivan Pavlov, John B. Watson and Edward Thorndike, and especially by Watson's view that psychology should be an objective science and concern itself only with observable and measurable behaviour. Harlow's research, on the other hand, should be viewed in the light of John Bowlby's notion that the attachment between a child and its parents is based on the provision of comfort, while Bowlby in turn was influenced by the work of ethologists on innate predispositions in animals. The research by Bigelow and La Gaipa was, admittedly, not influenced by any particular key idea of their time. Instead it was the lack of research on children's friendship that prompted the two psychologists to carry out their pioneering research. However, the more recent studies on online friendships are very much influenced by a dramatic development in contemporary society, namely the arrival of computers and the internet in homes in the early twenty-first century.

In Part 2 you also learnt that research is sometimes influenced by chance circumstances. Skinner decided to test a partial reinforcement schedule because he ran short of food pellets. Harlow only came to study attachment in rhesus monkeys because the rat laboratory had been dismantled at the university where he worked, and he could not study intelligence in rats as he had planned. What is more, had he not noticed, purely by chance, that infant monkeys were distressed when the soft lining of the cage was removed during cleaning, he probably never would have embarked on the study of attachment.

The three chapters in Part 2 of *Discovering Psychology* offered you further tasters of the different sub-disciplines of psychology. Chapters 5 and 6 (just like Chapter 3 in Part 1) looked at research that belongs to the domain of *developmental psychology*, in that the studies looked at children's behaviour and their psychological development. Chapter 5 also introduced you to *evolutionary psychology*, which focuses on the application of evolutionary principles to explain human behaviour. In Chapter 4 you encountered an approach in psychology called *behaviourism*, which was one of several dominant schools of thought in the first half of the twentieth century, and one that involved animal research.

The chapters also offered further insight into the range of *methods* used by psychologists. In Chapters 4 and 5 you read about the use of laboratory experiments, but this time involving animals rather than human participants. In Chapter 5 you also learned about the importance of interviews and observations when studying attachment in humans. These two methods of collecting data have proved especially useful when exploring behaviour that cannot be studied experimentally, for ethical and other reasons. Chapter 6, on the other hand, highlighted the important role that qualitative data plays in psychological research. Although Bigelow and La Gaipa coded their qualitative data, thereby transforming children's textual responses into numbers, other approaches to studying friendship involve analysing children's accounts in ways that allow the individuality and uniqueness of each child's experience to be preserved.

The fact that psychologists may use very different approaches and methods when exploring the same topic is important to bear in mind, as this diversity within the discipline helps to build a more complete understanding of human behaviour and its complexity. For example, the exploration of the similarities between humans and non-human animals with regard to learning and attachment led to important insights into the evolved, or innate, aspects of human behaviour. At the same time, the work on human participants highlighted the importance of culture and environmental factors on behaviour, including attachment. Cross-cultural research on attachment, for instance, revealed that the evolved aspects of human behaviour invariably interact with outside influences, including culture. Specific attachment patterns (as well as assumptions about what constitutes optimal attachment) are products of culture and the environment, and not just of evolution. Also, rather than being simply determined by innate factors, human behaviour has been shown to be flexible and adaptive. It is therefore the interaction between the two influences — between nature (evolved or inherited predispositions) and nurture (the culture and the environment) that determines who we are and what we do.

Finally, there is something else that brings together many studies presented in Part 2. Research on conditioning animals, studies on the evolution of attachment and examinations of children's understanding of friendship all focused either on visible behaviour or on language produced during interactions or play. None of the studies discussed in the three chapters were concerned specifically with what happens in a person's (or an animal's) brain or what mental processes are taking place as they perform the various behaviours or interact with others. This is the focus of Part 3, where you will read about how psychologists investigate the basic mental functions and processes without which interaction with the environment would be difficult, if not impossible. This poses a broader question, namely how do psychologists explore something that they cannot directly observe? How do they investigate the inner workings of things such as language, attention and memory?

Part 3

Introduction

In several places in Parts 1 and 2 of *Discovering Psychology* you encountered the notion of *cognitive* processes. The word 'cognition' refers to a whole range of internal mental processes that allow us to take in, store and use information or knowledge about the world around us. These processes include attention, perception, memory, reasoning and language. Studying these processes can help us understand a range of everyday experiences, some of which you will read about in Part 3. In Chapters 7–9 you will learn about the processes involved in using language to communicate, why it is not a good idea to drive while using a mobile phone, and how it is that some might remember an event that never actually happened. As cognition is the focus of Part 3, let us look back at what you have read about it already, in Parts 1 and 2.

In Chapter 1 you were introduced to the notion of *cognitive style* – a particular way of structuring and processing information. Individuals high in dogmatism were said to possess a rigid and closed-minded cognitive style which means that they are swayed more by *who* is presenting the message (an authority figure, for example) than by *what* information it actually contains. So, a personality attribute (dogmatism) was associated with a particular way of thinking and reasoning.

In Chapter 3 you read that one mechanism which is thought to underpin social learning involves a change in a person's attitudes, beliefs and judgements about aggression and its appropriateness. This mechanism, which concerns a change in a person's thinking processes as a result of experience (for instance, desensitisation), was referred to as a *cognitive* mechanism.

Also, in Chapter 4 you read that behaviourism advocated a psychology that looked at what was observable and could properly be measured, namely behaviour. Behaviourism was therefore not interested in mental processes, or cognition, at all. However, other researchers looking at animal behaviour found it difficult to avoid using mental terms to explain learning. Furthermore, the complexity of human behaviour is difficult to account for without any recourse to mental processes. In humans, what counts as 'reinforcement' or 'punishment' depends on the way a person perceives and thinks about their environment.

From these three examples alone, you will have a sense of the importance of things that cannot be directly observed. What this suggests is that psychologists need to investigate not just what an individual *does*, but also what happens 'inside their head'.

Part 3 will begin to explore cognition by looking literally at what happens 'inside the head'. Cognitive processes are all located in a single organ: the brain. The specific focus of Chapter 7, by Frederick Toates, is the role that different brain regions play in controlling the ability to comprehend and use *language*. You will read about the discoveries made by two important nineteenth-century figures, Pierre Paul Broca and Carl Wernicke, who studied damaged brains and who identified two particular areas of the brain, one involved in the production of speech and the other in the comprehension of language. Since their pioneering work, a more complex model of how language is regulated by the brain has emerged. You will read about the technological advances that made it possible for researchers to 'see' inside the working brain, leading to new insights into how the brain controls language, and the ability of the brain to recover from damage.

Chapters 8 and 9 then move on to explore research that used experiments to look at two different cognitive functions: attention and memory. Chapter 8, by Helen Edgar and Graham Edgar, introduces the work of Donald Broadbent, who is recognised as one of the founders of modern cognitive psychology. Broadbent was interested in the cognitive process of *attention* and the fact that our ability to attend to stimuli in the environment is limited: we cannot attend to *everything* around us. Broadbent sought to develop a model that would describe and explain how the human mind processes information. Put simply, he was interested in the 'software' of the mind rather than the 'hardware' of the brain. In the chapter you will read about how Broadbent and other psychologists used experiments to create, test and revise a model of attention. You will also read about how this research can be applied to a practical real-world issue, namely the question of whether or not it is dangerous to use a mobile phone while driving.

The final chapter of Part 3 looks at research on human *memory*. Chapter 9, by Graham Pike and Nicola Brace, focuses on one particular aspect of memory, memory for events, and considers research that has relevance for those witnessing a crime. It is difficult to imagine a situation where remembering accurately is as important as when one is summoned to testify as an eyewitness to a crime. Understanding what sorts of factors influence memory of events can provide valuable information for the legal profession. What is more, it can also contribute to our understanding of how memory operates more generally. The chapter discusses the work of Elizabeth Loftus and colleagues, and describes some widely cited experiments on leading questions and false memories. The chapter also introduces an important study by Sir Frederic Bartlett, tutor of Donald Broadbent and another important forefather of modern cognitive psychology.

Part 3 therefore takes you through different approaches to studying what happens 'inside the head', from different techniques for studying the brain to experiments testing ideas about attention or memory. In this part of the book, you will also learn about the relevance of research on brain function and cognition to a selection of real-life problems.

Chapter 7
Language and the brain

Frederick Toates

Contents

Aims and objectives

After reading this chapter you should be able to:

- describe what is meant by the term 'stroke' and understand the disturbances to language that often follow it
- explain what is meant by the assertion that a region of the brain is associated with a particular psychological function
- describe Broca's and Wernicke's contributions to our understanding of the relationship between the brain and language
- distinguish between Broca's aphasia and Wernicke's aphasia, with regard to brain regions and disruption to language
- explain what is meant by flexibility and plasticity of the brain
- outline how technical advances have enabled new insights into the psychology of language.

1   Introduction

This chapter is about understanding the brain and its role in language. On hearing the word 'language', most of us probably think first of listening to and understanding spoken words, or retrieving the right words from memory and uttering them using appropriate sounds. Listening and speaking are, however, not the only means of using language. There is written language of course, and sign language. Sign language, as used in communication with deaf people, is a form that does not involve either spoken or written words. An important question for psychologists has been whether the relationship between the brain and language is the same for any system of language, irrespective of its means of expression, and this is a question to which I shall return later on in the chapter.

A valuable source of insight into the link between language and the brain has been the study of what happens when things go wrong; that is, when language impairment occurs as a result of brain damage. Such damage can occur for various reasons, including traffic accidents and war wounds. But the most common cause in the UK is stroke.

1.1   The case of stroke

> Suddenly the light went out. Seven hours later I woke up in hospital. I couldn't move my right side, and my speech had gone.
>
> (David Diston, stroke survivor,
> quoted in The Stroke Association, 2009, p. 3)

In the UK, about 150,000 people suffer from a stroke each year. The term **stroke** refers to injury to the brain caused by an interruption of the blood supply to the cells in the brain. The body is made up of tiny components called cells and the brain itself contains billions of specialised cells called **neurons**. Each cell throughout the body, including neurons, requires a supply of nutrients and oxygen in order to survive and to perform its function. These are brought to each cell by means of blood travelling through the network of blood vessels. If deprived of this supply, there is a danger that a cell will die.

Stroke
A loss of supply of blood to a region in the brain, resulting in disruption of brain function.

Neuron
A type of cell involved in transmitting messages between different parts of the brain.

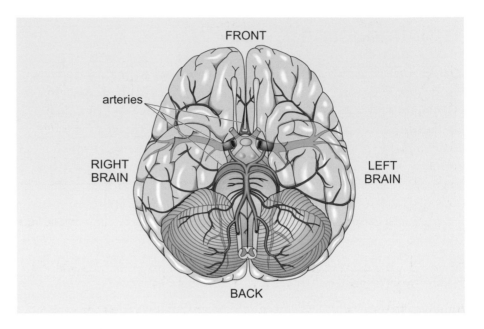

Figure 7.1   A drawing of the human brain (viewed from below) showing the blood vessels running through it

Figure 7.1 shows the network of blood vessels that supply nutrients and oxygen to the cells of the brain. If there is a loss of supply of blood to a region of the brain, the cells there will cease to function and can soon die. The resulting disruption of brain function is called a stroke.

A stroke can be caused by the blockage of a blood vessel, as when fatty substances build up on its wall, or when the wall of a vessel breaks (see Figure 7.2). Loss of function of the cells in a brain region means disruption to the feature of behaviour controlled by that region. So, if the region controls an arm, loss of its blood supply will disrupt the ability to raise that arm. If the region controls language, then there will be difficulty in understanding spoken words, or speech will be lost or slurred. In some cases, the disruption is so extensive that several such features of behaviour or functions will be disturbed.

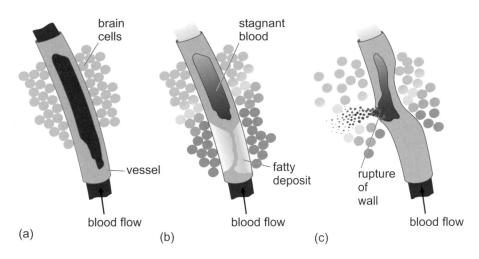

Figure 7.2 The basis of a stroke: (a) intact vessel; (b) a blood vessel blocked by fatty substance; (c) rupturing of vessel wall

Although not all victims of stroke will exhibit the same symptoms, most will experience some disturbance to language and to the movement of the arm and/or facial muscles. This is why The Stroke Association (2009, p. 6) gives the guidance to act FAST when you suspect that someone has suffered from a stroke, where FAST is not only advice on speed but also an acronym for the Face-Arm-Speech Test:

F Facial weakness: Can the person smile? Has their mouth or an eye drooped?

A Arm weakness: Can the person raise both arms?

S Speech problems: Can the person speak clearly and understand what you say?

T Test these symptoms.

Activity 7.1

If you see someone having a stroke, the priority is to get them to a hospital as soon as possible. The doctor will seek to maximise the chances that the individual affected survives and returns to a functioning life. But where do psychologists come in? Spend a couple of minutes thinking about why psychologists might be interested in stroke and how they might become involved in the recovery process.

First, on recovery, stroke patients might find themselves disabled in terms of not being able to move limbs or speak. They might suffer psychological changes, including depression. Psychologists often help the rehabilitation of stroke patients by informing their therapy. Second, by studying the effects of a stroke, or another form of brain injury that affects behaviour or performance, psychologists can develop a better understanding of how behaviour and cognitive processes such as language and memory depend upon what goes on in the brain.

This chapter is primarily concerned with the latter issue and addresses two specific questions using the example of language. First, it examines how researchers arrived at the view that the brain forms the basis of psychological processes and, second, it explores how knowledge of the brain helps us to understand how these processes are controlled.

1.2   Understanding and misunderstanding

The effect of a stroke, in terms of disruption to speech and movement, is widely known. Other disorders also point to the brain. Disruption of memory, as in dementia, follows deterioration of the brain. The expression 'brain dead' seems to be synonymous with the end of life. The idea that the brain forms the basis of our thought processes and behaviour is so much a part of our understanding of the human condition that it is hard to imagine anyone could ever have believed otherwise.

However, the ancient Egyptians thought that the 'soul' was located in the bowels and heart (Finger, 2000). When preserving the bodies of their dead leaders, with all the reverence that was appropriate for their journey to the afterlife, the brain was unceremoniously extracted through the nostrils. Strangely enough, in spite of taking such a 'dim view' of the brain, the Egyptians recognised that injury to it could have various consequences, such as disruption to coordination between the eyes and the hands. Quite brilliantly, they accurately observed that damage to one side of the brain usually had more serious consequences for the opposite side of the body.

To associate the mind with the brain requires taking a journey of several hundreds of years and to the other side of the Mediterranean. Some 400 years BC in ancient Greece, the followers of Hippocrates (the man widely regarded as the father of medicine) hit upon the truth. By carefully observing human bodies in illness and health, and scrutinising the development, spread and course of different illnesses, they challenged the notion that illness was a punishment sent by the gods. Rather, they explained illnesses in natural terms. 'Madness' and epilepsy were, for instance, described as manifestations of abnormality of the brain.

If abnormalities of behaviour are seen as afflictions sent by the gods, people can argue that these are punishments for wrongdoing. If they are instead understood as the product of unusual brain activity, then perhaps people are more likely to show tolerance. In seventeenth-century America, however, uncontrolled twitching and jerking was seen as evidence not of divine punishment but of possession by demons. Those with this condition, particularly women, risked execution as witches. It is now believed that these unfortunate people suffered from Huntington's disease (Vessie, 1932). This disorder of brain regions involved in controlling the muscles is inherited. Those suffering from the condition in America apparently all derived from a family group who emigrated in 1630 from Bures in Suffolk.

1.3   Phrenology

In modern times, the interest in the brain dates back to the late eighteenth century, when the Viennese doctor Franz Joseph Gall proposed that different parts of the outer region of the brain serve different roles or functions. He argued that each part of the brain has responsibility for the control of a particular behaviour or feature of mind. He was not the first to state this belief, the credit going to a Swedish Christian mystic, Swedenborg, but Gall was the first to gain wide recognition for advancing it.

According to this view, memory, for example, would be stored in one brain region, whereas a different region would be responsible for romantic love. This theory was called **phrenology**. Gall devised a phrenology map which proposed the **functional anatomy** of the brain. The term 'anatomy' refers to the structure of the body, so the anatomy of the brain is a description of its structure involving its appearance and the location of such things as contours and blood vessels. The word 'function' refers to what different bits of the brain do, or the role they play, with regard to behaviour, cognitive processes or individual characteristics. So, the phrenology map charted the brain regions and their roles, identifying, for example, parts involved in 'language' or 'benevolence' (see Figure 7.3).

Phrenology
The study of the contours of the head and trying to link this to the function of the various regions of brain. In large part, it is now discredited.

Functional anatomy
A description of the regions of the brain in terms of the function that they serve in the control of cognitive processes, characteristics and behaviour.

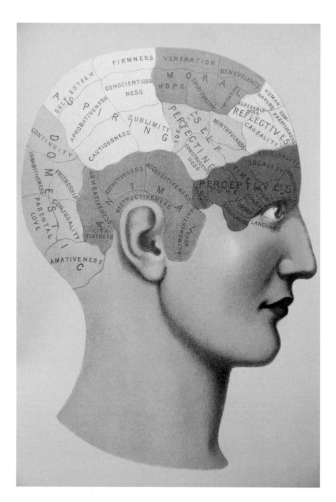

Figure 7.3 A phrenology map

Gall challenged two prevailing views. First, the religious authorities in Austria objected to his attempts to link personality characteristics to a material substance, namely the brain. They preferred to see them as features of an immaterial soul. Second, there was a disagreement with those who did accept that the brain was the basis of mental processes, but who argued that the *whole brain* contributed equally to every psychological activity (Graves, 1997).

Gall's idea contained a considerable amount of truth. Distinct bits of the brain do serve different functions. A given region of the brain tends to be associated with the same function in different individuals. This means regions can be labelled in terms of what they do. However, a region is rarely responsible for *just one* function. Rather, it is now known that regions of the brain interact or work together in determining psychological processes.

Gall also went 'to excess' in applying his approach. He found people whose behaviour deviated from the norm (e.g. geniuses, the mentally ill and murderers), compared their heads with those of so-called normal individuals, and claimed to have found differences that explain deviance. Gall asserted that unusual visible features of the head corresponded to unusual structures of the brain and thereby to the production of unusual behaviour. So, for example, a particularly amorous lady friend was said to have an abnormally large 'amorous region' of her brain, visible on the contours of the skull. Such unwarranted speculation led phrenology into disrepute. Nevertheless, the idea that different brain regions serve different roles was a sound one. Gall had rightly noted, for example, that loss of speech can arise from damage to the front half of the brain (Schiller, 1979). This leads us to the important contributions of Pierre Paul Broca and Carl Wernicke to our understanding of the relationship between the brain and language. Their work is described in the next section.

Summary

- It is now widely accepted that the brain forms the basis of cognitive processes and behaviour.
- In stroke, a disruption to behaviour, including speech, can arise from damage to a part of the brain.
- The study of brains damaged by stroke can give insights into the normal functioning of the brain.
- Phrenology was a theory that associated particular parts of the brain with specific psychological functions. It stood in opposition to two views: (a) that psychological processes are *not* rooted in the brain; and (b) that all parts of the brain have equal responsibility for different psychological processes.

2 Two dominant figures: Broca and Wernicke

Understanding the links between brain and langauge owes much to two dominant figures, Broca and Wernicke. Although neither of them was a psychologist, they were a major influence on the development of **neuropsychology**, which is a branch of psychology concerned with the relationship between the brain and psychological processes.

2.1 Pierre Paul Broca

Pierre Paul Broca was born in 1824 in the small French town of Sainte-Foy-la-Grande. On leaving school, he studied medicine in Paris. Broca made contributions in a wide range of medical and related fields but I shall concentrate only on his contribution to the study of language.

Influences on his scientific career included François Leuret, one of Broca's teachers of medicine. Leuret studied the folds ('grooves and ridges') that are clearly visible on the outer surface of much of the brain (see Figure 7.4). He advocated the view that their pattern is not haphazard. A study of the brains of humans and other species revealed a pattern that was consistent for and characteristic of each species.

Neuropsychology
The sub-discipline of psychology concerned with studying the structure and function of the brain, and therefore the relationship between the brain and psychological processes.

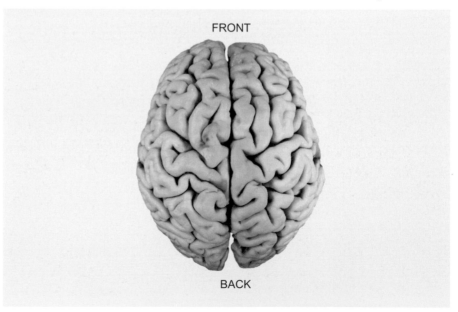

Figure 7.4   The outer surface of the brain (shown from above)

Another of Broca's teachers reiterated the belief of Gall that speech was impaired by damage specifically to the *front* half of the brain. This was based upon the frequent observation that damage to the front of the brain was associated with disruption to speech while damage to the rear tended to leave speech unaffected. However, the evidence for the latter proved to be less sound – some researchers found that disruption to speech sometimes occurred even when damage was to the rear part of the brain.

Those who were sceptical that the front part of the brain is involved in speech cited the case of Phineas Gage, a man who possessed what might be the most famous brain in all history (the candidate for second place will be described in a moment). In 1848, Phineas Gage was working on the construction of a railway in Vermont, USA when an explosion sent an iron bar through part of the front of his brain (see Figure 7.5). Miraculously Gage survived and, although he suffered from changes of personality, his capacity for language, in terms of understanding and articulation, was left intact.

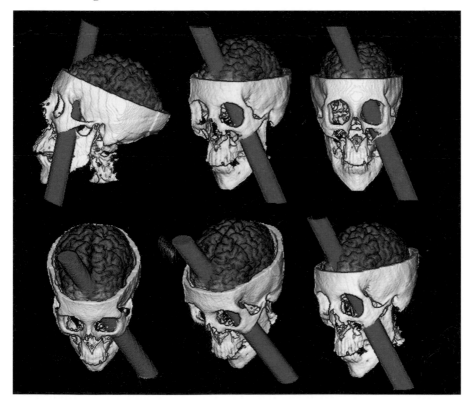

Figure 7.5   A reconstruction of the damage to the brain of Phineas Gage

Based upon such evidence, a more nuanced claim emerged: the effect of brain damage depends upon the *exact site of damage* within the brain. So, speech could be disrupted while such actions as walking or non-speech-related movements of the mouth and tongue would remain intact. This was believed to be because damage to certain parts of the brain led to specific impairments related to speech, while other functions were left unimpaired.

Broca and other researchers studied the brain by dissecting the brains of deceased people. They were especially interested in the outer layer of the brain, termed the **cortex** (see Figure 7.6).

Cortex
The outer layer of the brain.

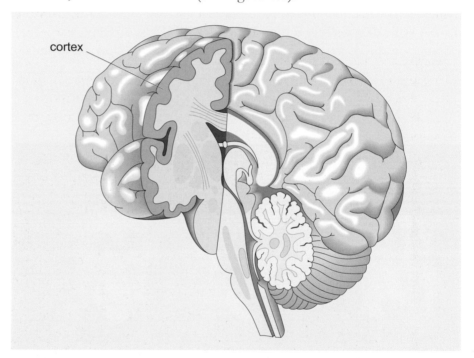

cortex

Figure 7.6   The brain, in part cut away to reveal the cortex. The cortex is formed of grey matter with white matter lying underneath

Broca made his most famous observation, which is the focus of this chapter, in 1861 while examining the brain of a 51-year-old man, Mr Leborgne, who died while under the care of Broca at the Bicêtre hospital in Paris (Broca, 1861). This unfortunate man had been without the capacity of speech for the last twenty-one years of his life and there was impairment in his ability to move his right arm. To any question, he gave the spoken response 'tan', and thereby acquired the name of 'Tan' in the hospital. By means of the gestures that the patient made with his left hand and its individual fingers, Broca concluded that Mr

Leborgne was able to understand speech. At autopsy, Broca noted disruption to tissue in a region on the *left* side of the brain towards the front (see Figure 7.7). The left and right sides of the brain (as shown in Figure 7.1) are commonly referred to as the left and right **hemispheres**. Broca concluded that this specific location in the left hemisphere was responsible for speech production.

Hemisphere
The left and right hemispheres are the left and right sides of the brain.

Observation of other patients with loss of the ability to speak followed, and the autopsies demonstrated a similar disruption to the same area of the *left* side of the brain. In several cases studied by Broca, there was also disruption of the ability to move the right arm, the significance of which will become apparent later. Then, as now, it was rare that damage to the right hemisphere of the brain led to major disruption of speech.

Underpinning Broca's conclusion was a very basic principle, the **principle of localisation**. According to this principle, different regions of the brain have responsibility for different psychological functions. Also, Broca was suggesting that the brain is asymmetric in respect of function: speech is controlled by a region in the left hemisphere only.

Principle of localisation
The principle that psychological functions can be associated with particular regions of the brain.

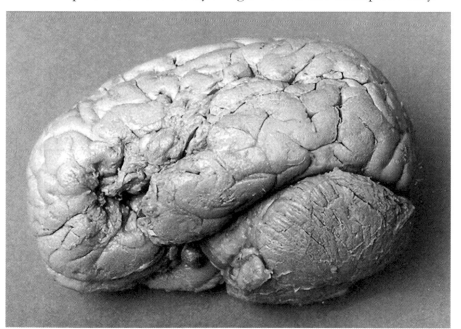

Figure 7.7 The brain of Mr Leborgne

Activity 7.2

Take a moment to look at Figures 7.5 and 7.7 in more detail. Compare the site of damage to the brains of Phineas Gage and Mr Leborgne. As you can see, the damage to the brain of Phineas Gage is to an area further to the front, compared to the hole in the brain of Mr Leborgne. This might explain why Phineas Gage's language ability was intact.

Between 1861 and 1865, Broca became more confident about his findings concerning the localisation and asymmetry in the functioning of the brain, especially as more and more evidence from deceased patients confirmed that there was asymmetry in the control of speech, and that disruption of speech production was associated with damage to the left brain. However, Broca's hypothesis of asymmetry went against the then widely held view that the brain had to be symmetrical in both its structure and function (Buckingham, 2006). From a religious perspective, a perfect act of creation demanded perfect symmetry, so the brain had to be symmetrical too.

Aphasia
Impairment to language or language disorder.

Subsequently, the brain region that Broca identified as being involved in speech production acquired the name of 'Broca's area' (see Figure 7.8). A disruption to language caused by damage to the brain is generally referred to as **aphasia**, so impairment resulting from damage to Broca's area has become known as Broca's aphasia. This particular type of aphasia consists of an inability to articulate speech fluently, so that language may consist only of disjointed words. Normally, writing is also disrupted. Understanding of language can, however, be near to normal.

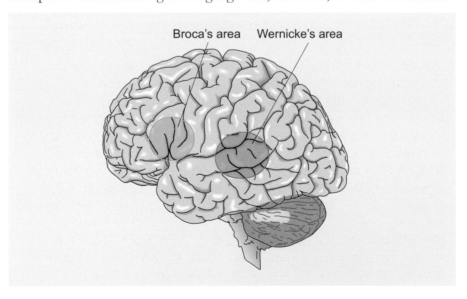

Figure 7.8   The left hemisphere of the brain, indicating Broca's and Wernicke's areas

Box 7.1   The nature of discovery

Progress in science and personal fame depend not just on making original observations and having clever ideas. It is also important to be in the right place at the right time, to have a university position and to get one's findings published in a reputable journal.

Although Broca's name is universally associated with the formal discovery of the principle of asymmetry, one of his fellow-countrymen appears to have made this observation considerably earlier than Broca. Marc Dax was a doctor in Sommières, a small community about twenty miles from Montpellier. Dax died in 1837, some twenty-four years before Broca made his groundbreaking observations.

Much later, it was claimed that, in the year before his death, Dax had presented a paper to a conference of doctors from the south of France, in Montpellier. In this paper, he apparently described his twenty-five years of observations of an association between loss of speech and disruption of movement in the right arm. Dax had concluded that in all such patients damage was to the left side of the brain. He observed that patients who lost speech did not lose all tongue movements, as in paralysis of the muscles controlling the tongue. They could move their tongues but could not exploit such movement in the service of speech. The problem, as Dax correctly reasoned, was an inability to organise the sequence of muscular actions that underlie speech.

Alas, Montpellier is 'not Paris' and Dax was a small-town doctor, so the paper did not attract wide attention. In fact, it has proved impossible to verify that Dax actually presented his paper at the conference in Montpellier (Buckingham, 2006). He might have shown it to just a few colleagues. So, how did he finally come to national attention? In 1863, twenty-six years after his death, his son, Dr Gustave Dax, brought his father's paper to the Academy of Medicine in Paris, where somewhat belatedly it received attention. However, by the time its contents were publicised two years later, Broca's name had already become associated with the discovery. Hugh Buckingham (2006, p. 618) wrote: 'Once again in science, we have likely witnessed another case where a previous investigator actually hit on a concept first, only to lose credit to a later researcher who more properly "framed" the hypothesis in a detailed, all-encompassing publication.'

2.2 Carl Wernicke

Carl Wernicke was born in 1848 in Germany and studied medicine in Breslau. He later served in the psychiatric department of Breslau university hospital. Like Broca, he made original contributions in a number of areas of medicine and psychiatry. Wernicke was interested in the new discoveries on language coming from Paris. From the careful study of patients, he identified another region of the brain, the disturbance of which also led to a disruption of language. However, while Broca was interested in patients who exhibited impairment in speech production, but who could understand language, Wernicke focused on those who experienced a breakdown in the ability both to understand speech and to formulate coherent sentences. He discovered that this impairment was associated with damage to a different area, located towards the middle of the outer surface of the left hemisphere of the brain. Predictably, this region of the cortex became known as 'Wernicke's area' (see Figure 7.8), and impairment associated with damage to this area is referred to as Wernicke's aphasia.

Wernicke's aphasia manifests itself as a breakdown in the ability to understand speech and to formulate coherent, meaningful sentences. Patients are often able to utter words, the grammar can often be correct, but sentences are deficient in meaning.

Wernicke's name has gone down in history for his account of the nature of disruption to speech. But there are indications that, as with Broca, others had earlier realised that speech could be disrupted by damage to the area later to take Wernicke's name. Indeed, one such person appears to have been none other than Dr Gustave Dax, the man who had advanced his father's claim to have discovered the asymmetry of the brain (Finger and Roe, 1999).

Wernicke's fame did not arise only from the discovery of the role of a specific region of brain, important as this was. In addition, he suggested that the control of behaviour, such as language and speaking, depended upon the *interaction* of identifiable regions of the brain (Pillman, 2003). Wernicke proposed that the area bearing his name and Broca's area must be linked and interact with one another to produce language. Wernicke's area is near to the part of the cortex that analyses sounds and is involved in understanding speech. Broca's area, on the other hand, is involved with the process of articulation of speech. Only together do they act to produce normal language processing.

Summary

- Broca articulated the principle of localisation.
- Broca found that damage to a region in the left hemisphere of the brain caused disruption to the production of speech. This area came to be called Broca's area and the resulting speech deficit became known as Broca's aphasia.
- Wernicke discovered that an area of the left brain nearer the back disrupted the comprehension of speech. This area became known as Wernicke's area and the resulting language deficit became known as Wernicke's aphasia.

3   The assumption of localisation of function

The fundamental assumption underlying the work of Broca and Wernicke was that identifiable parts of the brain can be associated with particular aspects of cognition and behaviour. Closely associated with this is the idea that one can gain useful information from studying damaged brains, including how 'normal', undamaged brains function. Also, Wernicke put forward the view that, in order to understand how the brain works, researchers need to study how its various parts *interact*.

3.1   Support for localisation of function

Following Broca and Wernicke, an increasing amount of evidence from people with brain damage pointed to particular parts of the brain being associated with particular psychological functions. When the damage is in the left hemisphere, for example, there is likely to be a disruption to the production of speech or comprehension of the spoken word, or both. Similarly, disruption to the control of limbs resulting from brain damage will affect the opposite side of the body to the site of brain damage. The same applies to the loss of sensation (e.g. of touch). All of these findings provide support for the notion of localisation of function.

Ever since Wernicke's and Broca's pioneering work, researchers have worked on identifying areas of the brain associated with particular functions. For instance, they identified a specific area of the cortex involved in motor (muscular) movement. This research confirmed what Ancient Egyptians had already suspected, namely that muscle movements on the left side of the body are controlled by the right hemisphere of the brain and vice versa. This is why Broca's patients, who had damage to the *left* side of the brain (Broca's area), often had difficulty moving the *right* arm.

Motor homunculus
A functional map of the motor cortex showing the regions of the body over which each region of motor cortex exerts some control.

The area of the brain that controls muscle movement is known as the motor cortex (see Figure 7.9(a)). Yet even within this area, there is further specialisation. Figure 7.9(b) is an illustration of what is known as a **motor homunculus** – a functional map of the motor cortex. It shows each part of the body and the corresponding part of the brain that exerts some control over that body part. It exemplifies the principle of localisation.

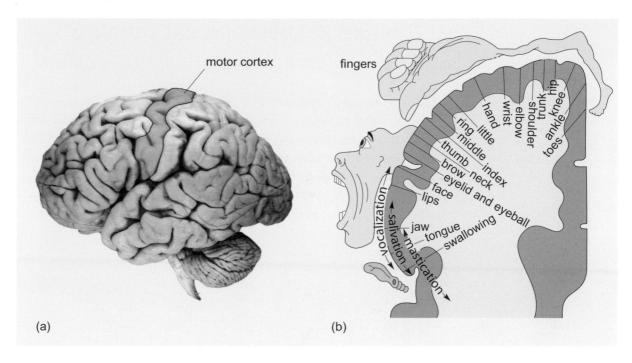

Figure 7.9 (a) the left side of the brain, highlighting the motor cortex; (b) a section of the motor cortex and the motor homunculus

---

Activity 7.3

Look at Figure 7.9(b) and examine the motor homunculus and the relationship between brain region and body part.

- Consider each region of the brain and each body part in terms of the amount of brain devoted to it. What could be the possible significance of this?

- What is the significance of the location of Broca's area relative to the parts of the motor homunculus?

Some regions of the body (e.g. the fingers) have disproportionately large regions of the cortex devoted to their control, whereas other parts (e.g. the hips) have relatively small areas. This reflects the relative degree of sensitivity of control that is exerted over the different body parts. Broca's area is adjacent to that part of the motor cortex concerned with controlling the mouth and tongue. Broca's area interacts with this part of the motor cortex, sending 'instructions' for movements of the mouth and tongue in articulating speech.

3.2   Limits to localisation of function

The evidence from brain damage and studies of the motor homunculus provide support for the principle of localisation of function. However, this evidence largely relates to control over parts of the body and certain sensations. Could the principle of localisation be extended to the whole range of behaviour and cognitive processes? Was Gall right in that areas of the brain responsible for complex emotional processing, as in compassion or romantic love, could be similarly identified? Researchers did indeed subsequently find that parts deeper than the cortex were involved in the regulation of sensations such as anger or erotic arousal (remember that the cortex is just the top layer). However, brain surgery raised some doubts about localisation of function regarding the control of human emotions, and this will be outlined next.

The brains that provided so much evidence for Broca and Wernicke received their damage from such causes as sword wounds, tumours or stroke. Another source of information relevant to localisation arose later in cases where parts of the brain were surgically cut or even removed. There were two reasons why this was done. The medical need to remove diseased brain tissue, as when trying to halt the progress of a cancerous tumour, is surely uncontroversial. By contrast, what is highly controversial is the technique of psychosurgery, which was practised extensively between the 1930s and the 1950s as a treatment for different types of mental illness. The rationale behind this was that by removing selected brain tissue or simply making targeted surgical cuts (usually to the region at the front of the brain), the working of the brain would alter with subsequent benefits for the person receiving the operation.

The results of psychosurgery were mixed. Human emotions and psychological functioning are subtle and doubtless arise from numerous brain regions acting in concert. It has proved very difficult to associate surgical intervention at a particular region with a particular desired outcome, such as to lift chronic depression or anxiety. In fact, undesirable outcomes such as total apathy were far more common. So, the results of psychosurgery suggested that there was no simple relationship between specific areas of the brain and emotions such as anxiety and anger. This is why it is rarely used today.

The poor results of psychosurgery therefore cast some doubt over the claim that there is always a close link between a particular part of the brain and a specific feature of behaviour. The link between brain and psychological processes is more complex than localisation of function suggests. In the late twentieth century, researchers sought to understand how the brain areas worked together as a whole to control behaviour and cognition, as you will learn in Section 4.

3.3   The use of analogies

Psychologists have suggested that analogies can prove useful in understanding brain and behaviour. An analogy is when something unfamiliar or difficult to understand is explained by comparison to something that is familiar. Analogies of different forms are very commonly used to convey ideas to others.

Which analogy you find useful will depend upon what you are most familiar with already. People who are familiar with computers might like to draw analogies between the brain and a computer. Someone else might prefer an analogy with another type of electronic device, such as a radio. Every radio set consists of different components: a battery, a receiver, a speaker, the dials and buttons, as well as a whole host of circuits and wires. Each component corresponds to a specific function: power supply, capturing a signal, emitting sound, switching between stations, etc., but all components interact or work together to capture the message transmitted from a radio station far away.

While you might think that this analogy captures the essence of localisation of function, the British psychologist Richard Gregory used this same analogy to highlight the need to be very cautious when speculating about what damage to individual brain parts can tell us about the brain (Gregory, 1961). Suppose that we carefully remove a component from a radio that was hitherto functioning normally. Immediately, the radio starts to emit an awful howling sound. No one would conclude that the normal role of the component within the radio was to suppress howling. Rather, the howling arises from the way that all the remaining components interact.

The same applies to the brain. The fact that damage to a part of the brain causes a particular symptom does not imply a direct correspondence between that brain part and the symptom. Damage to one part also interferes with the working of other regions of the brain and upsets a complex system. This is why drawing conclusions from studies of patients with brain damage is difficult.

The analogy with the radio, although illustrative, is of limited usefulness. Not only is the brain more complex than a radio, but it is also a living organism. If you remove a component from a radio, the rest of the radio presumably remains the same, even after weeks. You could replace the component and expect the radio to work the same as before. However, if part of the brain is missing, damaged or removed, there is a tendency for the remainder of the brain to compensate for the missing part. This flexibility or *plasticity* of the brain will be described in Section 4.4. First, some relatively new technological developments in brain research will be examined, which have allowed psychologists and those from other, related disciplines to 'see' what is going on in the living brain.

Summary

- Following Broca and Wernicke, further evidence pointed to localisation of function: particular parts of the brain having responsibility for particular behaviour. Disruption following brain damage exemplifies this.

- The motor cortex is a strip of brain that is involved in the control of movement of the various parts of the body. The motor homunculus shows the relationship between the regions of the motor cortex and the parts of the body over which they exert some control.

- The results of psychosurgery suggested a more complex relationship between the brain and certain psychological processes than implied by localisation of function.

- Caution is needed when using findings from research on damaged brains to explain normal brain functioning.

4   Recent developments in neuropsychology

Recent advances in brain surgery have provided significant new avenues for examining brain structures and their role in language. I am not talking about psychosurgery, a practice that is somewhat out of favour, but other forms of surgery to remove tumours or blood clots, or to relieve the symptoms of epilepsy. In most instances, brain surgery involves opening a section of skull, which enables the surgeon to operate on a piece of brain tissue. The procedure can be performed under local anaesthetic. The brain functions normally during the operation and the patient can hear and speak to the surgeon (Penfield and Roberts, 1959). This is useful because during surgery different areas can be stimulated electrically and the effect on the patient's behaviour or abilities noted. This enables the surgeon to 'work around' the key areas of the brain and keep the adverse effects of surgery to a minimum.

So, how has this new type of brain surgery contributed to our understanding of language? During surgery, if the brain region underlying the production of speech is stimulated in a particular way, the patient will be unable to speak. You might intuitively think that stimulation equals action and that the patient would be triggered to speak excessively and utter random expressions. But this is not the case. Speech is the product of complex patterns of activity in neurons in, among other regions, Broca's area. Artificial stimulation disrupts these patterns of activity and inhibits speech. By contrast, stimulation of parts of the motor cortex does indeed trigger such reactions as involuntary jerking of a limb.

Brain surgery enabled scientists to develop a more sophisticated map of the brain, and confirm many of the earlier findings derived using less sophisticated methods. But it also demonstrated that it is not actually possible to map the brain precisely, or to define the borders of Broca's or Wernicke's area in a way that would apply to every patient. Brains are not just complex, but to some extent each patient requires his or her own functional map.

In addition to learning from brain surgery, there are a number of other ways of exploring the relationship between the brain and psychological processes. Relatively recent advances in technology and medicine have provided a rich array of techniques that have enabled psychologists to gain a much better understanding of how the brain controls language. Techniques for studying neurons give new insights into how the brain can reorganise itself following damage. Next, I will describe a number of these techniques and what they reveal about language.

4.1 Techniques for studying the brain

One technique developed just after the Second World War is the 'Wada technique' (named after the Canadian neurologist Juhn A. Wada who invented it). It involves an anaesthetic being injected into the artery that supplies blood to one hemisphere of the brain. The anaesthetic temporarily impairs the activity within just this hemisphere. Hence, during the short period when the anaesthetic is effective, the activity of the non-injected hemisphere acting alone is revealed. Disruption to speech can be observed in response to requests, for example, to name objects shown to the individual. Each hemisphere is usually tested in turn. This technique reveals that usually, but not always, the left hemisphere is dominant for language, just as Broca and Wernicke had shown. Sometimes, however, both hemispheres share responsibility for language, and very occasionally the right hemisphere is dominant. The test is not really a research tool as it is not very precise. Instead, it is done prior to brain surgery, so that the surgeon can get an estimate of the likely disruption of the operation to the patient's cognitive processes.

A more recent technique is magnetic resonance imaging (MRI), which involves looking at the detailed structures of the brain. A person is placed in an MRI scanner, and a detailed image of their brain is taken using magnetic waves. It is similar to an X-ray but a lot more sophisticated. The technique can show up contrasts between different components of the brain, such as blood vessels, fluid-filled spaces and different kinds of underlying collections of neurons, as well as any diseased tissue. It can also be used by researchers to look in fine detail at the deeper structures of the brain without surgery. If there is damage to deep brain structures, there is usually a build-up of fluid and these fluid-filled spaces are visible on the scan. Without using a knife, different sections through the brain can be selected and viewed, rather as if the brain had been literally sliced.

MRI can be applied to deceased brains, as well as living brains. Recall that Broca identified a clearly visible lesion on the cortex of the brain of Mr Leborgne (see Figure 7.7). A second patient, Mr Lelong, showed a similar lesion at the same location. Traditionally, Broca's area was defined in terms of damage to this outer layer of the brain. Other researchers suggested that Broca's aphasia could also arise from damage to deeper structures of the brain. Broca said little about the possible role of lesions to deeper structures in his two patients, and there was a good reason for this: he did not subject the brains to dissection. Rather, they were placed in alcohol to be preserved intact for posterity in a Paris museum. After well over a hundred years of resting in alcohol, the two brains have been subject to penetrating examination using an MRI scanner (Dronkers et al., 2007).

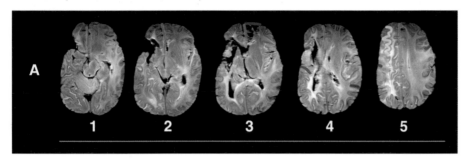

Figure 7.10   MRI scan of the brain of Mr Leborgne (from above) showing several sections through the brain at different depths. (Source: Dronkers et al., 2007, p. 1437, Figure 4)

Figure 7.10 shows the results of the MRI scan of Mr Leborgne's brain. As you can see, there is clear damage, visible in all five sections, to the area to the front of the left hemisphere, which has come to be known as Broca's area. Crucially however, the scan, especially the third section, also shows that the damage to Mr Leborgne's brain extended below the cortex. What this suggests is that the extent of the damage cannot be determined simply by observing the outer surface. The main benefit of the MRI scanner is that it allows researchers to look below the outer surface without actually dissecting the brain. Dronkers et al. (2007, p. 1441) who scanned the two brains wrote: 'Fortunately, Broca had great foresight in preserving these historic brains and in some ways, Leborgne and Lelong can speak to us more eloquently now than they could over 140 years ago'.

Whereas magnetic resonance imaging looks at the *structure* of the brain, a different technique known as functional brain imaging looks at the activity of the brain. As described in Section 1, the brain is made up of billions of cells or neurons. When a region of the brain is active (i.e. processing information), there is a high level of activity in the neurons in that area. This means that these areas will require more oxygen and energy and therefore an increased blood flow. So, the more activity there is in a region of the brain, the greater will be the need for blood. The adjustment in blood supply occurs naturally and automatically. Each region signals its need for blood and the vessels supplying each region dilate or constrict in diameter accordingly.

By monitoring the amount of blood flow to each region of the brain, it is possible to identify which areas are most active under different conditions. So, suppose an experimenter sets a task of listening to spoken language and repeating what is heard. Greatest activity should be seen in the areas underlying the processing of speech or the production of spoken words. By contrast, if the task were to consist of examining a picture, a high level of activity should be seen in regions of the brain concerned with processing information coming from the eyes. Triggering anger in the participants (and, yes, this is done occasionally!) should trigger a flow of blood to brain regions underlying emotion.

fMRI

Functional magnetic resonance imaging is a technique that allows the blood flow in the brain to be monitored while the individual undertakes a particular task.

One way of monitoring blood flow is to undertake functional MRI or **fMRI**. Here, an individual is placed in the MRI scanner and asked to undertake a specific task or undergo a specific sensory process. For example, they can be asked to perform a variety of language tasks, each involving a different aspect of language. Differences in blood flow to brain regions can then be monitored.

In another functional imaging technique, investigators inject into the blood a small amount of a harmless radioactive tracer, known as a 'label'. The apparatus can detect the tracer for a short period following injection. The increase in blood flow in regions where there is high activity will manifest itself on the image as high density of the tracer.

4.2 Tracing the links between brain regions that contribute to language

The development of techniques for tracing pathways in the brain has enabled a clearer understanding of how different brain regions contribute to language, and how they work *together*.

Figure 7.11 shows some of the interactions between the brain regions involved in understanding and performing speech (Geschwind, 1972). Suppose that a person is asked to listen to words and then repeat them aloud. First, auditory information arrives in the auditory cortex, where analysis of sounds occurs. This information is passed to Wernicke's area where sounds are linked to words, and their meaning is processed; that is, language comprehension takes place. For the person to repeat the sounds, appropriate information must then be conveyed to Broca's area. Note the pathway termed the *arcuate fasciculus*. This consists of a bundle of neurons along which information about the words that the person has heard is conveyed. At Broca's area, information on the sounds heard is processed further and instructions relevant to speech production are conveyed to the face area of the motor cortex, where commands to the facial muscles are made. From the motor cortex, signals are sent to those muscles that control the mouth and tongue, etc., so that the sound is produced. This flow of information is summarised in Figure 7.11b.

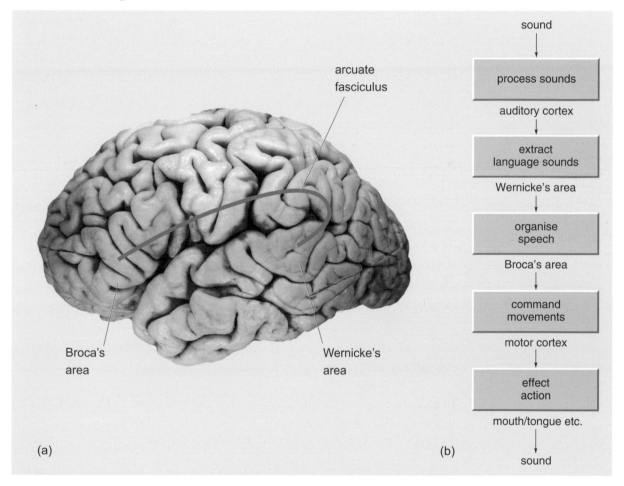

(a) (b)

Figure 7.11   Flow of information involved in language comprehension and production: (a) the left side of the brain highlighting the arcuate fasciculus; (b) the processes involved in repeating a word

In describing the interactions between the brain regions, I have spoken of signals ('information') being transmitted from one region to another;

for example, from Wernicke's area to Broca's area. However, you have also read such phrases as 'Wernicke's area where sounds are linked to words, and their meaning is processed'. Psychologists would say that a brain area such as Wernicke's performs 'information processing': it receives information on raw sounds and, acting with other brain areas, extracts meaningful speech from this. Exactly how this happens, no one is entirely clear about, but the following analogy might be useful. A computer performs information processing. Suppose that you ask it to add up a series of numbers. You feed in the numbers, press the right button and the computer does information processing which provides you with the answer: the sum. The brain's processing is a bit like that, except it is vastly more complex than a computer! You might be able to determine what parts of the computer were involved in the computation but without knowing exactly how it is done.

The description in this section of how the regions in the brain work together to control language is, however, somewhat simplistic. Recall that magnetic resonance imaging of the deceased brains of Mr Leborgne and Mr Lelong revealed that damage was not limited to Broca's area, but extended to other structures, some of which were located below the cortex. This suggests that the pathway involved in language is likely to be more complex and to involve even more brain regions than the above description suggests.

Functional magnetic resonance imaging has also revealed that the flow of information between the areas of the brain involved in language processing is more complex than Figure 11b suggests. Broca's area, for instance, is active not just during speech production, as Broca had suggested, but also during comprehension of speech. Also, electrical stimulation of Broca's area does not just disrupt speech production but can also impair speech comprehension (Fadiga et al., 2006).

4.3   Language beyond speech

Most of the discussion of language and the brain so far has focused on spoken language, the kind that manifests itself as *sound* coming through the ears (input) and *sound* from the mouth (output). There is more to language than speech, however, and this issue raises some interesting questions (Bellugi et al., 1989). Are the brain processes that underlie language *necessarily* tied to sound? Is the ability to hear spoken language necessary for the development of these brain regions in childhood? In Section 3.1, I drew your attention to the proximity of Broca's area to the regions of the motor cortex involved with movement of the mouth. This is because in most people there is correspondence between language and speech. But in sign language, for instance, language is linked to movements of the arms and hands. So, would the brain region of the left hemisphere termed 'Broca's area' also underlie the organisation of sign language? Alternatively, would there be a functional equivalent of Broca's area adjacent to the regions of the motor cortex that control the arms and hands?

Functional magnetic brain imaging conducted to address this question shows that Broca's area is activated in a similar way for individuals who use only sign or only spoken languages. In people who are able to express themselves in both spoken and sign language, there is a similar activation of Broca's area regardless of which of the two they use (Emmorey, 2006). Similarly, electrical stimulation of Broca's area disrupts expression of sign language, in the same way that it disrupts spoken language. Finally, damage to this region through stroke or injury disrupts the expression of sign language (Bellugi et al., 1989).

What about Wernicke's area? As noted in Section 2.2, Wernicke's area is adjacent to the region of the cortex processing sounds. This raises the question of whether damage to this area would also disrupt the understanding of sign language, and indeed it does (Hickok et al., 2002).

All this evidence points to common features in the organisation of spoken and sign languages. In both cases, there is a predominant involvement of the left hemisphere and similar regions, among them Broca's and Wernicke's areas.

4.4   Investigating flexibility

Figure 7.11b shows in simplified form how language understanding and speech are organised in most people. That is to say, given normal life circumstances, these are the processes involved in language comprehension and production. However, this diagram does not mean that the processes are inevitably fixed and unchanging. Sometimes there can be radical reorganisation within the brain, relative to the 'basic design'. As a general principle, disruption to the normal process underlying speech can be the trigger to reorganisation within the brain. Furthermore, undergoing speech therapy, even in patients with serious aphasia, can often restore part of the lost function. This ability of the brain to adapt is known as **plasticity**. You can apply another analogy

Plasticity
The property of the brain that it can alter its structure in the light of experience.

here: a plastic object is not rigid in its structure but, rather, its shape can be changed according to the pressure placed upon the object.

Consider the following example. While conducting his research on language impairment, Broca reported the case of a woman who appeared, from her autopsy, to have been born without the region of brain that later came to be known as 'Broca's area'. Nonetheless, she showed normal speech. Broca reasoned that, in her case, the intact right half of the brain had taken over responsibility for speech.

Box 7.2   Why do it this way?

People whose brains are different in some way have always been a source of great interest to researchers. You have already seen the insight Broca and Wernicke gained from investigating brain damage. The interest is no less these days, even with the advent of powerful technology to aid the understanding of brain function. Of course, it hardly needs saying that investigators cannot inflict deliberate damage on human brains in order to see what the consequences are. Therefore, they must be confined to accidents of nature, such as people born with parts of the brain missing and losses of brain parts as a result of war, accidents, etc. In neuropsychology, detailed explorations of single patients are described as 'case studies'. Also, unlike in the nineteenth century, today the patients' anonymity is protected and they are usually identified simply by their initials. Of course, the results of research involving a single patient cannot be generalised, but they nevertheless provide useful insight into the workings of the brain, especially when researchers stumble on an unusual case, such as when the brain compensates for a missing region and so function is not as badly impaired as it might have been.

Modern techniques of imaging, which were unavailable to Broca, have proved invaluable in studying the flexibility of the brain. If Broca's patient were alive today, she could be studied using an fMRI scanner to see which part of the brain is active when she is processing language. It could be that she indeed developed an equivalent of Broca's area in the right hemisphere, or alternatively that intact parts of the left hemisphere might have taken over some of the role of the hemisphere's missing regions (Crosson et al., 2007). The fact that the woman was born without Broca's area is important, as the brain is better able to reorganise at a younger age than in older years. Young brains are still developing and have a greater capacity to show plasticity.

Figure 7.12 shows the connections within a group of neurons. Suppose that some of the neurons in the brain are damaged (for example neuron A in Figure 7.12b) and wither as a result (Figure 7.12c). This damage can trigger growth in other intact neurons, which leads to the development of new links that compensate for the loss (Figure 7.12d). This growth and the emergence of a new connection represent a fundamental reorganisation.

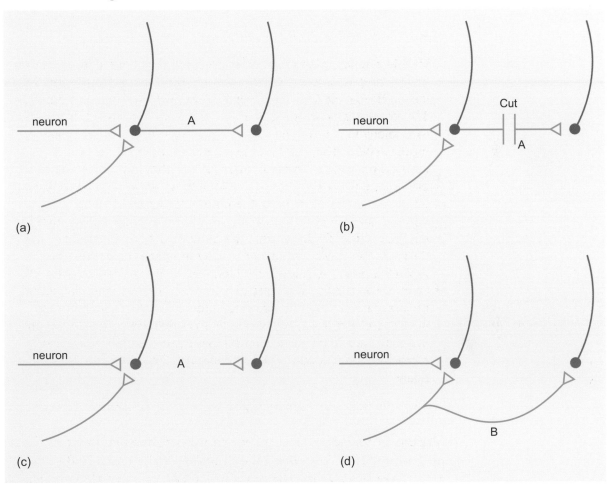

Figure 7.12   Changes in connections between neurons: (a) set of connections in which A is intact; (b) damage done to A; (c) A withers; (d) a new link is formed (link B)

Summary

- Temporary disruption of particular brain regions can reveal which of them are involved in language.
- Imaging techniques reveal structures of the brain and which parts of the brain are most active under different conditions.
- The same brain regions are involved in controlling different forms of language, such as sign language and spoken language.
- The term 'plasticity' refers to the ability of the brain to adapt and alter its structure in the light of experience.

5   Contemporary relevance

5.1   A two-way street

The chapter started by describing stroke and its consequences in terms of disruption to language and other functions. So what is the relevance of the research described in Sections 2–4 to understanding stroke? Over the years, stroke patients have provided psychologists with valuable evidence about the link between the brain and psychological functions. But have these discoveries helped people with stroke in any way?

The basic principle of localisation first described by Broca means that we can understand why strokes that affect the left hemisphere are more likely to disrupt language compared with strokes that affect the right hemisphere. Understanding that the left hemisphere has major responsibility for the right half of the body allows us to understand why strokes that disrupt speech are often associated with disruptions to movement of limbs or sensations corresponding to the right side of the body. Stroke patients have proved to be a valuable source of information in confirming the validity of these early observations. At the same time, knowing the basic localisation of function enables doctors not only to diagnose stroke more easily, but also to determine, on the basis of visible symptoms (speech impairment, paralysis in the arm, etc.), which brain region is likely to be affected.

Research on plasticity, or the brain's capacity to reorganise, has also yielded results. By studying the survivors of stroke, researchers have been able to map the reorganisation of brain function and monitor its progress using brain-imaging techniques. For example, changes in brain activity that happen as one hemisphere acquires a new capacity after damage to the other hemisphere can be followed over a period of time. Shifts within a single hemisphere from the damaged regions to intact regions can similarly be detected (Crosson et al., 2007).

This research has proved valuable in developing novel techniques for treating stroke symptoms. There is a wide armoury of different techniques to help the rehabilitation of stroke patients, and they need to be employed with an understanding of the processes that underlie the plasticity of the brain. As a general principle, gradual retraining is necessary in order for the brain to be able to reorganise (Crosson et al., 2007). In the case of loss of speech, such retraining would normally be specific to speech.

Computer technology has provided a technique in which patients are encouraged to interact with a 'virtual environment' on a computer screen (Rand et al., 2009). For example, they visit a virtual supermarket, select items, load a trolley, ask for information and listen for announcements on bargain offers. They are provided with instant feedback on each action that they take (e.g. a spoken request for information yields the appropriate answer). It enables a graded transition back to real-world activities, which might otherwise at first appear daunting to the patient.

Another technique is based on the understanding that the right half of the brain is particularly involved in the control of the left half of the body (Crosson et al., 2007). If speech is impaired by damage to the left brain, steps can be taken to encourage the right brain to take over control of speech. One way to attempt to do this is to get the patient to point with his/her left hand while trying to utter expressions. The logic is that activation of the right hemisphere by pointing with the left hand could spread to activation of potential speech processes in the right hemisphere.

Music can play a vital role in helping stroke patients. One recent study found a particular improvement in the use of the limbs as a result of learning the basics of playing a musical instrument, such as hitting a drum with drumsticks (Altenmüller et al., 2009). This gives immediate feedback of sound for an action. Possibly the technique could prove useful for the rehabilitation of speech.

The technique of 'melodic intonation therapy' (MIT), to help stroke patients, consists of daily sessions of therapy over seventy to eighty days (Schlaug et al., 2009). The rationale for MIT is the observation that, if asked to sing a familiar song, patients who suffered a stroke in the left brain and who have seriously disturbed speech can often produce a correct sequence of words. They would not otherwise be able to speak these same words. The assumption is that either the right hemisphere or both left and right hemispheres underlie the ability to sing. So, patients are trained to sing very short and carefully selected sentences. Simultaneously with singing, they are asked to pace this with rhythmic tapping by their left hand. The assumption underlying the tapping is that this serves as a pacemaker to areas of the right hemisphere with some basic potential for spoken language. It could be that there is a natural coupling between brain areas underlying the control of hand movements and speech. Hand gestures tend to accompany speech – even when speaking on the telephone! The sequence of words to be sung is gradually made more difficult. The expectation is that this will develop speaking capacity, which indeed it tends to do (Schlaug et al., 2009).

Research on the brain has made a contribution not only to our understanding of how the brain works and the role it plays in normal functioning, but also to helping stroke patients on their road to recovery. When dealing with patients recovering from stroke, however, it is important to bear in mind that disruption to specific functions such as speech and movement is one part of a bigger picture. The caring professions are increasingly accepting the need for holistic approaches to treatment. This is where psychologists have a crucial role to play. Stroke patients sometimes suffer from apathy, depression and problems with attention. This is bound to have repercussions for their rehabilitation. This is why techniques designed to facilitate the reorganisation of the brain must take into account the patient's motivation, their mood and their psychological well-being more generally (Altenmüller et al., 2009). Treatment and therapeutic intervention is therefore never just about the brain, but also about the person as a whole.

5.2 Conclusion

With a focus on humans, the chapter has demonstrated where links can be formed between the brain and psychological processes. A number of interacting brain regions that play a role in producing and understanding language can be identified. However, caution needs to be exercised in identifying a particular brain region with a particular function. The brain exhibits the property of plasticity such that, to some extent, it can reorganise itself following brain damage.

Summary

- Stroke patients can not only be helped by new research but they can also contribute to understanding how the brain works.
- Recovery of language ability in stroke patients is associated with plasticity in the brain that can be identified by using imaging techniques.
- Different therapeutic techniques have been devised to assist this recovery.

References

Altenmüller, E., Marco-Pallares, J. Münte, T.F. and Schneider, S. (2009) 'Neural reorganization underlies improvement in stroke-induced motor dysfunction by music-supported therapy', *Annals of the New York Academy of Sciences*, vol. 1169, pp. 395–405.

Bellugi, U., Poizner, H. and Klima, E.S. (1989) 'Language, modality and the brain', *Trends in Neurosciences*, vol. 12, no. 10, pp. 380–8.

Broca, P. (1861) 'Perte de la parole, ramollissement chronique et destruction partielle du lobe antérieur gauche du cerveau', *Bulletins de la Société d' Anthropologie*, vol. 2, pp. 235–8.

Buckingham, H.W. (2006) 'The Marc Dax (1770–1837)/ Paul Broca (1824–1880) controversy over priority in science: left hemisphere specificity for seat of articulate language and for lesions that cause aphemia', *Clinical Linguistics and Phonetics*, vol. 20, no. 7–8, pp. 613–19.

Crosson, B. et al. (2007) 'Functional MRI of language in aphasia: a review of the literature and the methodological challenges', *Neuropsychology Review*, vol. 17, no. 2, pp. 157–77.

Dronkers, N.F., Plaisant, O., Iba-Zizen, M.T. and Cabanis, E.A. (2007) 'Paul Broca's historic cases: high resolution MR imaging of the brains of Leborgne and Lelong', *Brain*, vol. 130, no. 5, pp. 1432–41.

Emmorey, K. (2006) 'The role of Broca's area in sign language' in Grodzinsky and Amunts (eds) (2006).

Fadiga, L., Craighero, L. and Roy, A. (2006) 'Broca's region: a speech area?' in Grodzinsky and Amunts (eds) (2006).

Finger, S. (2000) *Minds Behind the Brain: A History of the Pioneers and their Discoveries*, New York, NY, Oxford University Press.

Finger, S. and Roe, D. (1999) 'Does Gustave Dax deserve to be forgotten? The temporal lobe theory and other contributions of an overlooked figure in the history of language and cerebral dominance', *Brain and Language*, vol. 69, no. 1, pp. 16–30.

Geschwind, N. (1972) 'Language and the brain', *Scientific American*, vol. 226, no. 4 (April), pp. 76–83.

Graves, R.E. (1997) 'The legacy of the Wernicke–Lichtheim model', *Journal of the History of the Neurosciences*, vol. 6, no. 1, pp. 3–20.

Gregory, R.L. (1961) 'The brain as an engineering problem' in Thorpe, W.H. and Zangwill, O.L. (eds) *Current Problems in Animal Behaviour*, Cambridge, Cambridge University Press.

Grodzinsky, Y. and Amunts, K. (eds) *Broca's Region*, New York, NY, Oxford University Press.

Hickok, G., Love-Geffen, T. and Klima, E.S. (2002) 'Role of the left hemisphere in sign language comprehension', *Brain and Language,* vol. 82, no. 2, pp. 167–78.

Penfield, W. and Roberts, L. (1959) *Speech and Brain Mechanisms*, Princeton, NJ, Princeton University Press.

Pillman, F. (2003) 'Carl Wernicke (1848–1905)', *Journal of Neurology*, vol. 250, no. 11, pp. 1390–1.

Rand, D., Weiss, P.L.T. and Katz, N. (2009) 'Training multitasking in a virtual supermarket: a novel intervention after stroke', *The American Journal of Occupational Therapy*, vol. 63, no. 5, pp. 535–42.

Schiller, F. (1979) *Paul Broca: Founder of French Anthropology, Explorer of the Brain*, Berkeley, CA, University of California Press.

Schlaug, G., Marchina, S. and Norton, A. (2009) 'Evidence of plasticity in white-matter tracts of patients with chronic Broca's aphasia undergoing intense intonation-based speech therapy', *Annals of the New York Academy of Sciences*, vol. 1169, pp. 385–94.

The Stroke Association (2009) 'What is a stroke' [online], www.stroke.org.uk/document.rm?id=699 (Accessed 22 March 2010).

Vessie, P.R. (1932) 'On the transmission of Huntington's chorea for 300 years – the Bures family group', *Journal of Nervous and Mental Disease*, vol. 76, no. 6, pp. 553–73.

Chapter 8
Paying attention

Helen Edgar and Graham Edgar

Contents

Aims and objectives

By the end of this chapter you should be able to:

- begin to appreciate the application of research on attention to real-world tasks, specifically driving behaviour
- describe Donald Broadbent's research on the cognitive processes of attention
- outline the experimental approach of Broadbent and other psychologists, and discuss how these experiments informed the development of theories of attention
- recognise how experimental studies of attention have produced theoretical advances that can be used to understand real-world problems.

1 Introduction

We would like to begin this chapter with an anecdote from one of the authors (Graham), as it illustrates rather nicely why it is important to understand what 'attention' is, and how it works:

> A few years ago I was cycling through Cardiff. The road was clear and straight, the weather was fine, and visibility was excellent. On my left was a lay-by with a row of shops (see Figure 8.1). I was dimly aware of a car (a red Ford Fiesta) coming from the opposite direction and positioning to turn right into the shops' lay-by. I assumed that the driver was waiting for me to pass before turning, as I was moving quite fast. I then became acutely aware that they weren't waiting, they were turning in to me and there was nowhere to go on my bicycle. Actually, there was somewhere for me to go (without the bicycle), and that was straight over the bonnet of the car in a graceful arc, landing in the gutter on the far side. As well as being a personally painful experience, this is also one of the most common forms of accident (the so-called 'right-turn' accident), and I can vouch for that, as it has happened to me twice! What is also not uncommon is the explanation given by the driver of the car that they 'Didn't see me at all'. On the 'plus' side, I am proud to be one of a select band of psychologists that has succeeded in denting a car using only their head and a bicycle.

Figure 8.1 The road that left a lasting impression on one of the authors of this chapter

---

Activity 8.1

Plainly, the driver of the car that Graham crashed into was not aware of everything that was going on around them. You would probably agree that they were not 'paying attention'. Is that unusual? Are you aware of everything that is going on around you as you are reading this? Is the television or the radio on? Can you recall anything of the programmes that have been on while you were reading this? Are you aware of noises from outside (assuming you are indoors of course!)? Passing traffic? Try concentrating on noises and/or objects around you. Can you read this at the same time as paying attention to noises and/or objects, or to the TV or the radio? Probably not, which does suggest that, like the Fiesta driver, people have difficulty maintaining an awareness of all that is happening around them.

The activity you have just done involved the conscious allocation of attention. You were asked to attend to what was going on around you whereas, before that, you were (we hope) attending to the material in this chapter. You are most likely to be aware of how you allocate attention when you are consciously shifting it from one thing to another, as you were asked to do in Activity 8.1. But what *is* attention and do we always know what we are attending to?

1.1 What is attention?

One of the most widely used definitions of attention was provided by William James, more than a century ago. James is regarded as one of the founders of experimental psychology, who established one of the first ever experimental psychology laboratories in 1875. In 1890, James wrote:

> Every one knows what attention is. It is the taking possession by the mind, in clear and vivid form, of one out of what seem several simultaneously possible objects or trains of thought. Focalization, concentration, of consciousness are of its essence. It implies withdrawal from some things in order to deal effectively with others …

(James, 1890, pp. 403–4)

James's definition is interesting in that it openly acknowledges that **attention** is a term in general use and not just an element of psychological jargon (although it may be that as well!). People often talk about someone being 'absent-minded', or of being told to 'pay attention' to something. These terms suggest that attention is regarded as a capacity that can be directed to prioritise one aspect of the world over another (as you were doing in Activity 8.1).

Attention
A cognitive process involving the selection of information for further processing, such as the extraction of meaning.

James's definition also emphasises that people cannot attend to everything at the same time. If there are many competing stimuli, people tend to focus on only one or a few of them and are then *conscious* (that is, aware) of those few stimuli. This provides a clue to how some lapses in attention occur. If your attention is directed elsewhere, you may miss some of what is going on around you.

Reading this chapter is (or should be!) an example of 'sustained attention'. You maintain your focus of attention on the material in the chapter and attend relatively little to what is going on around you. As demonstrated in Activity 8.1, however, you can consciously shift your attention to other aspects of the world if you wish. But are all shifts of attention consciously controlled? Are shifts of attention always driven by the individual, or can certain stimuli 'grab' our attention? Indeed, it does seem that certain stimuli, such as loud noises and sudden movements, naturally attract our attention. Other stimuli, on the other hand, might attract our attention as a result of experience. For example, the attention of parents of young children will almost always be attracted by a child's voice saying, 'Oops'.

Designers of cars, aircraft and other complex systems are aware that it may be necessary to 'direct' the user's attention to certain places. Have a look at Figure 8.2. The cockpit of a modern aircraft can provide pilots with a phenomenal amount of information, most of which they need to be aware of only when something goes wrong. Designers try to use warnings to make sure that attention is directed to certain systems only when it is absolutely necessary. The same principle holds in driving. Most of the time you can ignore the petrol gauge in your car – except when the warning light comes on and then you really should attend to it. Given the fact that people can attend to only a limited number of things at any one time, it is necessary to be extremely cautious in the use of warnings, and it is easy to have too many. Indeed, one modern fighter aircraft has so many spoken warnings, which sound so often, that the warning system has become known among pilots as 'Nagging Nora'.

Figure 8.2   The cockpit of a modern civil airliner. All of the information provided by the displays (and there is quite a lot of it) may be needed at some point – but thankfully not all at the same time!

1.2   Attention and driving: the effect of using a mobile phone

You should have the idea by now that attention is a precious resource. If you attend to one thing, then you have fewer attentional resources to spare for other things. This can cause problems if resources are squandered on some tasks at the expense of other, more safety-critical, tasks. For example, improvements in technology have significantly increased the number of tasks that you can do while driving. Perhaps the most obvious example of this multitasking is the use of mobile telephones while at the wheel of a car. Once the technology for mobile phones had advanced to the stage where they were relatively small, they quickly became very popular. Indeed, a report on mobile phone use while driving estimated that in 2004, at any given moment in the day, 8 per cent of drivers on US roads were using their mobile phone (Glassbrenner, 2005).

So, does using a mobile phone while driving impair driving performance? The discussion so far suggests that it might, and the law in the UK agrees. Using a hand-held mobile phone while driving was made illegal at the end of 2003. Looking again at James's definition of attention, it seems that using a mobile phone will almost certainly take precious cognitive resources that could perhaps be better directed elsewhere to improve the user's driving. But does using a mobile phone really make that much difference to driving? Donald Redelmeier and Robert Tibshirani (1997) looked at the mobile-phone records of 699 drivers who had been involved in a driving accident. They found that 24 per cent of these drivers were using their phone within the ten minutes prior to the accident. Given Glassbrenner's findings described earlier, this suggests that drivers on mobile phones are over-represented in the accident statistics – whilst 8 per cent of the general driving population were estimated to be using their phone at any one time, this group comprised 24 per cent of the accident population. These figures suggest that there is a strong association, or correlation, between mobile-phone use and the likelihood of having an accident.

One has to be cautious, however, about drawing firm conclusions from correlational data. Just because there is a correlation between mobile phone use and driving accidents does not necessarily mean that the phone use contributed directly to the accident. As David Strayer and colleagues (2006) point out, it may simply be that the people who use

You were introduced to the term 'correlation' in Box 3.2, Section 3, Chapter 3. Issues relating to correlational data were also discussed in Section 5, Chapter 5.

phones while driving are simply more prone to risky behaviour, so that their driving is more dangerous with or without a mobile phone.

Although correlational studies cannot establish a causal link between mobile-phone use and decrements in driving performance, experimental studies could look at the effect of using a mobile phone while driving; for example, by comparing two situations that are matched as closely as possible except for the fact that the participant is using a mobile phone in one situation and not in the other. This also allows an investigation of just what aspects of driving performance might be affected by phone use. One such study (Brookhuis et al., 1991) found that driving while using a mobile phone actually *decreased* the amount of swerving by the driver, but *increased* the driver's reaction time to a change in speed of the car in front. In the context of the discussion so far, it is possible that the drivers directed their attention to the vigilance task (maintaining lane position) but this was at the expense of detecting a sudden change in the situation (e.g. the car in front braking). This study emphasises that attention has a number of interacting components, including (in the case of driving) maintaining vigilance and detecting changes.

Are we consciously aware of where we are allocating attention and how it is being 'shared out'? A study entitled 'Sorry, can't talk now... just overtaking a lorry: the definition and experimental investigation of the problem of driving and hands free car phone use' (Boase et al., 1988), found that mobile-phone use significantly impaired the performance of the nine drivers who took part in the study. The interesting aspect of this study is that interviews with these nine drivers revealed that none of them believed their performance had been affected by the use of a mobile phone. They appeared to be unaware that the attention they were paying to their phone may have impaired their driving.

The title of the Boase et al. paper was remarkably prescient of an actual accident that took place in the UK some years later. A Royal Society for the Prevention of Accidents (RoSPA) report cites the case of a driver overtaking another vehicle at up to 90 miles per hour in heavy rain. The overtaking driver lost control, hit a tree, and was fatally injured. When the police checked the dead driver's phone they found a text message three pages long that had been received two minutes before the crash. The coroner's report included the phrase, 'A message had been accessed, it may have diverted his attention' (RoSPA, 2002, p. 11).

Summary

- Attention is a complex cognitive process which involves focus or concentration on certain stimuli in the environment.
- There are limits on how much we can attend to at any one time.
- These limits have implications for a range of real-world tasks, including driving.

2 The psychology of attention

2.1 Donald Broadbent and the beginnings of experimental cognitive psychology

The previous section outlined what attention is and discussed some studies on driving that were relevant to a real-world problem. This applied stream in psychological research is part of a tradition that is strongly associated with one of the founders of modern cognitive psychology, Donald Broadbent. This section will consider the early contribution of Broadbent and others to our understanding of attention.

Figure 8.3   Donald E. Broadbent (1926–1993)

As well as being a famous cognitive psychologist, Broadbent was a pre-eminent figure in the development of the discipline of applied psychology. In 1943, aged just 17,Broadbent joined the Royal Air Force (RAF). It was this experience in the air force that sparked his interest in psychology (Weiskrantz, 1994). During flight training and operations, incidents occurred that, in Broadbent's opinion, could have been avoided if the capabilities of the operators had been considered in the design of the equipment. Specifically, Broadbent was interested in how the design could be driven by an understanding of the capacities and limitations of the operator, rather than designing the equipment and then hoping the operator could get to grips with it somehow.

One specific problem that piqued Broadbent's interest was the design of the AT6 aircraft, which had two levers close together under the seat; one of them pulled up the flaps (a manoeuvre needed when landing) and the other pulled up the undercarriage. Several pilots made the mistake of pulling the wrong lever during a landing manoeuvre, and lifted the wheels instead of the flaps, thus damaging a very expensive aircraft!

Broadbent's experiences in the RAF inspired him to read psychology at Cambridge, after he was demobilised in 1947. When he graduated he started work on a project sponsored by the Royal Navy to look at the effects of noise on performance. Broadbent went on to explore, using experiments, what happens when 'listeners characteristically are confronted with a multitude of signals arriving more or less simultaneously, but can react to only a limited sub-set' (Weiskrantz, 1994, p. 36). How is this choice made? How do they preferentially select only some incoming information? In 1958, he published a book titled *Perception and Communication* where he described his limited capacity model of attention. Broadbent used a diagram, a simplified version of which is shown in Figure 8.4, to describe human information processing as a system with a finite limit for the intake and storage of information. Broadbent's model was relevant to many of the everyday problems discussed in Section 1. Indeed, the notion of the limited capacity of our attentional system is present in James's original definition of attention (1890, p. 4), in that the process of attention 'implies withdrawal from some things in order to deal effectively with others'.

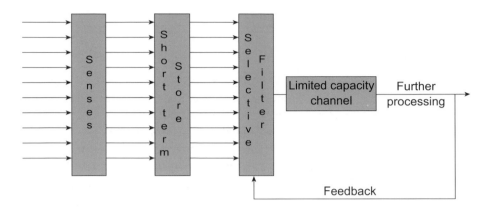

Figure 8.4   A simplified version of Broadbent's information-flow diagram
(Source: modified from Broadbent, 1958, p. 299, Figure 7)

According to Broadbent's model, information about our environment enters the first system (labelled 'Senses') in *parallel* via the different senses (e.g. the eyes and ears). These 'inputs' are then stored briefly before being filtered through the selective filter. The information may be filtered on the basis of the physical properties of the stimulus, such as the intensity of the sound. Alternatively it may be filtered using feedback from memory stores, prior experience and expectations. For example, sounds recognised as warning signals would be selected for further processing. Information then exits the filter in *series* (only one piece of information at a time), through the **limited capacity channel,** to be processed by other systems. The boxes in the diagram represent the different systems that process information, and the arrows indicate the flow of information through those processing systems.

Broadbent suggested that things such as multitasking (i.e. performing more than one task at the same time) could be achieved only by rapid switching amongst inputs, as there was a limit to how much information could flow through the systems. Broadbent's model was rather vague as to what lies after the filter, although it indicates that there are processes that govern which inputs should be selected and when to change the selection. This **information-processing model** constituted the first testable model of attention, and Broadbent's approach actively encouraged others to conduct experiments that would test it.

Limited capacity channel

A channel through which filtered and attended-to information passes for further processing, such as storage in memory. It is 'limited' as regards the amount of information it can deal with at any one time.

Information-processing model

A hypothetical model depicting how information taken in by the senses might be processed in the brain.

Box 8.1   Influences on the work of Donald Broadbent

In 1947, Broadbent was accepted by Pembroke College, Cambridge to study experimental psychology. At that time the department head was Sir Frederic Bartlett, who had been involved in wartime research into human performance and was ideally placed to encourage Broadbent's interest in applied psychology. Bartlett strongly believed that psychology should strive to address real-life problems, but also that psychological theories should be derived from experimental research. Broadbent strongly supported this view and went on to champion it throughout his career.

After graduation, Broadbent was employed by the Royal Navy to study the effects of noise on performance. This research was carried out at the Applied Psychology Unit at Cambridge (APU), because the noise involved was considered to be too distracting for other staff in the naval research laboratory. Broadbent then moved on to study the effects of noise on vigilance tasks in gunnery and air traffic control systems, where operators were bombarded by many simultaneous incoming messages (signals) but could react to only a limited subset of those signals.

An engineering approach to psychology had been established at Cambridge by Kenneth Craik, the first director of the APU, who died just before Broadbent joined the university. Broadbent was nevertheless able to study Craik's manuscripts, which compared human information processing with artificial information-processing systems such as computers.

Broadbent's use of a flow diagram to depict his model of attention clearly demonstrated the influence of Craik's ideas. He used ideas and terminology from emerging fields concerned with computer systems and information processing. Broadbent liked this way of depicting processes that went on in the brain and which he could not observe directly.

See Chapter 4 for a discussion of behaviourism

In his book *Perception and Communication* (1958), Broadbent laid down a framework for the understanding of attention, memory and comprehension that formed the basis of what is now called 'cognitive psychology'. At the time when *Perception and Communication* was first published, psychology, especially in the USA, was dominated by behaviourism. Experiments designed to study operant conditioning took no account of prior knowledge or experience and were therefore far removed from the complex real-life situations that Broadbent aimed to address.

Broadbent's abstract representation of human mental processes, the information-flow diagram, was to prove enduringly popular in what became known as cognitive psychology. His experiments showed how the new sub-discipline of cognitive psychology could address complex, real-world problems. The use of information-processing terminology and flow diagrams with boxes and arrows quickly became the accepted way to describe cognitive processes that could not be observed directly, and it is still used today. Note that Broadbent was not suggesting that the actual brain structures and systems could be ignored as irrelevant 'hardware'. It is just that he did not undertake physiological or neuropsychological studies of real brain systems. His information-processing theory did not seek to identify the brain structures underlying the attentional systems but to describe the processes involved and develop a theoretical model of attention.

2.2 The experiments underlying Broadbent's mode

Dichotic listening
When two different messages are presented simultaneously, one to each ear.

Broadbent's model of attention was developed and refined from a large body of empirical work. Perhaps the most influential experiments involved 'dichotic listening'. In a **dichotic listening** task, different stimuli are presented to the two ears simultaneously and the participant may be asked, for example, to recall all the material presented to one ear first, before recalling material presented to the other. The general principle of dichotic listening is illustrated in Figure 8.5.

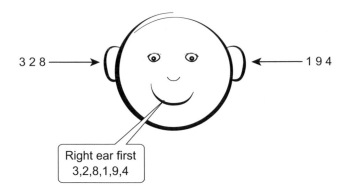

Figure 8.5   An example of a dichotic listening task. The three numbers shown on each side are presented simultaneously, and the task here is to report those presented to right ear first. The correct response is therefore: 3, 2, 8, 1, 9, 4

Dichotic listening experiments were designed to be analogous to the complex tasks Broadbent worked on early in his career. For example, gunnery and air traffic control personnel received many, often simultaneous, messages and had to select the appropriate ones to respond to. Dichotic listening simplifies these tasks to allow the isolation and investigation of one variable at a time in a controlled environment. Different aspects of the stimulus (a message or a task) that might be expected to affect performance (making it easier or more difficult to perform to a required standard) were manipulated in a series of studies. In addition to the similarity to complex, real-world tasks, the use of auditory stimuli had another practical advantage: while we can move our eyes to control what we see, it is much harder to move our ears (especially if the stimuli are delivered via headphones!). From a theoretical point of view, dichotic stimulus presentation provides a simple and elegant way of taxing the human information-processing system so that filtering becomes necessary and unavoidable. Broadbent and one of his contemporaries, Colin Cherry, made extensive use of dichotic listening in their experiments. Some of these experiments will be described in detail as they demonstrate how the model shown in Figure 8.4 was developed and refined by a series of linked experiments, each one providing a little extra information to help complete the theoretical jigsaw.

Previous studies had shown that when participants were presented with three digits to one ear and another three digits to the other ear simultaneously, they could repeat all six digits from memory, but normally all three from one ear were recalled before those from the other. These results led Broadbent to deduce that there is a mechanism, which cannot be observed directly, that can only pass information serially (one item after another) and another mechanism which can store information from two (or more) channels simultaneously (i.e. can handle information 'in parallel'), but that the latter is limited with respect to how much information it can store and how long for.

In order to test his theory, Broadbent (1954) undertook a series of experiments designed to see whether, for example, expectations had an effect on the allocation of attention and subsequent recall. Participants were presented with two sets of digits simultaneously, one set to each ear. They were then asked to write down the digits from memory, beginning with those in an ear chosen by the experimenter. More mistakes were made on the second set of digits when participants knew in advance which set they would have to report first (left or right). This suggested that attention was directed to the chosen ear and the material from the other ear was not always retrieved accurately as it had not been selected for attention.

The results from these experiments showed that participants reported the material they processed first more accurately than the later material, which may have been lost from the brief memory store by the time the participant got around to reporting it. This finding was true for simultaneous presentation of stimuli (as shown in Figure 8.5) as well as for successive presentation (where one set of stimuli follows on from the first set of stimuli). Broadbent (1957, pp. 2–3) wrote: 'We can listen to only one voice at once, and the first words we hear are the best recalled.'

Activity 8.2

Try dichotic listening for yourself.

Listen to two conversations at the same time; one on the telephone (do warn the person on the other end of the line first!) and the other with someone in the same room as you (someone talking on the radio or television will do).

You are likely to have found it difficult to follow both conversations at the same time. This is what would be predicted by Broadbent's model.

Other experiments using dichotic listening sought to investigate the effects of delay on recall. The results were consistent with Broadbent's prediction that any delay in recovering items from the limited-capacity storage mechanism reduced the efficiency of recall.

Irrelevant stimuli were also considered. The presentation of irrelevant material (for instance, letters) to the *same* ear as the 'target' stimuli (numbers) made the task of reporting the target stimuli almost impossible. Broadbent noted that this is in stark contrast to a finding by Cherry (1953) that participants were able to ignore irrelevant material when the target stimuli were presented to *one* ear and the irrelevant material to the *other*. Cherry's experiment also provided support for the notion that filtering can be done on the basis of simple physical features (for example, according to the location or intensity of the sound) but that, if irrelevant items cannot be discriminated on the basis of such physical features, they will then interfere with the processing of the target items. (We will return to this experiment in Section 3.)

The experiments conducted by Broadbent and also by other psychologists were used by Broadbent to test and refine specific aspects of his information-processing model. By systematically manipulating different variables, a slightly different aspect of the process was investigated. Taken in isolation, the results of individual experiments could be open to at least two different interpretations, but each successive experiment narrowed down the possible number of interpretations, thereby increasing the confidence with which conclusions could be drawn about the workings of human attention.

Summary

- Donald Broadbent proposed a very influential model of attention.
- His research and his interest in real-world problems were informed by his experience with the RAF.
- For his model, Broadbent drew on the then emerging fields concerned with information and computer systems.
- His use of information-processing terminology and flow diagrams to describe cognitive processes that could not be observed directly is still popular today in cognitive psychology.
- The model was developed and refined on the basis of the results from dichotic listening experiments.

3 The development of Broadbent's model

3.1 The work of Colin Cherry: early indications that meaning may be important in allocating attention

A contemporary of Broadbent was Colin Cherry. Like Broadbent's work, Cherry's focused on how psychological theory and the insight it provides could be applied to practical problems. Cherry agreed that incoming stimuli *can* be filtered on the basis of simple physical characteristics, such as voice intensity. However, after carrying out a number of studies, he suggested that sometimes the incoming stimuli (e.g. the messages presented to each ear) is analysed more fully *before* a decision is made about which one is attended to. Specifically, stimuli are sometimes filtered according to their meaning. Cherry drew this conclusion from the observation that people can perform tasks such as listening to one speaker when others are speaking at the same time. He used the term 'cocktail party problem' to describe this ability to follow what one person is saying, when others are also speaking.

Could Broadbent's model be refined to incorporate Cherry's findings? Before looking at this and at Cherry's studies in more detail, it would be useful to clarify the role of the **hypothesis** when conducting experiments (see Box 8.2).

Hypothesis
A prediction or statement that is tested in an experiment or correlational study.

Theory
A set of propositions about a psychological phenomenon (e.g. attention) that forms the basis of a testable explanation.

Box 8.2 Why do it this way?

Experiments are generally conducted to *test a hypothesis*. A hypothesis is basically a prediction, phrased as a simple statement. Crucially, this statement may not be true, but it should be logical; it is set up as a starting point and an experiment is then conducted to see whether or not the statement is true. It's important to note that the aim of an experiment is *not* to 'prove the hypothesis true', but to gather *evidence* to decide whether it is *likely* to be true or not. A negative result can be as informative (although often not as satisfying for the experimenter) as a positive one.

The hypothesis is usually devised in the first place by looking at an existing **theory**. Theories allow one to make predictions that can be tested using a suitable method. These predictions are phrased as hypotheses. For example, you can do an experiment to test a

---

hypothesis, revise the theory from which it was derived, (or not, depending on how the experiment turned out) and generate further hypotheses. This is known as the **cycle of enquiry**.

One of the very first studies of the effects of using a phone while driving provides an example of hypothesis testing. This was a study conducted by Ivan Brown et al. (1969) at the Applied Psychology Unit in Cambridge while Donald Broadbent was the director. This was 'cutting edge' research at that time, as demonstrated by the fact that the mobile phone had to be simulated for the study, as there were none in general use. Interestingly, the simulation used the equivalent of a hands-free mobile phone.

Brown et al. proposed that performing two tasks simultaneously, driving and telephoning, would be challenging for a person. Not only might using a telephone interfere with steering or gear changing, but attention would need to be switched between the demands of the two tasks. You may remember that Broadbent suggested that multitasking could be achieved only by rapid switching amongst inputs. The hypothesis Brown et al. tested was similar to: '*Using a mobile phone will affect performance on a driving task*' (the actual wording is more precise and beyond the scope of this box!). Participants were required to drive round a test track and judge whether or not they would be able to pass through gaps of varying sizes, some smaller and some bigger than the actual width of the car.

Two measures of performance (dependent variables) used in the study were:

speed (time taken to complete the circuit)

accuracy (how well the driver judged the width of the gaps).

There were two conditions of particular interest in this experiment. In the experimental condition the driver drove round the test track while answering questions on the mobile phone, and in the control condition the driver drove the same route without using the phone. These two conditions resulted from the manipulation of the independent variable – the use or not of a mobile phone.

Other variables – for example, age, driving experience and gender – were controlled by having the *same participants* take part in both conditions (phone and no phone). Controlled variables are the factors that are kept constant in the experiment, so that only the variable being investigated in the experiment influences the observed result. If other variables that might have an effect are not controlled (i.e. they are not kept the same across both conditions),

Cycle of enquiry
The way in which the questions that research addresses are often derived from theories or explanations, and the findings of that research then generate new questions or refinements to theory or explanation.

You read about the controlled nature of experiments in Chapters 2 and 3 of Part 1.

then it is not possible to say whether the observed effect is due to the manipulation of the independent variable and the results of the study will not be valid. An alternative approach is to try to ensure that any variables that cannot be controlled act randomly across the conditions. For example, it is possible that some things might distract the drivers (birds flying across the track, sunlight, etc.), but as long as they don't distract them more in one condition than another it should not affect the overall result.

With all these precautions in place, you now have an experiment that can provide a valid test of the hypothesis, 'Using a mobile phone will affect performance on a driving task'. The independent variable is whether or not the driver is using a mobile phone and the dependent variables are aspects of driving performance. If there is a difference in the dependent variables measured (speed and accuracy) between the two conditions, then you can say that the findings provide support for the hypothesis. In the Brown et al. study, driving time increased when participants were telephoning, and judgements regarding whether the width of the gaps were sufficient were impaired.

This is where it becomes important to control, as much as possible, for all variables other than the one manipulated (use of a phone). If another variable happened to differ across the conditions (e.g. you had all novice drivers in one condition and all experienced drivers in the other), then you could not be sure that a difference in the conditions was really due to the effect of your independent variable, or the other, *confounding* variable. If you did not control for driving experience, for example, you could not be sure that any difference was due only to phone use and not to driving experience.

Once you know whether your hypothesis is supported or not, you can then go back to the theory from which the hypothesis was derived, modify the theory if necessary, then generate another hypothesis and test it. For example, you might hypothesise that using mobile phones has a larger detrimental effect on the performance of drivers who are tired or stressed, and then design another experiment to test that. The more experiments you do, the more comprehensive the theory becomes (you hope!).

Cherry's (1953) work is a good example of using a *series* of experiments to develop a theory. The approach taken by Cherry of using spoken language in his experiments was very different from the majority of studies that had preceded his. Using natural speech as a stimulus required a different way of thinking about experimental design. Cherry approached this work by thinking about how a machine or filter might be designed to discriminate between continuous speech when more than one person is talking at once. First, he identified some of the factors that might aid this process:

1   the direction from which the voice originates

2   the presence of additional cues such as movement of the lips and gestures

3   characteristics of the voice such as pitch, speed and whether the voice is male or female

4   different accents and dialects

5   the ease with which it is possible to predict what the next item of information is likely to be, based on what has gone before; for example, this is much easier with continuous prose, such as complete sentences, compared with random words.

By recording two (interwoven) messages spoken by the *same* speaker, Cherry was able to control for factors one to four above, allowing him to isolate the effect of the fifth factor, namely meaning. The findings of the experiments looking at the importance of meaning are described next.

3.2   Cherry's experiments

Cherry (1953) carried out a series of experiments designed to determine exactly what information allows participants to separate out two spoken messages that are presented together. Remember that messages were spoken by the same speaker, so participants would not be able to distinguish between these messages on the basis of the physical characteristics described in points 2–4 above, such as the characteristics of the voice. The two messages were presented either as 'mixed' or as 'simultaneous' speech as described next (also illustrated in Figure 8.6):

- The presentation of *mixed* messages involved two different spoken messages about different subjects presented to *both* ears. That is, both ears heard both messages at the same time, giving the impression, as Cherry notes, of 'a babel'.

- The presentation of *simultaneous* messages involved two messages about different subjects, one presented to one ear and one to the other so that each ear heard only *one* of the messages (a basic dichotic listening task).

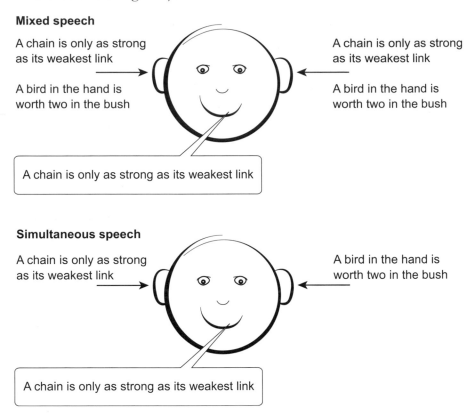

Mixed speech

A chain is only as strong as its weakest link

A bird in the hand is worth two in the bush

A chain is only as strong as its weakest link

A bird in the hand is worth two in the bush

A chain is only as strong as its weakest link

Simultaneous speech

A chain is only as strong as its weakest link

A bird in the hand is worth two in the bush

A chain is only as strong as its weakest link

Figure 8.6   Mixed and simultaneous presentation of natural speech

In the experiment, participants in the simultaneous speech condition were asked to repeat whatever message was presented in the right ear, while in the mixed speech condition they were asked to pick out and repeat *one* of the messages.

Cherry obtained the following results from the mixed speech condition:

- The different messages could be identified and separated by the listener even when they were not allowed to write anything down; that is, when verbal repetition of each message was the only response allowed. Participants found this task difficult, however, and the tapes were played up to twenty times.

- Writing the responses down made the task much easier. It was easier to separate out meaningful messages than nonsense ones (even if the nonsense ones obeyed normal grammatical rules), implying that the *content* of a message influenced participants' ability to attend to, and separate out, the two messages.

Using simultaneous speeches, Cherry found that:

- As regards to the message presented to the right ear (i.e. the message that they were asked to repeat), participants could easily report this message whilst another was being played in the other ear. (This finding was described earlier, towards the end of Section 2.)

- As for the message presented to the left ear (i.e. the message that they were instructed to ignore), the participants were unaware of its content to the extent that they did not 'notice' if the language spoken in the unattended message changed during presentation (for example, from English to German). Participants accurately reported whether or not the unattended message consisted of human speech, although specific words, phrases or the language used were not reported. If the speech was reversed (i.e. played backwards), this also was difficult to identify, with some participants reporting it as normal speech and others being able to say only that there was 'something queer about it'.

Activity 8.3

Imagine an experiment where exactly the same message is presented to both ears, but with a slight delay so this message arrives at the right ear before the left ear. Participants are asked to attend to the message presented to the right ear. Would you expect participants to notice that the same message was presented to the left ear?

Reflect on this for a moment before reading on.

This is precisely what Cherry did in a variation of his experiment. He presented participants with the same message to both ears, but with one following slightly after the other. The results showed that when the delay between the two messages was between two and six seconds, most participants did notice that the two messages were the same. This suggests that they were extracting meaning from the information that was directed to both ears, even the one to which they were not attending.

3.3   Implications of Cherry's findings for Broadbent's model

The results of these experiments provided support for the notion that material can be filtered on the basis of simple physical features, such as what ear the sound is played to. This was what Broadbent's model suggested. The findings from Cherry's experiment where a different message was presented to each ear (simultaneous speech condition) are consistent with Broadbent's model. Participants attending to one ear were often unaware of the language spoken in the other ear.

If, however, the material to be discriminated was all presented to both ears at the same time (mixed speech condition), then cues other than simple physical characteristics appeared to aid in attending to a particular message. Meaningful messages were easier to separate out than nonsense ones.

Also, if the messages to the two ears were actually the same message but one was delayed by a small amount, then most participants reported being aware that the unattended message was the same as the attended one.

Thus, Cherry's findings, while generally supporting Broadbent's notion of the filtering of material on the basis of physical characteristics, also imply that the *content* or meaning of a message can influence how attention is allocated. Findings such as these presented a paradox for Broadbent's model in that they suggested that some processing of the stimulus (such as content and meaning) could take place *before* it is selected for attention.

As Broadbent progressed his own research, he adapted his model of attention to accommodate as much of the new findings as possible. The model gradually became more complex. The version published in 1958 and shown in Figure 8.4 incorporated the idea that feedback from memory, prior experience and expectations can influence the workings of the selective attentional filter.

The modification of Broadbent's theories in the light of experimental evidence is a good example of the process that Broadbent believed experimental psychology should follow, namely that 'Data should determine theory rather than theory being used to search for particular data' (Weiskrantz, 1994, p. 35).

Summary

- Experiments are designed to test hypotheses that are derived from theory or previous experiments. The results of the experiments can then inform refinements to existing theories or help in the formation of new hypotheses.
- The experiments conducted by Cherry (1953) provided evidence that information may be filtered on the basis of its physical characteristics, as suggested by Broadbent.
- The findings of Cherry also suggested that meaning may be extracted before filtering takes place, and these results were incorporated into Broadbent's model.

4 Later developments in theories of attention

The work of Cherry provided early indications that *meaning* might also under certain circumstances be important with regard to which information was selected and attended to. This finding was confirmed by other studies reported next, which in turn generated alternative approaches to explaining attention.

4.1 Confirmation that meaning has an effect on the allocation of attention

Jeffrey Gray and Alexander Wedderburn (1960) presented different messages simultaneously, one to each ear as Cherry had done. The difference was that the messages were interspersed so that one particular message switched from one ear to the other, as illustrated in Figure 8.7.

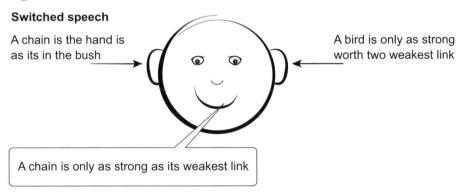

Switched speech

A chain is the hand is as its in the bush →

← A bird is only as strong worth two weakest link

A chain is only as strong as its weakest link

Figure 8.7   Switching of messages from one ear to ear

Gray and Wedderburn found that if participants were instructed to follow the meaning of the message, then they could do so even though this involved switching attention from ear to ear. Furthermore, Anne Treisman (1960) found that participants would switch attention from ear to ear to follow the meaning of a message even if they were instructed not to.

These studies thus suggest that filtering may, in some circumstances, occur much later in the processing system, after meaning has been extracted. But this filtering, on the basis of meaning, was taking place because there was not enough attentional capacity to properly process both messages. With so much information falling on our senses, early filtering on the basis of physical characteristics is desirable as this reduces the amount of information being passed along for further processing. However, later filtering is also desirable as there is a limit to how much information can be properly and fully processed, or in other words, to how much of the incoming information we can properly make sense of.

4.2   Limited processing resources are why we need attention

Regardless of whether filtering occurs early or late, what appears to be important is that there is a limit to the amount of information we can attend to. Daniel Kahneman (1973) suggested that our brains can process only a certain amount of information at any one time. That is, our cognitive resources are limited, and thus can be used to process only a limited amount of material. The implications of this assumption are clear and fit well with the studies we have already discussed; if you allocate cognitive resources to one task, then you will have fewer to spare for other concurrent tasks. Thus, filtering, whether early or late, acts as a way of reducing the drain on the *central* cognitive resources that are used to fully process information, for example, when learning something to remember later on.

Activity 8.4

Let's demonstrate the notion of a limited capacity, i.e. that there is a limit to our cognitive processing resources. Pick two pages from a book that are of similar length and that you have not yet read. Read the first page and time how long it takes you to read it. Now try to read the second page but, while you are doing it, try saying out loud the seven times table. See how long it takes to read the second page.

Did you find that it took you longer to read the second page? Can you remember as much from it as from the first page? According to Kahneman, the second page should have taken longer and you should remember less of it because saying the seven times table takes cognitive resources that you would otherwise use to process the material you are trying to read – and the task becomes more difficult.

The studies described so far in this chapter (including those of Cherry) can be explained on the basis of the allocation of limited-processing resources and, indeed, Kahneman based his limited-capacity theory on the research available at the time. The development and testing of the theory did not end there, however. At the time of writing this chapter, Kahneman's 1973 book had been cited more than 4000 times by other authors, many presenting data supporting, refining, or challenging Kahneman's original ideas. As you have seen in the discussion of hypothesis testing, this is how theories develop and are refined or rejected. A theory such as the limited-capacity theory of Kahneman is not an end point of research, but simply a point in a cycle of enquiry whereby theories are constantly tested and refined.

4.3 The neurophysiology of attention

Kahneman's theory has stood the test of time. More evidence has been provided as different techniques have been developed that were not available to the likes of Broadbent, Cherry and Kahneman. One widely used technique is that of functional magnetic resonance imaging (fMRI). Functional MRI is of great interest to psychologists because it can be used to detect localised changes in blood flow in the brain. This, in itself, would be of limited use except for the finding that changes in blood flow appear to immediately follow, and are closely associated with, increases in brain activity. Thus, fMRI can be used to give an almost real-time picture of brain activity.

You read about fMRI in Chapter 7, Section 4.1.

Functional MRI has been widely used in the study of attention and, in particular, how changes in attention are reflected by changes in brain activity. A study by Sabine Kastner et al. (1998) compared the brain activity generated by viewing multiple visual stimuli with brain activity generated by viewing one of those stimuli in isolation. Examples of the stimuli are shown in Figure 8.8.

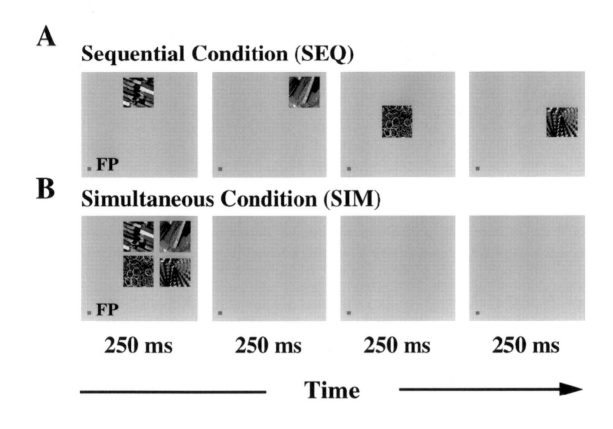

A

Sequential Condition (SEQ)

.FP

B

Simultaneous Condition (SIM)

.FP

250 ms   250 ms   250 ms   250 ms

Time

Figure 8.8   An example of the stimuli used by Kastner et al. (1998). Four complex images were presented either sequentially (A) or simultaneously (B)

According to Kahneman's theory, viewing multiple stimuli simultaneously should place a greater load on the individual's information-processing system than presenting a single item. Kastner et al. found that the level of brain activity in response to the lone stimulus (the sequential condition) was higher than when the same stimulus was viewed as part of a group (as in the simultaneous condition). Thus, it appears that processing resources are limited and, if spread across a number of stimuli, then each stimulus has less processing devoted to it than when one stimulus is presented in isolation. Kastner et al. also found that, if participants viewed all the stimuli together but were instructed to *direct attention* to only one of the stimuli in the group, then brain activity associated with this 'attended-to' stimulus increased, and that activity associated with the other ('non-attended-to') stimuli decreased. The results of this study are certainly consistent with the notion that attention involves the allocation of a limited pool of resources (as suggested by Kahneman), and the idea that if more resources are directed to one location (i.e. attention is 'paid' to that location), then fewer are available for use elsewhere. In other words, the more tasks you perform simultaneously, the fewer resources are available for each one. Attention refers to the process by which those resources are allocated.

Functional MRI studies, in conjunction with other research techniques for investigating brain function, have helped to show how different areas of the brain are involved in different aspects of attention (Kastner and Pinsk, 2004). For example, there is a posterior system (so called because the relevant areas are mostly at the back of the brain) that appears to be responsible for selecting, and hence attending to, objects, based on features such as position, shape or colour – very much the sort of physical properties that Broadbent and Cherry thought were used for early filtering of incoming stimuli. In addition to this system, there is also an anterior system (involving areas at the front of the brain) that appears to control *which* of the features mentioned above will be used as a cue to direct attention. There is a third region (mostly to the front of the right hemisphere) that appears to be involved in allowing attention to be maintained on a particular set of stimuli (Coull et al., 1996). Studies such as these have provided some evidence for which brain regions are responsible for controlling attention.

So, is the notion of an attentional 'filter' still valid? The first thing to note is that Broadbent used the term 'filter' simply as a *metaphor* for what was happening in the brain. It is an elegant and convenient way of conceptualising what is happening when we try to process incoming information. The term 'filter' simply encapsulates the notion that some information gets through and some does not. What later studies have done is to increase our understanding of why filtering may be necessary, how filtering is done and which brain regions are responsible. Thus, we can still say that, especially when there is a lot of it, some incoming information is filtered out by our attentional systems. What has changed since Broadbent's time is that we now have a far greater understanding of the mechanisms and complexities of that filtering process.

As usual, a word of caution is necessary. Breaking the attentional system down into its component parts is a useful and necessary way of studying it and, indeed, is an inherently 'scientific' way of doing so. But labelling parts of the process (e.g. 'filter' and 'channel' as in Figure 8.4) somehow makes them appear more solid and discrete. It is important to emphasise that these processes interact and overlap, not only with each other, but also with other processes within the brain, such as those concerned with perception, knowledge and emotion. Broadbent explicitly addressed these interactions, and later studies have helped to show how complex they can be, and how they can influence performance in the real world.

Summary

- Further evidence has supported the notion that meaning may be extracted before material is selected for further conscious processing, and hence that filtering may occur later on in the information-processing system.
- Kahneman's limited-capacity theory proposed that there are limited cognitive processing resources to make sense of incoming information.
- There is evidence that several different brain regions are responsible for controlling attention.

5 Attention in context

5.1 Automatic and controlled attention

From the studies discussed so far in this chapter, you may be wondering how anyone ever manages to do anything at all because their cognitive resources appear to be so limited. There is, however, another aspect of attention that, so far, we have not really considered. Throughout this chapter, we have been developing the idea that, when you pay attention to something, you become consciously aware of it. But, as we will consider in this section, it appears to be possible to process information and make responses without being conscious of the underlying processing.

Activity 8.5

Think about a journey you make regularly, or a task that you perform every day. You will probably find that you have a general recollection of the journey, for example, to the extent that you remember the route, and things along it, very well. This is a memory built up over many repetitions of the journey. But how about details of a specific journey? For example, do you remember how many red cars you saw? Can you remember if you saw any red cars?

Did you find that you could not remember the details of a specific journey? Perhaps you could recall a journey where you set off on a route that is supposed to deviate at some point from a regular route, such as the trip to work, only to find that you followed the regular route anyway! You can probably recall examples where you reached the end of a regular journey, almost without any recollection of that journey. It was as if you were working automatically and your cognitive resources were allocated elsewhere (perhaps thinking about work or what to cook for dinner later).

This apparent distinction between processes that we are aware of and those that appear to happen automatically has led to the development of 'two-process' theories of attention, such as that proposed by Richard Shiffrin and Walter Schneider (1977). Two-process theories suggest that there are, broadly, two types of attention. The first is the one that we have been discussing throughout this chapter: conscious (or controlled) attention. **Controlled attention,** as the name suggests, can be directed

Controlled attention
The conscious allocation of resources to the processing of specific stimuli.

and controlled by the individual who is aware of the information that is being attended to. The cost of this type of processing is that it draws on cognitive resources and, as has already been demonstrated, this limits the amount of information that you can consciously attend to. The second type of attention is referred to as **automatic processing**. Again, as the name suggests, this occurs automatically, below the level of conscious awareness. Many aspects of a driving task, including route finding over familiar routes, can be controlled by automatic processes. The advantage of using automatic processes is that large amounts of material can be processed without drawing on scant cognitive resources. The cost is that automatic processes are difficult to stop, precisely because they are not 'controlled'. This is how you can end up in the wrong place at the end of a journey – your driving is being controlled by an automatic process while your conscious attention is directed elsewhere.

Automatic processing
The automatic processing of stimuli that occurs without conscious awareness.

5.2   Attention and experience

Odmar Neumann (1984) suggested that an automatic process requires appropriate stimuli from the environment that then trigger the skills required to complete the task at a level below that of conscious awareness. Thus, when driving a familiar route, the familiar stimuli along the route trigger the appropriate automatic responses that have been learned over many repetitions of the journey. Little conscious control is required and, as a result, at the end of the journey we may have little conscious recollection of it.

Furthermore, Neumann suggested that automatic processes are not entirely uncontrolled, but are controlled at a level below conscious awareness. Individuals can allocate attention to specific information; for example, they can determine which part of their environment to allocate attention to by moving the eyes. Daniel Gopher (1993) argued that appropriate allocation of attention is a cognitive skill in itself, and one that can be improved by training and experience.

Studies of driving support the notion that experience may affect the allocation of attention. Geoffrey Underwood (2007) looked at the visual scanning patterns of drivers and found that, whereas experienced drivers adapted their scanning patterns to road complexity, novice drivers did not. The change in scanning patterns was even more pronounced in trained police drivers. Experienced drivers may not be aware that they are doing it, but they are changing the way in which they allocate attention, depending on the driving conditions.

Top-down processes
When experience, expectations and/or stored knowledge influence the allocation of resources to certain stimuli.

If experience affects the way in which people gather information, this implies a possible involvement of so-called **top-down processes**, whereby allocation of attention may be influenced by (for example) expectancies and knowledge. Indeed, this interaction between incoming information (flowing bottom-up) and higher-level influences acting top-down in the control of attention was addressed by Broadbent in the work we have already discussed. You may remember from Section 2 that Broadbent's model included the possibility that feedback from information stored in memory, prior experience and expectations could influence the selective filter.

5.3 Back to the real world

Returning to the notion of applying theories of attention to real-world problems, the authors of this chapter conducted a study (Edgar and Edgar, 2007) that demonstrated the influence of expectations on the allocation of attention. A war game was conducted on an extensive 1:300 scale terrain model, as shown in Figure 8.9, using physical scale models of tanks and other forces. Participants' awareness of aspects of the situation was measured. For example, one participant demonstrated an impressive awareness of the broad strategic sweep of the battle but no awareness *at all* of some basic physical features, such as the fact that his own forces were coloured grey while those of the enemy were coloured green. Such a lack of attention to basic physical characteristics resulted in this participant attempting to open fire on his own troops in a 'friendly fire' incident. This player appeared to allocate attention according to what he thought *should* be there, based on his expectations (enemy troops), rather than allocating resources to what *actually* was there (his own troops).

This finding demonstrates that although on many occasions our expectations may usefully direct us to the more relevant stimuli in our surrounding environment, at times our expectations can also result in us overlooking important aspects of the situation that are relevant to the task at hand.

Figure 8.9   Using a 1:300 scale terrain model to reveal the attentional basis of friendly fire

So, what was going on in the head of our errant Fiesta driver described in the anecdote that began this chapter? It is likely that the driver was following a route that he had done many times before and was therefore on 'automatic pilot'. Furthermore, he almost certainly was not *expecting* to see a cyclist. Thus, although the driver's visual system may well have *detected* a cyclist, the stimulus was not salient enough to attract his attention and so he did not become *aware* of the danger and carried on as if there were no cyclist. Rather like the friendly-fire incident just described, it appears that the driver was responding to what he believed should be there, not what actually was there. The failure of the Fiesta driver to attend to an oncoming cyclist demonstrates how little of the world around us we are really aware of at any one time.

5.4   Conclusion

The evidence presented throughout this chapter suggests that people have limited attentional resources and can rarely process all of the information impinging on their senses. This is why using a mobile phone in a car is a bad idea. Using a phone requires vital cognitive resources that could be better used elsewhere when driving.

This chapter also suggested that there are two broad aspects to trying to understand attention. The first is the theoretical interest in how the human brain takes in and processes (or doesn't process) information, which helps us gain a better understanding of how the human mind works. The second aspect relates to the *use* of this understanding to explain how things work in the 'real world' and, crucially, to make things work better, such as improving the way information is presented to pilots and drivers, and designing effective early warning systems.

The development and testing of a theory alongside the *application* of that theory to real-world problems was the approach advocated and practised by Donald Broadbent. After all, a theory that cannot be applied in practice needs to be treated with extreme caution! We hope that, after reading this chapter, you can appreciate why Broadbent's systematic approach to experimental research and theory development has formed the foundation for much later work and why he is, justifiably, regarded as one of the key figures in the development of modern cognitive psychology and in the establishment of psychology as a scientific discipline.

Summary

- As well as conscious attention, there can be automatic processing of information, which operates below the level of conscious awareness.

- Automatic processing does not draw on our limited cognitive resources.

- Top-down processes may operate so that expectations, knowledge and experience can influence allocation of attention.

References

Boase, M., Hannigan, S. and Porter, J.M. (1988) 'Sorry, can't talk now … just overtaking a lorry: the definition and experimental investigation of the problem of driving and hands free car phone use' in Megaw, E.D. (ed.) *Contemporary Ergonomics*, London, Taylor and Francis.

Broadbent, D.E. (1954) 'The role of auditory localization and attention in memory span', *Journal of Experimental Psychology*, vol. 47, no. 3, pp. 191–6.

Broadbent, D.E. (1957) 'Immediate memory and simultaneous stimuli', *The Quarterly Journal of Experimental Psychology*, vol. 9, no. 1, pp. 1–11.

Broadbent, D.E. (1958) *Perception and Communication*, London, Pergamon.

Brookhuis, K.A., de Vries, G. and de Waard, D. (1991) 'The effects of mobile telephoning on driving performance', *Accident Analysis and Prevention*, vol. 23, no. 4, pp. 309–16.

Brown, I.D., Tickner, A.H. and Simmonds, D.C.V. (1969) 'Interference between concurrent tasks of driving and telephoning', *Journal of Applied Psychology*, vol. 53, no. 5, pp. 419–24.

Cherry, E.C. (1953) 'Some experiments on the recognition of speech with one and two ears', *Journal of the Acoustical Society of America*, vol. 25, no. 5, pp. 975–9.

Coull, J.T., Frith, C.D., Frackowiak, R.S.J. and Grasby, P.M. (1996) 'A fronto-parietal network for rapid visual information processing: a PET study of sustained attention and working memory', *Neuropsychologia*, vol. 34, no. 11, pp. 1085–95.

Edgar, G. and Edgar, H. (2007) 'Using signal detection theory to measure situation awareness: the technique, the tool (QUASA^{TM}), the test, the way forward' in Cook, M., Noyes, J. and Masakowski, Y. (eds) *Decision Making in Complex Environments*, Aldershot, Ashgate.

Glassbrenner, D. (2005) *Driver Cell Phone Use in 2004: Overall Results*, Research note DOT HS 809 847, US Department of Transportation, National Highway Traffic Safety Administration (NHTSA), Washington, DC; also available online at www-nrd.nhtsa.dot.gov/Pubs/809847.PDF (Accessed 25 March 2010).

Gopher, D. (1993) 'The skill of attentional control: acquisition and execution of attentional strategies' in Kornblum, S. and Meyer, D.E. (eds) *Attention and Performance XIV: Synergies in Experimental Psychology, Artificial Intelligence and Cognitive Neuroscience*, Cambridge, MA, MIT Press.

Gray, J.A. and Wedderburn, A.A.I. (1960) 'Grouping strategies with simultaneous stimuli', *Quarterly Journal of Experimental Psychology*, vol. 12, no. 3, pp. 180–4.

James, W. (1890) *Principles of Psychology*, Vol. 1, New York, NY, Holt.

Kahneman, D. (1973) *Attention and Effort*, Englewood Cliffs, NJ, Prentice-Hall.

Kastner, S., De Weerd, P., Desimone, R. and Ungerleider, L.G. (1998) 'Mechanisms of directed attention in the human extrastriate cortex as revealed by functional MRI', *Science*, vol. 282, no. 5386, pp. 108–10.

Kastner, S. and Pinsk, M.A. (2004) 'Visual attention as a multilevel selection', *Cognitive, Affective, and Behavioral Neuroscience*, vol. 4, no. 4, pp. 483–500.

Neumann, O. (1984) 'Automatic processing: a review of recent findings and a plea for an old theory' in Prinz, W. and Sanders, A.F. (eds) *Cognition and Motor Processes*, Berlin, Springer-Verlag.

Redelmeier, D.A. and Tibshirani, R.J. (1997) 'Association between cellular-telephone calls and motor vehicle collisions', *New England Journal of Medicine*, vol. 336, no. 7, pp. 453–8.

Royal Society for the Prevention of Accidents (RoSPA) (2002) *The Risk of Using a Mobile Phone While Driving*, Birmingham, RoSPA; also available online at www.rospa.com/roadsafety/info/mobile_phone_report.pdf (Accessed 24 March 2010).

Shiffrin, R.M. and Schneider, W. (1977) 'Controlled and automatic human information processing: II. Perceptual learning, automatic attending and a general theory', *Psychological Review*, vol. 84, no. 2, pp. 127–90.

Strayer, D.L., Drews, F.A. and Crouch, D.J. (2006) 'A comparison of the cell phone driver and the drunk driver', *Human Factors*, vol. 48, no. 2, pp. 381–91.

Treisman, A.M. (1960) 'Contextual cues in selective listening', *Quarterly Journal of Experimental Psychology*, vol. 12, no. 4, pp. 242–8.

Underwood, G. (2007) 'Visual attention and the transition from novice to advanced driver', *Ergonomics*, vol. 50, no. 8, pp. 1235–49.

Weiskrantz, L. (1994) 'Donald Eric Broadbent, 6 May 1926–10 April 1993', *Biographical Memoirs of Fellows of the Royal Society*, vol. 40, pp. 33–42.

Chapter 9
Witnessing and remembering

Graham Pike and Nicola Brace

Contents

Aims and objectives

After studying this chapter you should be able to:

- describe the different types of memory and provide examples of episodic memory
- discuss the reconstructive nature of episodic memory
- appreciate the methodological and ethical challenges facing those who research eyewitness memory
- describe how research on the misinformation effect has moved on into research on false memories
- appreciate the impact of psychological findings on police practice and interviewing guidance.

1   Introduction

The last chapter introduced you to the notion of limited capacity, particularly that there are limits to our capacity to attend to the world around us. As you will see in the current chapter, there are also limits to our capacity to remember. Even if we are able to direct all our *attention* to an event, it is not necessarily the case that we will be able to *remember* all that happened.

Like attention, memory is important in all aspects of everyday life. This chapter, as well as exploring memory more generally, looks specifically at the question of eyewitness memory – people's ability to remember crimes, car accidents and other important events. As you will see, eyewitnesses experience great difficulties when it comes to remembering a crime. Not only do they forget a lot of what happened, but they sometimes also remember things that didn't happen at all. For instance, the 2010 TV series called *Eyewitness*, which the BBC produced in collaboration with The Open University, studied the memories of witnesses for staged, but very realistically enacted, crimes such as a violent attack in a pub and a heist from a security van. The differences between their accounts and what actually took place were astounding. For example, they disagreed on who perpetrated the attack in the pub; indeed, one witness confused the attacker and the victim. In the case of the heist, one witness reported seeing a car reverse round a corner and the criminals leaping out, although the incident involved no so such event. Another witness described in some detail the sunglasses that one of the gunmen was wearing, even reporting the brand. However, not only was the man in question not wearing any sunglasses, he was in fact wearing a balaclava.

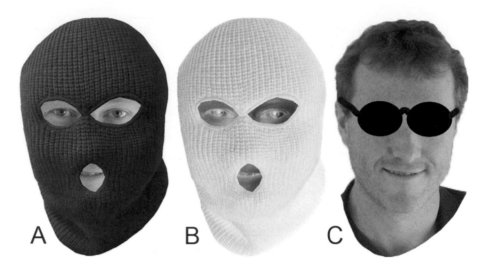

Figure 9.1 From balaclava to sunglasses: the gunman wearing the dark balaclava (image A) may have been misremembered by the witness as having dark rather than light eye patches (image B), leading them to recall the perpetrator as having worn sunglasses (image C)

To understand why eyewitnesses tend to make such fundamental errors, we first need to find out more about how human memory works. This chapter will explore memory and examine why our memory of events is often incomplete, and also how it is that we sometimes we report remembering events that never happened at all.

1.1 Types of memory

We have a friend called Jim who has often been described as having a very good memory. If you want to know who sang an obscure pop song from the 1980s or the name of a character from a television series, Jim is your man. You probably know someone like Jim, but even if you don't you probably equate the phrase 'good memory' with someone who can readily bring to mind a large number of facts.

Semantic memory
Remembering factual information.

Procedural memory
Remembering how to perform actions.

Prospective memory
Remembering actions that need to be completed in the future.

Memory for facts, which is referred to by psychologists as **semantic memory**, is actually only a small part of our memories, which also include:

- **procedural memory**: remembering how to perform certain actions (e.g. ride a bicycle)

- **prospective memory**: remembering that you need to do something in the future (e.g. that tomorrow you need to pick up the dry-cleaning)

- **episodic memory**: remembering an event that happened in the past (e.g. a football game or a play)
- **autobiographical memory**: a type of episodic memory that relates to events that are of personal relevance to the person doing the remembering (e.g. first day at school).

Another way of categorising memory is to look at the type of task that remembering actually involves. For example, exams that are designed to test the memory of a student routinely use two different types of question. The first type consists of essay questions or any other format that asks a question without providing the answer. These questions require the student to *recall* some of the material that they learned and memorised. The second type is multiple-choice questions, which both ask a question and provide the answer (among a series of incorrect answers). This type of question requires the student to *recognise* the answer. In everyday life we use recognition memory almost constantly. As long as we can perceive objects, places and people, our mind automatically (at least most of the time) recognises what we are seeing. For instance, we can tell from memory that the person standing in front of us is our mother and that she is standing in front of a tree. Memories that are recalled tend to occur mostly in conversations, particularly when we are describing something from memory. Witnesses are routinely asked to use both recall and recognition memories as part of a police investigation. For example, recognition memory is used if the witness is asked to identify the perpetrator of the crime from a line-up, and recall memory is used when the witness is asked to give a statement of what they saw.

As well as there being different types of memory and remembering, it is also possible to describe memory as happening through three distinct stages. The first is **encoding**, which involves processing information from the physical senses into memory. The second stage is **storage**, which involves the information that was encoded being stored in memory until it is needed again. The final stage is **retrieval**, which is when the information is brought from memory to be used again. For example, when studying you try to encode the information you read in a textbook, store it until your exam and then retrieve it when answering a question.

Another way of looking at these three stages is by using computers as an analogy. When you enter some text into your word-processing software, the computer encodes the information. Once you select the

Episodic memory
Remembering events that happened in the past.

Autobiographical memory
Remembering events that are of personal relevance.

Encoding
Processing information received from one of the senses into memory.

Storage
Storing information in memory.

Retrieval
Recovering information that is stored in memory.

'save' icon it stores it so that it can be retrieved at a later date, whenever you chose to 'open' that file.

This chapter will concentrate on how people recall an *episodic* memory, in that it will look at witnesses describing a crime from memory. This also means that subsequent sections will focus on the *retrieval* stage. There is a practical reason for this. The police interview eyewitnesses only after a crime has taken place. By that time they have no influence on how the memory of the crime was encoded or stored. The police can only assist the witness to recall the event as accurately as possible. This is why applied research on eyewitness memory has focused extensively on the retrieval stage.

1.2   What are memories?

The different ways of classifying memory, described in Section 1.1, provide part of the answer to this question. Regardless of the specific type, memory essentially involves information from one of the senses (e.g. vision or hearing) being encoded and stored so that it can later be retrieved. But in relation to human memory, this is only part of the answer.

One way of describing human memory is to look at what it is not. Let's return to the computer analogy. To some extent computer and human memory are similar, as both involve the encoding, storage and retrieval of information. However, computer memory:

- is based in one or more discrete components, usually the computer's hard drive and memory chips
- is perfect, in that (barring such things as viruses and spilt coffee) the information that is encoded, stored and retrieved is exactly the same
- does not require the computer to be able to understand the 'meaning' of the information being stored.

By comparison, human memory:

- *is stored throughout the brain*. Although it is possible to identify certain brain structures that are important to particular parts of the memory process, the 'memories' themselves seem not to be stored in any one particular region, but are instead distributed throughout the brain.
- *is imperfect*. If a computer read this chapter, if it was either scanned as an image or typed in as a word-processor file, it would be able to reproduce every word in this chapter in the correct order. Imagine

the results if I asked you to do the same task! Critically, the computer would reproduce the same information no matter what the conditions were under which it was asked to do so. As you will see, human memories seem to change significantly as a result of how they are retrieved.

- *often requires understanding the meaning of the information.* Although a computer would be able to reproduce every word in this chapter, there is no real sense in which it could be considered to have understood the information contained in the words. However, if I asked you to recall this chapter, it is likely that most of what you would remember is what the words and sentences *meant*. Indeed, without being able to deduce this meaning it is likely you would remember very little at all. To think of it another way, imagine this chapter was written using ancient Egyptian hieroglyphics: how much do you think you could remember? Of course, it matters little to the computer what language is used, because the computer just remembers the characters and their order, not what they mean.

The differences in the performance of computer and human memory provide hints as to the extremely complex role that memory has to play in human life. Unlike the computer, humans need to make sense of their environments and that requires creating meaning of the world. Most of the time any inaccuracies in our memories will go unnoticed and are unlikely to have any particularly negative consequences. On occasion, though, people encounter a situation where errors of memory can have adverse consequences. One such situation is in an exam, where failure to remember facts can lead to a poor mark. Another situation is where the police rely on the memory of an eyewitness to discover what happened in a crime. As you will see in Section 1.3, people not only forget information but sometimes also remember things that didn't happen.

1.3   Reconstructing memories

To say that when presented with a page of text people remember the meaning of the words rather than every actual word seems obvious. However, deciding exactly what the meaning of the text is requires that it is first interpreted, and how it is interpreted depends on who the person doing the interpreting is. You can imagine that different people may well interpret the same basic information, whether this information is a page of text, a picture or a real-life scene, in very different ways.

That information can be interpreted differently poses a particular problem in the case of eyewitness memory, as the police need witnesses to describe what happened accurately. To demonstrate some of the errors people make when trying to remember, we will take a look at a famous study conducted in 1932 by Sir Frederic Bartlett. Bartlett taught Donald Broadbent at Cambridge and, like Broadbent, is considered by many to be an important figure in the history of cognitive psychology. The study involved asking a group of British participants to read and remember a Native American folk tale called 'War of the Ghosts'.

Figure 9.2   Frederic Bartlett (1886–1969)

Activity 9.1

The 'War of the Ghosts' story used by Bartlett is reproduced below. To experience the task faced by Bartlett's participants, read the story through once, attempt to recall as much of it as you can, and then answer the specific questions that we have provided after the story. Do not reread the story before you have tried to recall it and attempted the questions.

Box 9.1   War of the Ghosts

One night two young men from Egulac went down to the river to hunt seals and while they were there it became foggy and calm. Then they heard war-cries, and they thought: 'Maybe this is a war-party'. They escaped to the shore, and hid behind a log. Now canoes came up, and they heard the noise of paddles, and saw one canoe coming up to them. There were five men in the canoe, and they said:

'What do you think? We wish to take you along. We are going up the river to make war on the people.'

One of the young men said, 'I have no arrows.'

'Arrows are in the canoe,' they said.

'I will not go along. I might be killed. My relatives do not know where I have gone. But you,' he said, turning to the other, 'may go with them.'

So one of the young men went, but the other returned home.

And the warriors went on up the river to a town on the other side of Kalama. The people came down to the water and they began to fight, and many were killed. But presently the young man heard one of the warriors say, 'Quick, let us go home: that Indian has been hit.' Now he thought: 'Oh, they are ghosts.' He did not feel sick, but they said he had been shot.

So the canoes went back to Egulac and the young man went ashore to his house and made a fire. And he told everybody and said: 'Behold I accompanied the ghosts, and we went to fight. Many of our fellows were killed, and many of those who attacked us were killed. They said I was hit, and I did not feel sick.'

> He told it all, and then he became quiet. When the sun rose he fell down. Something black came out of his mouth. His face became contorted. The people jumped up and cried.
>
> He was dead.
>
> (Bartlett, 1932, p. 65)

Now write down on a separate sheet all you can recall of the story. Once you've done this, try to answer the questions below *before* looking at the story again.

1 How many men from Egulac went down to the river?

2 When they heard war-cries, what did they hide behind?

3 What was the name of the town the warriors went to? Was it:

   (a) Katana

   (b) Lakaka

   (c) Malaka

   (d) Kalama

4 Had the men from Egulac caught any fish before they heard the war-cries?

Now you can look back at the story to see how much you recalled and whether you answered the questions correctly.

You may well have found that you could answer the questions even if you did not recall that part of the story earlier, particularly question 3, where you were also presented with the answers (and therefore had to *recognise* rather than *recall* the answer). Specific questions such as those above can help us remember extra information because the question itself contains information which prompts our memories, or in other words leads us to remember more. Question 4 demonstrates one danger with such **leading questions**, as the information contained in the question is false, as the story states that the men were hunting seals, and not fish. As you will see, this type of false information can influence what we remember.

Leading questions
Questions that suggest or imply an answer.

When Bartlett studied how well people could remember the 'War of the Ghosts' story, he discovered that not only did people fail to recall the whole story, but they often recalled elements of the tale either incorrectly or indeed recalled something that was not part of the story at all. For example, some participants recalled there being a boat, rather than a canoe, and one reported that the death at the end was the result of a fever and that the person was foaming at the mouth. Bartlett suggested that these changes were a result of the participants interpreting the story, and, as the participants came from a Western culture, they tended to interpret the events from a Western viewpoint. So, for example, to the participants in Bartlett's study, the event in the final paragraph resembled an epileptic seizure, so 'something black' coming from a person's mouth was remembered as the culturally more familiar phenomenon of 'foaming at the mouth'. In other words, participants were not remembering exactly what they had read, but were *reconstructing* the meaning of the text in the light of their own culture.

The task used by Bartlett is fairly unusual, particularly as it involves people from one culture trying to remember a story from another culture. For that reason we cannot necessarily conclude that memory is always subject to the distortions reported by Bartlett, particularly when we are dealing with everyday scenarios. Another way of saying this is that the task used by Bartlett was not particularly *ecologically valid* in relation to everyday memory. Nonetheless, Bartlett's work is extremely important in demonstrating that the memories we retrieve may not be a particularly good match for the original event. Also, it shows that we remember information in ways that make it meaningful to ourselves. Most of the time, people are unaware that memory involves reconstruction and most of the time it matters little if an event is recalled accurately or not. However, as you will see in the next section, there are occasions when errors in recall can have serious consequences.

You read about ecological validity in Section 4.2 of Chapter 5.

Summary

- There are different types of memory, including semantic, procedural, prospective, episodic and autobiographical memory. Recalling an event, such as a crime, involves episodic memory.

- Memory can involve recall or recognition, and is often described as involving the stages of encoding, storage and retrieval.

- Remembering can involve reconstructing what was experienced in the light of our expectations, knowledge and experiences, which can lead to errors and even to memories of things that never happened.

2 The Loftus and Palmer (1974) study

Errors in our memory often tend to go unnoticed in everyday life and, even if noticed, they tend not to be that important. It is also rare for a situation to arise that requires us to remember a past event in particular detail, as usually all we need to recall are a few meaningful elements. Last week I (Graham) celebrated my friend Hayley's birthday. I can remember that I picked up an Indian takeaway on the way, that I took my two collies (as my friends love dogs), and that another friend, Gemma, spent quite a bit of the evening looking for badgers in the garden. I cannot remember who was in the Indian restaurant and, beyond the fact that Gemma had a straw hat, I could not tell you what anyone was wearing. Such detail is just unimportant. However, what if it had turned out that the Indian restaurant had been robbed just after I was there, or one of my friends had gone missing that night? The police would want to know as much as possible and I would suddenly be in a position where I was expected to remember very specific details.

Just as trying to recall the details of the 'War of the Ghosts' story can be considered to be outside the everyday experience of the participants, witnessing and trying to recall what happened in a crime is also outside the everyday experience of most of us. One key difference between recalling an event as part of everyday life and recalling a crime in a police interview is that the latter requires us to remember as many details as possible in response to questions. In 1974, Elizabeth Loftus and John Palmer published two experiments that examined what effect the specific wording used in questioning had on the information remembered by a participant. The research, which was supported by the US Urban Mass Transportation Administration, and has become one of the most famous and often-cited psychological studies ever conducted, is described next.

2.1 Reconstruction of automobile destruction

The first thing to note about this study is the title chosen by the authors, 'Reconstruction of automobile destruction: an example of the interaction between language and memory', and particularly that they used the word 'reconstruction' prominently. That memories are 'reconstructed' rather than remembered exactly as the original event occurred was the conclusion Bartlett reached following his research conducted forty years previously. Loftus and Palmer were building on the work of Bartlett, and examining how the reconstructive nature of memory interacts with the specific language used in questions designed to probe recall.

The study conducted by Loftus and Palmer is an example of applied research, in that it seeks to address a particular issue that has arisen in the 'real world' rather than an issue arising from academic theory. As the results of applied research need to be relevant to the 'real world', it is important that the studies conducted use stimuli and tasks that are a good match for real-world situations. The applied problem being studied by Loftus and Palmer (1974) concerns how accurately a witness can describe what happened in an automobile collision, particularly how the questions they are asked might affect what they remember happening.

If you have ever been involved in or witnessed an automobile collision, you will know that the speed of the vehicles tends to be a key part of any subsequent investigation, whether by the police or by insurance companies. The problem is that very often the only information about the speed of the vehicles comes from those that witness the collision, and people tend not to be particularly good at estimating vehicle speed. As an example of this, Loftus and Palmer cite evidence presented by James Marshall (1969) that involved asking Air Force personnel to estimate the speed of a car that was moving at 12 miles per hour (mph). Even though the participants knew in advance that they would be asked about the speed of the car, estimates ranged from 10 mph to 50 mph.

Loftus and Palmer suggest that, given this very large range in estimates, it is likely that there are variables that could influence the estimate given by an individual and that the specific phrasing of the question used to elicit the estimate could be one such factor. Loftus and Palmer's rationale for choosing the phrasing of the question came from legal studies and rules relating to leading questions.

2.2   Experiment 1: estimating speed

To study this issue, Loftus and Palmer conducted an experiment in which forty-five students were each shown seven film clips of vehicle collisions taken from driver education films.

Figure 9.3   A recent replication of Loftus and Palmer (1974)

Following each clip, the participants were asked to complete a questionnaire, which first asked them to give an account of the accident and then asked specific follow-up questions including a question on what speed the cars were going.

Four of the clips were staged collisions at particular speeds (20 mph, 30 mph and two at 40 mph), and these were first used to determine how accurate the participants' estimates of speed were. The **mean** estimated speed for each of these four clips is presented in Table 9.1.

Mean
An average that is calculated by adding together all the items to be averaged and then dividing the total by the number of items.

Table 9.1   Mean estimates of speed in Loftus and Palmer's (1974) experiment

Actual speed of vehicles (mph)	Mean estimate of vehicles' speed (mph)
20	37.7
30	36.2
40	39.7
40	36.1

Activity 9.2

Have a look at the data in Table 9.1. Does anything strike you as unusual about the mean estimates of speed? Try looking for trends in the data. For example, do the numbers increase or decrease in each column?

The actual speed of the vehicles (left-hand column) increases towards the bottom of the table, and in fact doubles from 20 mph to 40 mph. However, the mean estimates of speed do not increase and instead do not vary much at all. This suggests that the estimates of speed given by the participants did not tend to increase as the speed of the vehicle increased and instead participants gave an estimate of about 37 mph whether the vehicle was travelling at 20 mph or 40 mph! In other words, the participants were not very good at estimating speed, just as Marshall had previously noted.

Loftus and Palmer examined the effect that the specific phrasing of the question had on estimates of speed by varying the key verb that was used in the question. The question asking participants to provide an estimate of speed was: 'About how fast were the cars going when they hit each other?' The question was constructed so that the key verb 'hit' could be replaced with an alternative. In all, five different verbs were used, namely:

- hit
- smashed
- collided
- bumped
- contacted.

Each participant was asked the same question using the same verb for each clip they saw. So, each verb was used with a total of nine participants. If we were to describe this experiment in terms of the variables used, we could say that the independent variable (the variable manipulated) was the phrasing of the question, and that the dependent variable (the variable measured) was the estimate of speed provided by the participant. The authors calculated the mean speed reported for each of the five questions, and these are presented in Table 9.2.

Table 9.2   Mean speed reported by key verb used in Loftus and Palmer's (1974) experiment

Key verb	Mean speed reported
hit	34.0 mph
smashed	40.5 mph
collided	39.3 mph
bumped	38.1 mph
contacted	31.8 mph

So, although the participants saw exactly the same collisions, using the verb 'smashed' resulted in speed estimates that were on average 8.7 mph higher than when the verb 'contacted' was used.

2.3   Experiment 2: did you see any broken glass?

The results of Experiment 1 show that although the actual speed of the vehicles seems to have little effect on the estimates given, the particular phrasing of the question does have a marked effect. Loftus and Palmer identified two possible interpretations of this finding.

- Participants are uncertain whether to say 30 mph or 40 mph, for example, and are swayed in their decision by the verb used, so that, for example, 'smashed' biases them toward 40 and 'contacted' toward 30.

- The phrasing of the question causes a change in the participant's memory of the collision, so that using the verb 'smashed' results in their memory being of a faster collision than when 'contacted' is used.

In many respects the second explanation is the more interesting. If correct, it tells us something profound about human memory – namely that a memory may be reconstructed in accordance with the wording of the question.

To explore which one of the two interpretations of the findings was more likely, Loftus and Palmer conducted a second experiment. They wanted to find out whether the wording of a question could lead participants to reconstruct a memory of an event so as to include entirely novel elements. In other words, they wanted to see if they could get participants to remember details that never actually happened.

In this experiment 150 participants were shown a short film depicting a fairly low-speed vehicle collision that did not result in any broken glass. Each participant then completed a questionnaire similar to the one used in Experiment 1. Again, the critical question was the one relating to the speed of the vehicles, but this time only three variations were used, with each variation being given to fifty participants:

- About how fast were the cars going when they smashed into each other? (The 'smashed' condition)

- About how fast were the cars going when they hit each other? (The 'hit' condition)

- No question about the speed of the vehicles. (The control condition)

A week after viewing the film, the participants returned and, without seeing the film again, were asked a series of ten questions about the collision. The key question was 'Did you see any broken glass?', to which the participant had to answer either 'yes' or 'no'. This question is misleading, as the film did not show any broken glass. The authors expected that those participants previously given the question containing the verb 'smashed' would be more likely to report broken glass than those in either the 'hit' or control condition.

You were introduced to the definition of a control condition in Section 2.3 of Chapter 3.

The results of this experiment revealed that participants in the 'smashed' condition provided higher estimates of speed (mean estimate 10.46 mph) than those in the 'hit' condition (mean estimate 8.0 mph). In Table 9.3 you can see how the participants in each condition responded to the question about the presence of broken glass.

Table 9.3 Distribution of 'yes' and 'no' responses to the question 'Did you see any broken glass?' in Loftus and Palmer (1974), Experiment 2

Response	Verb condition		
	Smashed	Hit	Control
Yes	16	7	6
No	34	43	44

Looking at Table 9.3, it is clear that more than twice as many participants in the 'smashed' condition erroneously reported broken glass as participants in the other two conditions (16 in the 'smash' condition and only 6 or 7 in the other conditions). One important thing to note about the data presented in Table 9.3 is that in every condition far more participants responded 'no' than 'yes', which shows that most participants' memories were accurate even when asked a question that was intended to mislead.

2.4   Integrating memories

As using the verb 'smashed' led to both higher speed estimates *and* more participants remembering broken glass, one might be tempted to conclude that this experiment simply shows that people with higher estimates of speed are also more likely to remember broken glass. To test whether this is the case, Loftus and Palmer conducted additional analysis on their data and found that, while it may be the case that people in the 'smashed' condition gave higher estimates of the car's speed, the estimate of speed does not fully explain the effect of the question on the recall of broken glass. In other words, use of the word 'smashed' seems to have had an effect above and beyond that of increasing the estimate of speed.

In interpreting these findings, Loftus and Palmer suggested that a memory can consist of both information encoded while watching the actual event *and* information encoded when retrieving the memory. These two sources of information can be integrated into one memory, so that a person is unable to tell the two sources apart. In this case, some participants were integrating the suggestion that the collision involved two vehicles 'smashing' into one another and that there might have been broken glass, into their memory of the actual collision.

Post-event information
Knowledge provided about an event after it has taken place.

Since Loftus and Palmer (1974) published their research, many further experiments have been conducted in this area and the term **post-event information** has been developed to refer to information that may be incorporated into a memory of an event after it has happened. Likewise, the term **misinformation effect** has come to be used to refer to the errors that can occur in memory as a result of post-event information, such as being asked a leading question that suggests something that didn't happen. As you will see, providing post-event information can have a powerful effect on memory, and in regard of misinformation, it can result in people remembering things that never happened!

Misinformation effect
Errors in memory caused by incorrect post-event information.

Summary

- Loftus and Palmer (1974) conducted two experiments to explore factors that influence memory for the details of a car accident.
- They found that the way in which a question was phrased influenced what was recalled.
- They proposed that information recalled about an event may contain the original information encoded plus information provided at the time of recall.

3   Method: applied experiments

The experiments conducted by Loftus and Palmer (1974) are examples of applied research, in that they were clearly designed to investigate an issue of relevance to accident investigation and witness interviewing more broadly. However, simply attempting to answer an applied question is only part of what constitutes applied research. In addition, it is important to design the study in such a way that the results obtained can be usefully and meaningfully applied to the area in question. Constructing experiments that achieve this is quite a complex and difficult task.

3.1   Ecological validity, consequentiality, practicality and research ethics

One of the differences between applied and theoretical research is that the former needs to try to match the conditions of the real-world situation being studied as closely as possible. Psychologists use the term 'ecological validity' to refer to this matching of experimental and real-world conditions. Consider two experiments designed to test eyewitness memory. In the first experiment a 'live' crime is staged in front of unsuspecting participants, who are then taken to a police station to be interviewed about what they saw, and several weeks later attend an identification parade to try to identify the perpetrator. As this experiment is a good match for what would happen to witnesses in a real crime and real investigation, it can be said to have high ecological validity. The second experiment involves showing participants photographs of a scene at a restaurant and instructing them to remember as much of the scene as they can, and then giving them multiple-choice questions to test their memory. As the conditions in this second experiment are a poor match for those of a real crime and investigation, it can be said to have low ecological validity.

Figure 9.4   Two ways of researching eyewitness memory: participants in a laboratory viewing a video of a staged crime and participants observing the staged event live in a side street

Ecological validity is just one of the factors an applied researcher needs to bear in mind. Consider the high ecological validity eyewitness experiment described in the previous paragraph. The participants see a live crime and are interviewed by the police, just like a witness, but their experience is the same as that of a witness only if they are not told that they are taking part in an experiment until *after* the experiment is finished. If at any point during the experiment the participants learn that the crime and the investigation are staged, then they will realise that their actions will have no real consequences. A real witness knows that any evidence they provide could lead to someone being either prosecuted or released, but a participant in an experiment knows that any consequences are limited to the results of the experiment. Thus, *consequentiality* is a key difference between experimental research and the real world, even if the research has high ecological validity.

Of course, an experiment can have both high ecological validity *and* consequentiality if the participants do not realise that they are taking part in an experiment. The problem with this suggestion is that it involves deceiving the participants and, particularly if the study is one of witness memory, exposing them to a potentially stressful and therefore harmful situation. Such deception is unethical as it violates the ethics principles that participants must give their informed consent and have the right to withdraw from the research at any point.

You read about informed consent and the right to withdraw in Chapter 2, Section 3.1.

When designing an applied experiment, the task of the researcher is to do their best to achieve high ecological validity and adhere to ethics guidelines, while also considering what is practical. This last factor, *practicality*, tends to play a crucial role in applied research, if only because there tends to be only a very limited amount of time and research funding available. For example, to achieve high ecological validity in eyewitness memory research, it would seem sensible for researchers to hire actors and use live staged crimes. However, live staged crimes are not always practical and tend to be very expensive. The other problem with live events is that if you have to restage them (to add more participants to your experiment, for example), it is very hard to replicate the first event exactly – and it is important that all participants see exactly the same thing. It is for these reasons that most eyewitness memory research, like that of Loftus and Palmer (1974), uses video rather than live events, and has a researcher to test or interview the participants rather than an actual police or insurance investigator. Likewise, a lot of applied research is conducted in the laboratory or classroom, rather than 'in the field'.

Activity 9.3

As research ethics require participants taking part in an eyewitness memory study to be informed that they are taking part in research, they cannot be made to think they are participating in a real police investigation. Can you think of any way that some degree of consequentiality could be built into such a study?

If you're stuck for ideas, consider 'who' the participants are, 'how' they are recruited and 'what' they are told about the research.

What type of thing did you come up with? Below we have listed some of the techniques eyewitness memory researchers have employed:

- telling participants that the results of the study will inform expert testimony given by the researcher in court
- telling participants that the results of the study will be used to inform changes to police guidelines and practice
- using real police officers, possibly in a police station, to interview the eyewitnesses.

Did you think of any of the ideas in the list above? One thing you may have considered is rewarding the participants according to how well they performed. One problem with this is that it is difficult to design a reward structure that would mimic the actual experiences of being involved in a real investigation. Another problem is finding sufficient funds to give rewards substantial enough to influence behaviour.

3.2 Evaluating Loftus and Palmer (1974)

Consider the two experiments conducted by Loftus and Palmer with regard to their ethics, practicality, ecological validity and consequentiality. It would have been impractical (not to mention downright dangerous) to stage actual vehicle collisions, so the use of videos of collisions is as ecologically valid as possible. The only deception used in the study was not telling the participants that the verb in the key question would be manipulated, which is a very minor detail that would not affect the experience of the participant, so would seem irrelevant in terms of informed consent. That leaves consequentiality, which as we have seen is almost impossible to include in an experiment without seriously contravening ethical guidelines.

One way in which Experiment 1 did deviate from the experience of a real witness was that each participant saw seven collisions and had to answer questions about each one. In reality, a witness is likely to provide details about only one collision, so this element of the study can be considered to lack ecological validity. Another potential problem with the experiments is that of **demand characteristics**, a term that refers to the tendency of participants to behave in an experiment in the way they think the researcher wants them to behave. Recent research in this area (Ost et al., 2008) has drawn a distinction between *false reporting* and *false memories* – between whether post-event information actually alters what a person remembers or just what *they say* they remember – and has estimated that the rate of false memory is approximately only one-third of the rate of false reporting. In other words, it could be the case that twice as many participants *say* they remember something that didn't happen as the number who actually do *remember* it. It is possible, then, that at least some of the participants in Experiment 2 were simply saying they remembered broken glass because (even if unconsciously) that's what they thought the researcher wanted, but that their memories had not actually been changed.

Although demand characteristics are undoubtedly a problem, it is important to remember that Loftus and Palmer were conducting applied research and that a real witness in a real investigation may also behave, even answer questions, in the way they think the police officer wants them to behave, so in this case demand characteristics are replicating pressures that would be experienced by a real witness.

Demand characteristics The cues in an experiment that participants can use to work out how the experimenter expects them to behave.

Box 9.2   Why do it this way?

Although there are disadvantages to the type of experiment conducted by Loftus and Palmer, this technique also has several important advantages over other methods of exploring memory for vehicle collisions. One possible alternative would be to interview witnesses to real collisions. Although this does away with problems relating to ecological validity and consequentiality it has the disadvantage that the researcher would not know what actually happened in the collision, including what speed the cars were travelling at. As Loftus and Palmer have shown, just because a witness says the speed was 30 mph and that there was broken glass does not mean that this is accurate. Of course, if there were multiple witnesses you could compare accounts, but how would you ever know which was the accurate one? One method that would be ecologically valid *and* would have a record of what actually happened would be to interview spectators who had witnessed a crash in a motorsport event (so that accounts could be compared with video footage of the crash). The problem with this approach is the lack of control over the spectators. For example, different people *would* see different things if they saw the crash from different positions and there would be no way of preventing spectators from discussing the crash or even watching it on TV. This would mean that their memories would already have been contaminated by post-event information.

The type of applied experiment conducted by Loftus and Palmer therefore has the advantage that the researchers know exactly what happened in the events presented, and can ensure that all participants see the same thing and are not exposed to post-event information outside the experiment. In other words, an applied experiment allows the researchers to have considerable control over and knowledge of what happens in the study. Another big advantage of an applied experiment over, say, interviews or surveys of real witnesses is that an experiment allows the researcher to establish cause and effect, while other techniques are often limited to seeing whether two different variables are related or associated. As Loftus and Palmer used an experiment, they were able to conclude that the verb used in the question affected participants' recall of the event and their judgement of speed.

3.3   Elizabeth Loftus

Since the publication of the Loftus and Palmer (1974) study, Elizabeth Loftus has become a world-renowned psychologist, contributing a great deal to our understanding of human memory (despite being voted 'least likely to succeed as a psychologist' by her fellow graduate students!) and conducting many more experiments relevant to witness memory. Her PhD research concerned semantic memory and how people retrieved information such as the names of animals and, although she continued to research in this area for a few years, after moving from Stanford to the University of Washington (Seattle) she decided she wanted to conduct research with more social relevance. She managed to combine her expertise in memory with her interest in crime and legal issues by beginning research into witness memory. The 1974 article that she wrote with John Palmer brought her work to the attention of the legal community and led not only to invitations to address legal seminars but eventually to appearances as an expert witness. This initially proved to be a battle as such testimony was generally considered to be inadmissible in the USA in the 1970s.

Figure 9.5   Elizabeth Loftus

Memory is relevant to many criminal investigations and trials; indeed, any investigation involving a witness will also involve witness memory. One type of case that became of particular interest to Loftus involved what is known as 'recovered' memories, namely memories of childhood abuse that the victims remember only many years later after participating in counselling sessions. The debate centres on the accuracy of these memories. This debate intrigued Loftus and was to become the focus of a great deal of her research over the next few decades. In particular she was interested in whether it was possible to implant a memory of an event that never happened. The next section explores some of the research conducted by Loftus on this issue.

Summary

- The key focus of applied research is to address issues of real-life relevance, and therefore it needs to mimic real-world conditions as far as possible.
- Practical considerations and research ethics limit the extent to which research can achieve both ecological validity and consequentiality.
- Elizabeth Loftus is a leading figure in research on eyewitness memory.

4 False memories

The debate as to whether recovered memories are real or false memories has been as polarised as it has been vehement, and has become known as the 'memory wars'. One of the problems for psychologists studying this phenomenon is that, given the trauma and timescale involved, it is very hard to conduct an experiment to 'test' such memories. Loftus was able to find a way of investigating the issue of false memories that has become a standard tool in applied cognitive psychology, and which first occurred to her while she was driving past a shopping mall.

4.1 The 'lost in the mall' study

The pioneering study that followed was conducted by Elizabeth Loftus together with colleague Jacqueline Pickrell (Loftus and Pickrell, 1995), and is frequently referred to as the 'lost in the mall' study because participants were led to believe that they had been lost as a child when out shopping, either in a department store or in a shopping centre.

The study involved three phases. In the first phase, twenty-four participants worked through a booklet that contained four short stories about events from their childhood that had previously been provided by a parent, sibling or other older relative. Participants were asked to write down what they could recall, if anything, about each event in the booklet. If they did not remember the event, then they were to write 'I do not remember this'.

Of the four events depicted in the stories, three were true and one was false. The false story involved the participant getting lost, when aged about five years, during a shopping trip. The relative supplied details about a plausible shopping trip – for example, where this might have taken place – and also verified that the participant had not actually experienced such an event around that age. Each fabricated false event contained common elements such as 'lost for an extended period', 'crying' and 'found by an elderly woman'.

Figure 9.6   It is easy to get lost in a shopping centre

One to two weeks later, in phase two, the participants were reminded of the four events and then asked to recall as much as they could about them, regardless of whether or not they had previously provided that information in the booklets. They were also asked to rate the clarity of their memory for each event, and their confidence that if given more time they would remember more details. After a further one to two weeks, in phase three, the participants were again interviewed using the same procedure.

What did the findings reveal? The results showed that across all three phases the participants remembered about 49 out of the 72 true events (68 per cent). Of key interest, though, was whether or not they would claim to remember anything about the false event. In phase one, seven of the twenty-four participants wrote something about the false story in the initial booklet. In phase two, six of these seven continued to report something about being lost and they also went on to report either a bit or all of the false event in phase three.

False memory
A memory for an event that did not actually take place but was instead only suggested to have occurred.

In summary, then, 75 per cent of participants resisted the suggestion that they had been lost as child, but 25 per cent were led to believe that an entire event had happened to them. In other words, 25 per cent of participants formed a **false memory**. A key question is whether these false memories were in any way different from the real memories. Loftus and Pickrell (1995) found that participants used fewer words to describe false memories than they did true memories. In addition, the clarity and confidence ratings provided by the participants were also lower for false memories than for true memories. Below is an extract from the Loftus and Pickrell paper, outlining a false memory:

> During the second interview, she said,
>
>> I vaguely, vague, I mean this is very vague, remember the lady helping me and Tim and my mom doing something else, but I don't remember crying. I mean I can remember a hundred times crying … I just remember bits and pieces of it. I remember being with the lady. I remember going shopping. I don't think I, I don't remember the sunglasses part.
>
> She went on to remember that the elderly lady who helped her was 'heavy-set and older. Like my brother said, nice.'
>
> (Loftus and Pickrell, 1995, p. 723)

This extract nicely illustrates the sparse nature of many false memory reports. Other studies have also found that reports of real memories generally contain more detail, in particular sensory detail such as sounds and smells, than reports of false memories do (e.g. Schooler et al., 1986). The point, though, is that participants believe that the event did actually occur in their past, even though they report very little in relation to this false memory. Furthermore, with repeated suggestive interviews – that is, interviews that include leading questions – participants will recall the event in quite a bit more detail (Ost et al., 2005).

Activity 9.4

Reflect for a moment on why Loftus and Pickrell picked being lost as a child for the false event. Are there any ethical considerations?

Remember that Loftus was interested in researching whether memories recovered from childhood were real or false memories, so it was necessary to find something that adult participants might have experienced, in their childhood. Being lost as a child for a brief period of time is something that many might have experienced so this is a relatively plausible event. It was chosen because it was deemed to be 'safe' in that, although reasonably serious, it would not be traumatic, and so implanting such a memory should not cause harm to anyone.

Other researchers in the mid 1990s conducted similar studies, convincing adults that as children they had been hospitalised, or had experienced an accident at a family event, for example. In one particular study, some children were persuaded that when younger they had been to hospital to have a mousetrap removed from their hand (Ceci et al., 1994). Typically, around 25–30 per cent of adults who participated in such studies reported false memories, and if children were the participants then the percentage was higher. The rate of false-memory reporting has varied across studies and this is owing to differences in how plausible the suggested event was considered to be by the participants and also how the suggested event was presented to them.

One of the more unusual methods of planting a false memory is to show doctored photographs (see Figure 9.7). The photograph on the left is the original, which has been doctored in the image on the right to show a different background. The doctored photograph could be used to plant a memory of a trip on a boat.

Figure 9.7   Doctoring photographs: a means of implanting false memories

4.2   False memories and food preferences

Loftus and Pickrell found that false memories were less detailed and less clear, but in what other ways may a false, implanted memory be different from a real memory? One way of exploring this question is to consider whether a false memory can influence behaviour in the same way that a real memory can. Several studies have considered whether a false memory can influence attitudes and actions, and explored whether being told of a bad experience with some object meant that the object was avoided later on. As memories about food are relatively easy to manipulate and are not traumatic, several studies have implanted the false suggestion that participants had become ill after eating a certain food when they were children and then looked to see if that food was avoided in the future.

One such study was undertaken by Elke Geraerts et al. (2008). It involved 180 first-year undergraduates at a university in the Netherlands, who were told they were taking part in a study called 'Food and personality'. In phase one, they were asked about their experiences and preferences regarding food. This included finding out whether they had got sick after eating egg salad before their tenth birthday, and also how much they liked to consume different foods, including egg salad.

In phase two, one week later, 120 of these participants were given the false suggestion that as a child they had been ill after eating egg salad. The remaining sixty participants acted as a **control group** and were not given this false suggestion. The experimenters implanted the false memory by giving the participants false feedback about their responses in phase one; among other things, the 'false suggestion' group were told 'You got sick after eating egg salad'.

Control group
Participants who are allocated to the 'baseline' or control condition.

Following this they were again asked about food preferences, allowing Geraerts et al. to see if there had been changes in how confident participants were as to whether they had been sick after eating egg salad as a child. Participants were also asked to indicate whether they had a specific belief or memory from before age ten about a number of different events, one of which was being sick after eating egg salad.

The key question, though, was whether participants would act differently as a result of the false suggestion and start to avoid eating egg salad. To explore this, participants were taken to another room where they received a bogus debriefing, and as a treat were offered drinks and sandwiches. The sandwiches contained five different fillings, one of which was egg salad. Which type of sandwich was eaten by each participant was recorded by someone who was not aware of whether the participant was in the false suggestion group or in the control group.

Four months later, the same participants were asked to participate in what they thought was a separate study but in reality comprised the third phase of the same study. Many volunteered and during this study they were invited to eat up food that would otherwise be thrown away. You won't be surprised to learn that the food comprised five different types of sandwich, one of which was egg salad. After the food was removed they were again asked about their food preferences and whether they had a specific belief or memory about being sick after eating egg salad.

The results showed that none of the participants had realised the study was about false memories. Of those participating in all three phases of the study:

- 35 were classified as believers as their confidence that the event had happened increased and they reported a memory or belief that the event had taken place.
- 54 were non-believers as their confidence about the critical event remained the same or decreased.
- 50 were control participants.

The findings are summarised in Figure 9.8.

Activity 9.5

Inspect the graph for a moment. Did these three groups (believers, non-believers and control) differ in the number of egg-salad sandwiches they had eaten? Which group changed most from Phase 2 to Phase 3?

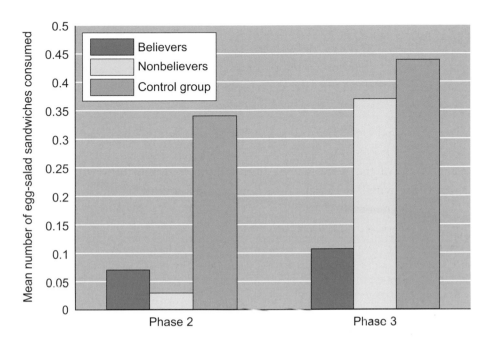

Figure 9.8   Mean number of egg-salad sandwiches consumed in the second and third phase

In the second phase, both believers and non-believers ate fewer egg-salad sandwiches compared with control participants. In the third phase, believers ate fewer egg salad sandwiches than did both non-believers and control participants, and it was the non-believers group who changed most across the two phases. Providing false feedback acted in the short term to deter both believers and non-believers from eating egg-salad sandwiches, probably because the notion of being sick after eating egg salad was fresh in their minds. This false feedback had no longer-lasting effect on non-believers, who ate a similar number of egg-salad sandwiches as the control group in phase 3. Geraerts et al. suggested that believers, having contemplated the egg-salad event, had created memories about being ill after eating egg salad as a child and this false belief influenced their eating behaviour four months later, so that this group continued to eat far fewer egg-salad sandwiches than the control group.

So, there is evidence to suggest that false memories relating to food can have repercussions for later eating behaviour. Research is now looking at the influence of other types of false memory on other behaviours. If false memories behave like real memories in influencing behaviour, you might be wondering whether there is a way of telling whether a particular memory is true or false. This is one of the biggest challenges facing memory researchers. Although on average false memories tend to be less detailed and contain less sensory information, this and other more complex methods for distinguishing between true and false memories have not been found to be sufficiently reliable for use in the courtroom. Moreover, Bernstein and Loftus (2009) suggest that:

> In essence, all memory is false to some degree. Memory is inherently a reconstructive process, whereby we piece together the past to form a coherent narrative that becomes our autobiography. In the process of reconstructing the past, we color and shape our life's experiences based on what we know about the world. Our job as memory researchers and as human beings is to determine the portion of memory that reflects reality and the portion that reflects inference and bias. This is no simple feat, but one worthy of our continued investigation.
>
> (Loftus and Bernstein, 2009, p. 373)

Summary

- Studies have found that some participants report memories that have been implanted by researchers; these are called false memories.
- Loftus and Pickrell (1995) pioneered research on false memories.
- Recent work suggests that false memories about being sick from egg salad affected some participants' eating behaviour, even after four months.

5   Questioning memory

The research conducted by Loftus and colleagues highlights how fallible and malleable memory can be. However, it is worth bearing in mind that memory is not always prone to inaccuracies. In any one study of false memory, only a minority of people were shown to be susceptible to suggestions made by researchers or to leading questions. This is important because it suggests that memories *can be* and often are accurate. This is why psychologists have conducted a great deal of research into developing methods for helping people to remember accurately. This chapter concludes by considering how best to help someone recall as much and as accurately as possible, and, as you will see, this is another area where psychology has had a significant impact.

5.1   Police interviewing

The most obvious piece of advice arising from research is to avoid the use of leading questions, and this is something that is taught to police officers during their training in many countries. The training provided to police officers in the UK is grounded in research, and guidance is provided on how best to interview and what tools might assist witness recall.

One such interviewing tool is that witnesses are asked to recall the event they saw without interruption. The police interviewer may start with what is called an **open-ended question**, which is a question that does not lead the witness in any way; for example, 'What do you remember about the event?' The idea behind this 'report everything' approach is that allowing witnesses to remember one thing, even something possibly irrelevant, such as the colour of the carpet, might cue or trigger the witness to recall something else about the event. Also, this encourages the police interviewer to hear the full story from the witness, and then later to ask questions that are compatible with the witness's own version of events.

Open-ended question
A question that does not suggest or imply an answer and usually invites the witness to provide as much detail as they can.

Figure 9.9   Interviewing technique is crucial for assisting witness recall

Interview training also covers a number of other tools designed to assist memory, which are known as mnemonic techniques. For example, police interviewers are instructed on how useful it can be to ask the witness to mentally reinstate the context of the event. This includes recalling the physical environment, such as the location in which the crime took place, as well as lighting conditions, smells, emotional reactions and feelings. You may have used this technique yourself when trying to find something you have misplaced by thinking back to when you last had seen or used the lost item.

This approach to interviewing is based on memory research, and the psychologists who brought together the relevant research to apply it to police interviewing were Ron Fisher and Ed Geiselman (e.g. Fisher and Geiselman, 1992). They proposed an interviewing procedure called the **cognitive interview**, which has not only been incorporated into the police training undertaken in England and Wales but has also informed NHS guidance on interviewing those involved in patient safety incidents.

Cognitive interview
A procedure for interviewing witnesses that draws on research on memory and incorporates a number of retrieval strategies.

5.2 Courtroom practices

The finding that our memories are prone to suggestion has also influenced courtroom practices. It is deemed acceptable to pose leading questions in the courtroom during cross-examination; for example, 'The car was dark blue, wasn't it?' This is because it is considered crucial by the legal profession that the accuracy of evidence obtained be probed, to allow any unreliable or dishonest witness to be exposed. The Youth Justice and Criminal Evidence Act of 1999 has, however, recognised that certain witnesses may be more susceptible to the effects of leading questions than others. This Act acknowledges the problems facing witnesses deemed vulnerable – because of their age or because of learning difficulties, for example – and who might find giving evidence at a criminal trial to be a particularly difficult experience.

Figure 9.10   Evidence via video link

Special measures have been introduced for such witnesses, one of which is to allow the police in England and Wales to record the initial witness evidence on video, which can then be presented to the court as evidence-in-chief. Guidance on how to interview witnesses for the purposes of criminal proceedings was provided, among others, by psychologists Ray Bull and Helen Westcott in the *Memorandum of Good Practice* (Home Office, 1992). This guidance was revised and expanded in *Achieving Best Evidence* (Home Office, 2002). The guidance promotes the use of open-ended questions (e.g. 'Please tell me what happened.') followed by specific, non-leading questions (e.g. 'What colour was the car?' if the witness has already mentioned a car), and to minimise or avoid forced-choice questions (e.g. 'Was the car black or blue?') or questions that have several parts. In Scotland, a steering committee worked with psychologists Amina Memon and Lynn Hulse to put together guidance on interviewing children and other vulnerable witnesses (Scottish Executive, 2003). This collaboration between psychologists and policymakers has helped to bring about improvements in the way evidence is elicited, in particular from vulnerable witnesses.

5.3   Conclusion

This chapter has focused on episodic memory, namely memory for events. You were introduced to the early work of Bartlett that highlighted the reconstructive nature of memory and the way in which people's knowledge, general beliefs and expectations may shape their recall of events. The malleability of memory has been explored further through Elizabeth Loftus's work on eyewitness memory. Together with other researchers' work, Loftus's research has shown not only that leading questions can lead to inaccuracies in recall but also that some participants can even be led to believe that an entire fictitious event took place earlier in their life.

In spite of the fallibility and malleability of memory, there are many episodes from our past that we will remember with a high degree of accuracy, and any errors are unlikely to have any significant impact. However, very occasionally people find themselves in a situation – such as witnessing a crime – when remembering accurately becomes especially important. For this reason, knowing how memory works in such unusual and often stressful circumstances, and understanding how interviewing techniques can help improve the accuracy of recall, has significant practical implications. Witness testimony represents an important area of applied research, in that psychological theories and experimental findings have made a significant contribution to law enforcement and the criminal justice system more generally.

Summary

- Research by psychologists on memory has been applied to witness interviewing, and the cognitive interview was designed for use in police interviews.
- Psychologists have also contributed to guidance on how to help vulnerable witnesses give evidence.

References

Bartlett, F.C. (1932) *Remembering: A Study in Experimental and Social Psychology*, Cambridge, Cambridge University Press.

Bernstein, D.M. and Loftus, E.F. (2009) 'How to tell if a particular memory is true or false', *Perspectives on Psychological Science*, vol. 4, no. 4, pp. 370–4.

Ceci, S.J., Huffman, M.L.C., Smith, E., and Loftus, E.F. (1994) 'Repeatedly thinking about a non-event', *Consciousness and Cognition*, vol. 3, nos 3–4, pp. 388–407.

Fisher, R.P. and Geiselman, R.E. (1992) *Memory Enhancing Techniques for Investigative Interviewing: The Cognitive Interview.* Springfield, IL, Charles C. Thomas.

Geraerts, E., Bernstein, D.M., Merckelbach, H., Linders, C., Raymaekers, L. and Loftus, E.F. (2008) 'Lasting false beliefs and their behavioral consequences', *Psychological Science*, vol. 19, no. 8, pp. 749–53.

Home Office (1992) *The Memorandum of Good Practice on Video Recorded Interviews with Child Witnesses for Criminal Proceedings*, London, Home Office.

Home Office (2002) *Achieving Best Evidence in Criminal Proceedings: Guidance for Vulnerable and Intimidated Witnesses, Including Children*, London, Home Office Communication Directorate.

Loftus, E.F. and Palmer, J.C. (1974) 'Reconstruction of automobile destruction: an example of the interaction between language and memory', *Journal of Verbal Learning and Verbal Behavior*, vol. 13, no. 5, pp. 585–9.

Loftus, E.F., and Pickrell, J.E. (1995) 'The formation of false memories', *Psychiatric Annals*, vol. 25, no. 12, pp. 720–5.

Marshall, J. (1969) *Law and Psychology in Conflict*, New York, NY, Anchor Books.

Ost, J., Foster, S., Costall, A. and Bull, R. (2005) 'False reports of childhood events in appropriate interviews', *Memory*, vol. 13, no. 7, pp. 700–10.

Ost, J., Granhag, P.A., Udell, J. and Roos af Hjelmsäter, E. (2008) 'Familiarity breeds distortion: the effects of media exposure on false reports of real life traumatic events', *Memory*, vol. 16, no. 1, pp. 76–85.

Schooler, J.W., Gerhard, D., and Loftus, E.F. (1986) 'Qualities of the unreal', *Journal of Experimental Psychology: Learning, Memory, and Cognition*, vol. 12, no. 2, pp. 171–81.

Scottish Executive (2003) *Guidance on Interviewing Children Witnesses in Scotland*, Edinburgh, The Stationery Office.

Conclusion

In the last three chapters of *Discovering Psychology* you read about the work of Pierre Paul Broca and Carl Wernicke on the relationship between the brain and language (Chapter 7), about Broadbent's experimental work on attention (Chapter 8), and about the applied research of Elizabeth Loftus and colleagues on eyewitness memory (Chapter 9). Research described in the three chapters has one thing in common: it explores cognitive processes – such as language, attention or memory – that take place in the mind and are therefore not directly observable. However, while Chapter 7 explored how a particular psychological function, namely language, is controlled by the brain, Chapters 8 and 9 focused largely on experimental work that was more interested in examining the limits of the human information-processing system, without looking into the underlying brain structures.

Another important point that emerges from the chapters is the relationship between an explanation, often formulated as a *psychological theory,* and *evidence.* As you have learned, theory (even if only a preliminary one) about how some process works informs a research hypothesis. By testing the hypothesis a researcher gathers evidence which then feeds back into theory. A theory is refined in the light of the new evidence, and new hypotheses are generated to test it further. This continuous process that links theory and research underlies the *cycle of enquiry.* For example, in Chapter 7, you read about Broca's and Wernicke's early findings about the neurological basis of language, which focused on two areas of the brain. Over the subsequent century their account of the control of language was refined (and continues to be refined even today), on the basis of *evidence* from a variety of studies. In Chapter 8, you read about Broadbent's model of attention developed on the basis of experiments using dichotic listening, and about how this model was tested and refined by the findings of further experimental work. Finally, as you read in Chapter 9, Loftus and Palmer's work consisted of a series of experiments that were necessary in order to assess and revise their own notions about how memory for events operates.

The cycle of enquiry raises once again an issue that you encountered in some of the earlier chapters: namely, that the work of a researcher in psychology is rarely complete. There are always theories to be tested, gaps in research to be filled, new questions to be answered and new insights revealed by new technologies and new techniques. Psychology has to be based on evidence and this evidence (as well as the theories that it helps to build) is subject to continuous evaluation and interpretation.

Another message conveyed in this last part of the book is that theories and research can have real-world relevance. In Chapter 7, you saw how research on the neurological basis of language revealed the plasticity of the brain. Understanding that there is the possibility of some recovery of function has led to the development of a number of therapeutic techniques designed to maximise recovery and alleviate some of the problems faced by those suffering from brain damage. Research on the limits of human attention (Chapter 8) and on how and why performing two tasks simultaneously causes interference has been used to address a number of real-life issues, from the effects of mobile-phone use while driving, to cockpit design and understanding the cognitive dynamic behind friendly-fire incidents on the battlefield. Finally, in Chapter 9, you read about the fallibility of memory. You were probably already aware of how easy it is to forget things, but may have been less aware of the possibility that memories could be so easily (and often unintentionally) distorted, or under certain circumstances even implanted. This has important implications for those rare situations when it is especially important to remember something we saw or experienced as accurately as possible.

These final three chapters also offered you a taster of further sub-disciplines of psychology. Chapter 7 introduced a particular area of biological psychology, namely *neuropsychology*, which is concerned with the relationship between the brain and different psychological functions. Chapters 8 and 9 introduced you to *cognitive psychology*, which explores how information is processed, and how knowledge is stored and retrieved.

What is particularly challenging to psychologists investigating cognitive processes is that they are dealing with phenomena, such as perception, attention, memory, thinking and language, that do not lend themselves to direct observation. One option, which you learned about in Chapter 7, is to look at how these processes are controlled by the brain. As you read in the chapter, psychologists have to be cautious about how they interpret the results of brain damage. The correspondence between damage in one area of the brain and the loss of a specific psychological function does not imply that this area is directly and solely responsible for regulating that function (remember the radio analogy). Only with the discovery of more recent techniques, such as brain imaging, has it been possible to gain a more accurate understanding of the complex nature of the relationship between the brain (and indeed different areas of the brain) and cognitive functions.

An alternative to looking at the brain – the 'hardware' behind cognition – is to devise models of the 'software' – namely, the human information-processing system. This is where analogies can be useful. Broadbent, for instance, drew on terms from the world of computers, and these terms provided him with a way of thinking about the relationship between different cognitive processes in humans. However, it is important to be aware of the limitations of analogies. As Chapter 9 highlighted, there are important differences between how a computer processes information and how a person does so.

Crucially, as you have read in Chapter 8, creating abstract models to represent cognition and examining the brain are not mutually exclusive approaches to studying how humans process information about the world around them. Experiments using brain-imaging techniques can help psychologists build a richer picture of how cognitive processes might operate.

Finally, it is worth noting that cognition does not exist in isolation from the issues discussed in Parts 1 and 2 of *Discovering Psychology*. Cognitive processes interact not only with one another but also with other aspects of the person and situation. In Chapter 7, you read about how therapeutic intervention to assist aphasia needs to acknowledge the other problems the individual may have, such as limited attention or apathy. The notion of a finite amount of processing resources, introduced in Chapter 8, does not preclude that our performance is likely to be influenced by factors such as stress or fatigue, or even by the mere presence of others. In Chapter 9, you saw that what we remember is influenced not only by factors within us but also by what is around us – by the way a question is phrased, by the information another person provides, and by the culture to which we belong. So, although psychologists seek to isolate and focus on a particular process or behaviour, they are aware that in reality this process or behaviour does not operate in isolation, but is part of the infinitely complex mechanism that is the human mind.

Final note

Nine chapters and several hundred pages after you embarked on this voyage of discovery, the time has come to take stock, reflect on the experience as a whole and consider what you have learned about psychology.

The main aim of the book has been to initiate you into the world of psychology. By exploring some of the most important and influential studies conducted by psychologists, the preceding chapters gave you a taster of the main areas of research and introduced you to the different methods used by psychologists to study the human mind and behaviour (and in some cases animal behaviour). You learned how a number of pioneering figures within the discipline formulated research questions and created innovative ways of answering them; how they developed, tested and refined theories about human behaviour, performance, personality characteristics, and mental states; and, most importantly, how they inspired successive generations of researchers to push the boundaries of human knowledge and further enhance our understanding of psychology. It is important to note, however, that what you read about in the chapters is just a snapshot of all the work carried out by psychologists to date, but one that nevertheless introduced you to a number of broader issues which are important for understanding what psychology is about.

So, when all the work examined in the preceding chapters is pulled together, what picture emerges of psychology?

One of the main tasks of *Discovering Psychology* has been to introduce you to what psychologists *do* and how they go about the tasks of discovering how the mind works or why humans (or other animals) behave the way they do. In reading the material presented in the chapters you probably noticed that psychology places important emphasis on research. Psychology is an evidence-based discipline. In everyday language, the term 'psychologist' is often used to describe someone who helps people address personal problems and issues. Having read the nine chapters of *Discovering Psychology*, you will now realise that there is more to psychology than this. Much of what we know about psychology has come from painstaking research using a whole range of methods: experiments, observations, questionnaires, interviews, case studies, to name but a few. Psychology, as a perpetually developing body of knowledge, has come about as a result of endless testing and refining of theories, ideas and methods, with the help of available technology – and occasionally luck. So, an important thing that distinguishes psychology from a purely philosophical enquiry about the human condition (of the kind that has been around since antiquity), or from everyday, lay theories about 'human nature', is this emphasis on *research* and *evidence*.

The emphasis on evidence and research makes psychology an inherently *dynamic* discipline. Every hypothesis tested and every prediction confirmed only yields more questions to be answered, and provides opportunities for further investigation. The *cycle of enquiry* that drives psychological research is a never-ending process. However, the dynamic nature of the discipline stems also from the fact that developments in society as a whole are constantly creating new challenges as well as new opportunities for psychological investigation. For example, the invention of complex electronic instruments, or even just the emergence, over the past hundred years, of the car as an everyday mode of transport, has highlighted the limitations of human attention which, all of a sudden, acquired importance that they did not have a century or two ago. The rising popularity of the internet since the 1990s has changed the way younger generations in particular interact with others, which in turn meant that many assumptions about social development and children's interactions with their peers needed to be revised. The rise of modern warfare has similarly posed new questions about obedience to authority and its potentially tragic consequences. All of these developments presented psychology with new challenges. At the same time, the evolution of science and technology – especially the invention of brain-imaging techniques, computers, video and audio recording devices, etc. – has provided psychologists with new opportunities, and has made psychology an even more fascinating, varied and sophisticated discipline.

Important in this respect is also the increasing awareness of the role of *ethics* in psychological research. The realisation over the past half a century or so that research must at all times preserve the dignity and safety of human participants and consider the welfare of animals used in experiments has imposed limits on what psychologists can do. The work of Harry Harlow, for example, is a clear example of why drawing these limits was both necessary and welcome. And yet, the emphasis on ethics in research has not brought psychological research to a halt. Instead, researchers have developed innovative ways of studying those aspects of behaviour that it would be unethical to explore in a traditional laboratory setting. Technology has proved useful here too, with computer simulation and virtual worlds providing exciting new opportunities for ethically responsible research.

So what has been the main finding of all this research and discovery? Part 3 of *Discovering Psychology* ended with a reference to the mind as an 'infinitely complex mechanism'. This sentence captures what is probably the most important message of this book. Our behaviour, personality characteristics, mental states and abilities, all of which define who we are and how we interact with the world around us, are the outcome of a complex interplay of a variety of different factors, processes and influences. We are as much a product of what we might refer to as *nature* – things like brain structures and innate aspects of behaviour which are passed on through the genes – as we are of *nurture* – for instance, learning, the influence of parents or peers, and more generally the effect of the environment. All of these different internal and external factors come together to create who we are and what we do. So, when trying to explain the human mind and behaviour, looking at any one of these factors is seldom enough. Answers are not to be sought just inside the brain, in abstract models of the human information-processing system, in some aspect of personality or in the influence of the environment. Rather, they are to be found in the interplay between the different elements that interact to produce the complex mechanism that we are. Although psychologists sometimes disagree about the relative importance of the different influences, there is general recognition that who we are and what we do is a result of a complex interplay of biological, cognitive and social factors. We are the product of an interaction between nature and nurture, internal and external influences. It is also worth noting that, in this context, debates and disagreements are not necessarily a bad thing. On the contrary – they are an intrinsic part of scholarly endeavour and an important driving force behind innovation and scientific advancement.

The increasing awareness of the complexity of psychology's subject matter and the development of the wide variety of methods that are used to study the human mind and behaviour have led to the emergence of more specialised sub-disciplines within psychology. In the chapters of *Discovering Psychology* you encountered a number of them: social psychology, cognitive psychology, neuropsychology, developmental psychology and the psychology of individual differences. This is not an exhaustive list. There are also many others, including clinical psychology and occupational psychology. There are also more complex combinations – developmental neuropsychology, evolutionary social psychology, etc. Within many of these sub-disciplines there are further distinctions on the basis of, for instance, the preference for qualitative or quantitative methods, or adherence to a specific theoretical perspective or tradition.

The existence of so many different divisions within psychology can leave one feeling somewhat overwhelmed. The important thing to remember is that none of the sub-disciplines exists in isolation. Imagine for a second that you are a developmental psychologist embarking on a project to study attention in very young children. To address this question you would need to acquaint yourself with the more general cognitive psychological research on attention in adults, of the kind you read about in Chapter 8. You might also find it useful to consult literature from neuropsychology that looked at the development, in early childhood, of specific brain regions that are implicated in regulating cognitive functions such as attention. You could also consult the work of clinical or educational psychologists and see whether findings from studies with children who are unable to concentrate for long (for example, those suffering from Attention Deficit/Hyperactivity Disorder) can help you shed light on normal development of attention. In this example, as is often the case, the different sub-disciplines work together to provide a more complete picture of a highly complex phenomenon.

Another theme running through the pages of *Discovering Psychology* is that psychological research is often informed by the desire to understand some real-life, everyday aspect of human (or animal) behaviour; or indeed by the need to shed light on and even solve some sort of practical problem. From understanding how the brain works and helping patients recover from brain damage, through working with the police on developing ways of obtaining accurate witness accounts, to understanding the psychology of perpetrators of genocide or the role of the media in aggression, researchers have always been responsive to the issues and concerns of the society and era that they inhabited. This is an important point because it shows that psychologists are not interested in the mind or behaviour for its own sake. In fact, a number of sub-disciplines within psychology have a distinctly applied focus, in that they look at how the understanding of psychology can be made relevant to what happens in courtrooms and prisons (forensic psychology), in the classroom (educational psychology), on the sports pitch (sports psychology) or in the workplace (occupational psychology).

And yet, it is also worth noting that when psychologists address practical concerns, they rarely do so in isolation from the broader world of academic enquiry. Psychologists are not the only researchers interested in human behaviour or psychological processes, nor is what they do always distinct from the work carried out in other disciplines or professions. Neuropsychologists, for example, work closely with the medical profession, and the lines that delineate the two disciplines are often blurred. Cognitive psychologists are working increasingly closely with computer scientists in pursuit of a more accurate understanding of the human information-processing system. In fact *cognitive science*, which is today a research area in its own right, emerged in recent decades as a product of this collaboration. Psychologists interested in innate aspects of human behaviour will often work together with zoologists and ethologists. You also learned that Milgram's work was not only influenced by the desire to explain a historical event, but that it also had an impact on how some historians interpret the conduct of perpetrators of Nazi crimes. Equally, it is today common for books or documentaries about famous historical figures to reflect on the person's childhood and their relationship with parents or parental figures. This is a manifestation of the subtle but enduring influence in contemporary culture of Sigmund Freud and his theories about the role of childhood relationships on adult personality.

This collaboration with other disciplines offers yet another illustration of psychology's importance in contemporary society. It shows that psychological research, together with other disciplines and professions, makes a difference and, as well as addressing practical problems, also influences the way in which people, and society as a whole, view and interpret events in the world. This continuing relevance of psychology goes a long way towards explaining why the interest in it remains so strong in the world today.

We hope that you enjoyed the material covered in *Discovering Psychology* and that it whetted your appetite for the discipline. Most importantly, we hope that it instilled in you the desire to pursue an interest in all things psychological!

Jovan Byford and Nicola Brace

Acknowledgements

Grateful acknowledgement is made to the following sources:

Figures

Figure 1.1: Copyright © Chris Barham/Daily Mail/Rex Features; Figure 1.2: Mary Evans Picture Library/SIGMUND FREUD COPYRIGHTS; Figure 1.3 left: Copyright © Popperfoto/Getty Images; Figure 1.3 right: Getty Images; Figure 1.4: Copyright © Imagno/Getty Images; Figure 1.5: Copyright © Janine Wiedel/Photofusion; Figure 1.6: Copyright © Underwood & Underwood/Corbis; Figure 1.7: Copyright © dpa/Corbis; Figure 1.7: Copyright © Bettmann/Corbis; Figure 1.8: Copyright © Yevgeny Khaldei/Corbis; Figure 1.9: Copyright © Farrizio Bensch/Corbis; Figure 2.1 top left: Copyright © Time & Life Pictures/ Getty Images; Figure 2.1 top right: Copyright © Steve Drew/EMPICS Sports/Press Association Images; Figure 2.1 bottom: Copyright © LOOK Die Bildagentur de Fotografen GmbH/Alamy; Figure 2.2: Courtesy of Alexandra Milgram; Figure 2.3: Copyright © Popperfoto/ Getty Images; Figures 2.4, 2.5, 2.6 and 2.7: Milgram, S (1974) Obedience to Authority, Harper & Row. Copyright © 1974 by Stanley Milgram; Figure 2.8: Slater, M et al (2006) 'A Virtual Reprise of the Stanley Milgram Obedience Experiments', PLoS ONE, No 1(1). Copyright © 2006 Slater et al; Figure 2.9: Courtesy of Yad Vashem – Holocaust Martyrs' and Heroes' Remembrance Authority; Figure 3.1: Copyright © picturesbyrob/Alamy; Figure 3.2 left: Copyright © Universal Pictures/Ronald Grant Archive; Figure 3.2 right: Copyright © Rockstar Games; Figure 3.3: Copyright © Time & Life Pictures/Getty Images; Figures 3.4 and 3.5: Copyright © Albert Bandura; Figure 3.6: Copyright © 2005 Bubbles Photo Library; Figure 3.7: Copyright © MBI/Alamy; Figure 3.8: Byron, T (2008) Safer Children in a Digital World: The Report of the Byron Review, Department for Children, Schools and Families. Crown copyright material is reproduced under Class Licence Number C01W0000065 with the permission of the Controller, Office of Public Sector Information (OPSI); Figure 3.9: Copyright © NetPics/Alamy; Figure 4.1: Courtesy of Frederick Toates; Figure 4.7: Copyright © Nina Leen/Time & Life Pictures/Getty Images; Figure 4.9: Copyright © Denkou/Alamy; Figure 4.10: Copyright © Matt Rourke/AP/Press Association Images; Figure 4.11: Copyright © Ashley Cooper/Corbis; Figure 5.1 top left, top right and bottom right: Copyright © John Birdsall/Press Association Images; Figure 5.1 bottom left: Copyright © Andres Rodriguez/Alamy; Figures 5.2, 5.3 and 5.5: Copyright © Nina Leen/Time & Life Pictures/Getty Images;

Figures 5.4 and 5.6: Copyright © Science Source/Science Photo Library; Figure 5.8: Copyright © Underwood & Underwood/Corbis; Figure 5.9: Copyright © Steve Back/Daily Mail/Rex Features; Figure 6.1: Copyright © Jerry Monkman/Narurepl.com; Figure 6.2: Copyright © Janine Wiedel Photolibrary/Alamy; Figure 6.3: Copyright © Sally and Richard Greenhill/Alamy; Figure 6.4: Copyright © Picture Partners/Alamy; Figure 6.5: by permission of William Corsaro; Figures 6.6 and 6.7: Copyright © John Birdsall/Press Association Images, photos posed by models; Figure 6.8: Copyright © Image Source/Alamy; Figure 7.3: Copyright © Mark Strozier/iStock; Figure 7.5: Damasio, H, Grabowski, T et al (1994) 'The return of Phineas Gage: clues about the brain from the skull of a famous patient', Science, Vol 264, No 5162; Figures 7.7 and 7.10: Dronkers, N F (2007) 'Paul Broca's historic cases: high resolution MR imaging of the brains of Leborgne and Lelong', Brain, Vol 130, May 2007, Oxford University Press. Copyright © 2007 by the Guarantors of Brain; Figures 8.1 and 8.9: Courtesy of Graham Edgar; Figure 8.2: Copyright © Justin Lane/epa/Corbis; Figure 8.3: Copyright © UK Medical Research Council used by kind permission; Figure 8.4: adapted from Broadbent, D E (1958) Perception and Communication, Pergamon Press; Figure 8.8: Kastner, S (1998) 'Mechanisms of directed attention in the human extrastriate cortex as revealed by functional MRI', Science, Vol 282, 2 October 1998. Reprinted with permission from AAAS; Figure 9.2: Copyright © UK Medical Research Council used by kind permission; Figure 9.5: Copyright © Jodi Hilton/Press Association Images; Figure 9.6: Copyright © Dave Thompson/PA Archive/Press Association Images; Figure 9.7: Courtesy of Nicola Brace; Figure 9.9: Copyright © Bubbles Photolibrary/Alamy; Figure 9.10: Copyright © David R Frazier Photolibrary Inc/Alamy.

Every effort has been made to contact copyright holders. If any have been inadvertently overlooked the publishers will be pleased to make the necessary arrangements at the first opportunity.

Index